Court Officials of the

DUCKWORTH EGYPTOLOGY
Series Editor: Nicholas Reeves

Burial Customs of Ancient Egypt
Wolfram Grajetzki

The Middle Kingdom of Ancient Egypt
Wolfram Grajetzki

Performance and Drama in Ancient Egypt
Robyn Gillam

The Royal Mummies
G. Elliot Smith

The Tomb of Hâtshopsîtû
Theodore Davis

The Tomb of Iouiya and Touiyou with the Funeral Papyrus of Iouiya
Theodore Davis

The Tomb of Siphtah with The Tomb of Queen Tîyi
Theodore Davis

The Tomb of Thoutmôsis IV
Theodore Davis

The Tomb of Tut.ankh.Amen (3 vols)
Howard Carter

The Tombs of Harmhabi and Touatânkhamanou
Theodore Davis

DUCKWORTH EGYPTOLOGY

Court Officials
of the
Egyptian Middle Kingdom

Wolfram Grajetzki

Drawings by Paul Whelan

Duckworth

First published in 2009 by
Gerald Duckworth & Co. Ltd.
90-93 Cowcross Street, London EC1M 6BF
Tel: 020 7490 7300
Fax: 020 7490 0080
info@duckworth-publishers.co.uk
www.ducknet.co.uk

A catalogue record for this book is available
from the British Library

ISBN 978 0 7156 3745 6

Typeset by Ray Davies
Printed in Great Britain by the
MPG Books Group

Contents

Figure of the 'overseer of sealers', Meru (stela, Turin 1447).
See pp. 81-2.

Preface

An essential element in Ancient Egyptian society was the royal court, the officials that surrounded the king. While modern historians still tend to focus on the king alone, these officials certainly contributed to or themselves made important decisions, led military campaigns and ruled the country. There are already several studies of individuals, of the royal court in general and of the relationship of court officials to the king and to other members of the administration. Nevertheless, modern written histories of Ancient Egypt still focus too narrowly on the king, although it is clear from better documented periods that courtiers must have played an important part in ruling the country. History was made not only by kings, but also by the men around the king and the rest of the population, the farmers and craftsmen. These people deserve their own consideration, to which I hope this book will contribute.[1]

The book is basically an expanded and more easily accessible version of my PhD thesis. Its main aim is to give new life to the tables, statistics and numbers presented there. The study is of the elite, the men at the top of Egyptian society in the Middle Kingdom. The term 'elite' is very widely used in archaeology, for example in the excavation of cemeteries to refer to the people with the largest and/or richest tombs, or in settlement archaeology where it is often stated that the biggest houses belong to the 'elite'. However, in modern sociology the term generally refers to the very small number of people at the top in a modern state who rule the country and society, perhaps only a few thousand at a time.[2] In Ancient Egypt, with its much smaller population, these people certainly formed only a small group at the top of Egyptian society, perhaps as few as fifty per generation. In recent times 'elite' has too often been used in Egyptology without a proper definition. It will generally be avoided here, with the exception of the title 'member of the elite', 'iry-pat', where 'pat' seems best translated as 'elite' but without the modern sociological meaning.

I am especially grateful to Paul Whelan who was interested in joining this project from the beginning and has provided the book with his excellent drawings. Their inclusion makes the book a unique guide to Middle Kingdom and Second Intermediate Period material culture and archaeology. I am also very grateful to him for his editorial work on the text.

For most officials discussed within the main text no references in the form of footnotes are provided. These references and the officials discussed are listed in an appendix at the end of the book. In the appendix a full bibliography to the main monuments of each official is given. If in the appendix more than one title for an official is mentioned, this refers to different stages in a career. The appointments are indicated with an arrow (→).

I would like to thank Nicholas Reeves for agreeing to include the book in his series and Deborah Blake from Duckworth for all her support; thanks also go to Sally-Ann Ashton (Cambridge), Ashley Cook (Liverpool), Vivian Davies, Marcel Marée, Susanne Woodhouse (BM, London), Chris Naunton (EES, London), Stephen Quirke (London) and Steven Snape (Liverpool). I am grateful to Gianluca Miniaci (Pisa) for taking pictures in the Cairo Museum and for providing information on objects there. Last but not least, special thanks goes to www.flickr.com, certainly the most important and useful picture archive that ever existed. Within a few years they have made high quality images of many museum collections and other objects available at a level never seen before.

Chronology

Only the more important kings are listed. Dates are all BC.

Early Dynastic Period, Dynasties 1-2	*c.* **3000-2800**
Old Kingdom, Dynasties 3-6	*c.* **2800-2250**
First Intermediate Period, Dynasties 7-11	*c.* **2250-2010**
Dynasty 11 (early)	
Antef II	2103-2054
Antef III	2054-2046
Middle Kingdom, Dynasties 11-13	*c.* **2010-1700**
Dynasty 11 (later, after unification)	
Mentuhotep II	2046-1995
Mentuhotep III	1995-1983
Mentuhotep IV	1983-1981
several lesser kings?	1981-1976
Dynasty 12	1976-1794
Amenemhat I; capital moves to Itj-tawy	1976-1947
Senusret I	1956-1911
Amenemhat II	1914-1879
Senusret II	1882-1872
Senusret III	1872-1834
Amenemhat III	1853-1806
Amenemhat IV	1807-1798
Sobeknofru	1798-1794
Dynasty 13	
Wegaf	*c.* 1794-1790
Sekhemkare Amenemhat V	*c.* 1790-1787
Nerkare	*c.* 1788
about 12 short reigning kings	*c.* 1788-1783
Sobekhotep I	*c.* 1783-1779
Khendjer	*c.* 1779-1775
3 short reigning kings, perhaps less than one year	
Amenemhat Sobekhotep II	*c.* 1774-1771
Sobekhotep III	*c.* 1770-1767
Neferhotep I	*c.* 1767-1756
Sobekhotep IV	*c.* 1756-1746
one or two kings	

Illustrations

Plates

(between pp. 66 and 67)

1. Deir el-Bahari, Tombs of Eleventh Dynasty court officials (photo: Paul Whelan).
2. Relief found in the mastaba of Siese at Dahshur (from J. de Morgan, *Fouilles à Dahchour en 1894-1895*, Vienna 1903, pl. XIV).
3. Stela of the vizier Zamont (Cairo CG 20102; photo: Gianluca Miniaci).
4. Statue of the 'treasurer' Khentykhetyemsaef (Cairo CG 408; photo: author).
5. Stela of the 'deputy treasurer' Sehetepibre (Cairo CG 20538; photo: author).
6. Scarab of the 'steward' Senebtifi (Eton College ECM 1850; photo: N. Reeves).
7. Statue of the 'high steward' Nebsekhut (two views; Cairo CG 42039; photos: author and Gianluca Miniaci (the whole)).
8. Fragment (full view and view of the head) of a life-size statue, Khons temple, Karnak (photo: author).

Figures

All the drawings are by Paul Whelan unless otherwise stated. While there is no substitute for a drawing made directly from an object, for practical and logistical reasons the majority of illustrations in this book have been made from photographs. This is rarely a problem when using modern high resolution digital images, however for a number of drawings the only source material available has been old and often poor quality photographs. It is possible, therefore, that a drawing may miss a minor detail where it is unclear or 'invisible' on the original photograph.

Illustrations

1

Historical Background

Around 3000 BC Egypt developed into a unified kingdom with a ruler at the top, a large number of officials on several levels and a population of farmers and peasants at the base. The people around the king played a significant part at the royal court. They were often depicted on royal monuments and left their own important monuments all around the country. There can be no question that they occupied a central part in Egyptian history and it is also certain that some of them were the real power behind a weak or young king. The people around the king are often called 'high officials', but they were certainly much more; it seems more reasonable to call them 'politicians' or 'ministers'. These people are easy to identify on monuments as they had ranking titles (see p. 5). The function of these titles was to announce the position of an official in Egyptian society. People with these ranking titles are the subject of this book.

On the famous Narmer palette (*c.* 3000 BC) the king is shown on one side in a procession. Behind him is depicted a man bearing the sandals of the king and in front of him another one labelled 'tjet'. The meaning of this word is much disputed. Is it the name of the official, or his title?[1] Despite our uncertainty over the exact translation and meaning of this word, the monument shows that the king's officials were already regarded as an important part of royal representation at the beginning of Egyptian history. Many officials are known from the First, Second and Third Dynasties, and many of them were involved in organising royal estates and the food supply for the palace. There were certainly also local officials responsible for single towns or regions, but they are hardly visible, known only indirectly from some huge provincial tombs.

Writing was at this time mainly used at the palace and had not reached the provinces. In the Fourth Dynasty, around 2650 BC, if not before, more constant institutions developed. At the head of the administration there was now the vizier, often with the title 'overseer of all royal works', announcing that he was the main person in charge of building the king's pyramid. Other important titles at the royal court were the 'overseer of the double treasury', the 'overseer of the double granary' and the 'personal scribe of the king'.[2] These are all key designations, but it should be mentioned that they were not really offices in our modern

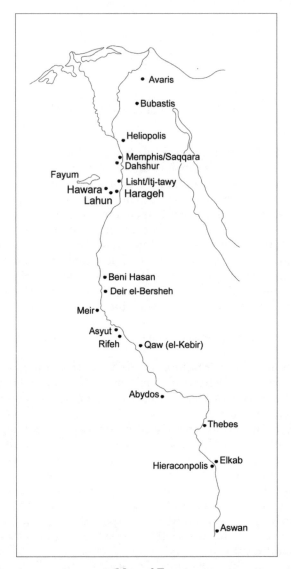

1. Map of Egypt.

sense of the word. A single high court official could bear one or several of these titles. This changed from one situation to another; the king might give one official many important titles, another only one or two. At the royal court of the Old Kingdom in Memphis there were also many officials without administrative titles, but with titles relating to the well-being of the king such as 'royal hairdresser' and 'royal nail cutter'. Physicians also played an important role at the royal court. This is clear not only from their big tombs in cemeteries at the royal residences, but also from their long lists of titles.

At the end of the Old Kingdom changes in administration are visible. There now appears to be a high number of viziers, suggesting that several of them acted at the same time. The provinces became stronger and there were viziers at certain places in the provinces. After the long reign of Pepy II the Old Kingdom disintegrated. Local rulers in the provinces started to act like small kings, independently of the official king at Memphis. Little is known about the administration at the royal court in this period, known as the First Intermediate Period. This may have nothing to do with missing monuments, but rather with problems of dating them and the officials mentioned on them. However, there are indications that elements of Middle Kingdom administration had already appeared in this period. At Heracleopolis, which seems to have been the capital of the northern part of Egypt after the Old Kingdom, many tombs were found. The officials buried here had high positions, perhaps at the royal court of the First Intermediate Period in the North. Their titles are similar to titles in Old Kingdom tombs, but new titles also appear. A certain Sehu, for example, was 'treasurer', a function not previously known from the royal court of the Old Kingdom.[3]

In the First Intermediate Period there appeared in the South, at Thebes, at about the same time (*c.* 2150 BC) a new line of rulers with the names Antef and Mentuhotep. These kings are known as the Eleventh Dynasty. Around 2000 BC the second king with the name Mentuhotep managed to unite the whole of Egypt after defeating the kings in the North. This is the beginning of the Middle Kingdom. King Mentuhotep II started a huge building programme, reorganised the administration and the royal court and placed new local governors at certain towns all over the country. Little is known about the administration and the royal court of the kings before Mentuhotep II, while the men that surrounded him are quite well attested. These people built huge tombs and left several inscriptions. Their names also appear in the funerary monument of the king.

The following Twelfth Dynasty was one of the strongest to rule over Egypt. Eight kings reigned over about two hundred years. For titles and administration, but also in terms of material culture and burial customs, it is possible to divide the period into several phases. It is especially noticeable in the early Twelfth Dynasty that many traditions of the Old Kingdom are still alive. Title strings in mastabas and rock-cut tombs often bear many phrases already known from that time, but which in the Middle Kingdom perhaps bear merely symbolical meaning. Examples of such titles are 'mouth of all people of Buto'[4] or 'pillar of the leopard-skin',[5] to name but two. Some officials even hold two or more important function titles at the same time, or at least they appear together on the same monument. This was common in the Old Kingdom,

but is not common in the early Middle Kingdom and disappears completely after Senusret III. There are, for example, Mentuhotep and Siese
who hold the titles 'vizier' and 'treasurer'. Ipi is 'steward' and 'treasurer', while Zanofret is 'high steward' and 'overseer of the double granary'.
Often lower officials bear no titles at all. After Senusret I, however, the
long title strings often became shorter, while lower officials now appear
with titles. Around the time of the reigns of Senusret II and Senusret III
many new titles appear in the administration and the long title strings
of Old Kingdom type fall completely out of use, or at least are no longer
visible on the monuments. It will be shown that there is also a clear difference from the early Middle Kingdom in the way officials are represented on monuments. The later Middle Kingdom lasts to the middle of
the Thirteenth Dynasty, until the reign of king Merneferre Iy or shortly
after. He is the last king attested in Upper and Lower Egypt and after
his reign, or at least in the following years, the political unity of Egypt
seems to have fallen apart. In the following Second Intermediate Period
few officials are known, but there is the impression that late Middle
Kingdom traditions continued.

This book deals with the Middle Kingdom and the Second
Intermediate Period. However, a high percentage of the officials covered
in this volume belong to the late Middle Kingdom, that is the late
Twelfth and Thirteenth Dynasties. This is for two reasons. In this period, scarab seals with names and titles were used, which provide us with
an almost complete picture of the court. Furthermore, a large number of
Middle Kingdom stelae were produced in this period. By contrast, few
tombs of officials are datable to the late Middle Kingdom; there are more
belonging to the early Middle Kingdom. This represents a significant
gap in the archaeological research. The Second Intermediate Period is
badly documented in terms of high court officials. Few stelae are datable to the period, scarab seals with name and titles were produced only
in Lower Egypt and just a handful of tombs are known.

Titles of officials are very important in understanding the Egyptian
court. However, there are many problems for Egyptologists attempting
a detailed understanding of titles. First of all, it is not always possible to
translate a title, and even when there is a translation, this does not necessarily provide a reliable guide to what an official did. While the title
'overseer of the house' might give a clue as to function from the translation, there are some problems in understanding a title such as 'mouth of
Nekhen'.

Most officials at the royal court and in the administration had one
or several titles. These titles generally expressed their function, but
they were also given as an honour or expressed certain responsibilities. In general terms it is possible to distinguish the following groups
of titles.

Titles

Function titles

The most important titles providing information on the holder and his duties are the function titles. On a monument, they normally appear directly before the name of a person. This title might come closest to describing the office or 'profession' of an official, although it must be admitted that it is often difficult to reveal the tasks of certain function titles. In general, it is dangerous to draw any parallels with the modern world about the use of titles. Function titles changed over time, so that those used in the early Middle Kingdom differed from the titles in use in the late Middle Kingdom or Second Intermediate Period.

Ranking titles

An official's ranking title provided information on his social status at the royal court. In the Middle Kingdom there were five of these titles. Their combination expressed the position of an official at the royal court. The most important title was 'iry-pat', perhaps best translated as 'member of the elite'. This title is known from the First Dynasty and was always exclusively given to a small circle of people around the king or to the highest officials in the provincial administration. The second important ranking title was 'haty-a', 'foremost of action', always placed after 'member of the elite' in the title strings. This title was also used by local governors and in this context is best translated as 'mayor' or 'governor'. With the meaning of 'mayor' the title was placed directly in front of the name or in front of 'overseer of priest' in inscriptions; as a ranking title it appeared after 'foremost of action' and before 'royal sealer', the third ranking title.

'Royal sealer' (khetemty-bity) is perhaps the most significant ranking title of the Middle Kingdom. The title is again known from the First Dynasty. In the later Middle Kingdom it became the most important one, expressing a high function at the royal court. While there were only a few people with the titles 'member of the elite' and 'foremost of action', this title became central to denote a royal official. After the Twelfth Dynasty 'royal sealers' in the provinces also appear sporadically and it seems likely that they had a special high position.

Finally, the fourth ranking title was 'semeher-waty',[6] 'sole friend' (of the king). The title rarely appears alone, but is most often found in a title string together with the other titles just discussed. There are a few exceptions where the title appears as the only ranking title in title strings. This might indicate a special social status outside the 'normal' court hierarchy. In the Thirteenth Dynasty and Second Intermediate Period the title becomes rare. Only the 'treasurer' bears the title regularly and it seems to be a sign of his higher position.

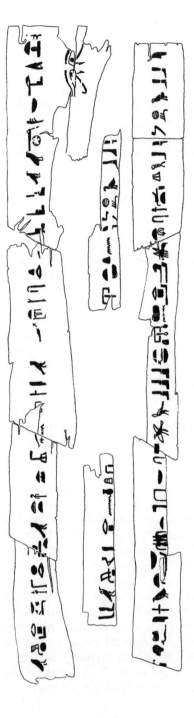

2. Fragments of the coffin belonging to the 'lector priest' Bebi, First Intermediate Period. 'Lector priest' is not a high title. However, Bebi bears the ranking titles 'member of the elite, foremost of action, royal sealer' and 'sole friend', common even for people of low status in this period. In the Middle Kingdom these titles were restricted to the upper levels of society.

1. Historical Background

These four are the classical ranking titles. They generally appear in a sequence and in the same order. Their combination is important. Someone stating on a monument that his only title is 'member of the elite' was at the top at the administration and second only to the king. Officials with the full sequence, 'member of the elite', 'foremost of action', 'royal sealer' and 'sole friend', were still important people, but lower ranking than the official bearing the single title. Interestingly, the title 'foremost of action' was rarely used as the sole ranking title, while 'royal sealer' became the most important sole ranking title in the late Middle Kingdom and Second Intermediate Period.

These ranking titles are important in identifying the people who were the highest officials in Ancient Egypt. They were the 'elite' of Ancient Egypt. Ranking titles are almost always combined with a function title, exceptions to this being extremely rare.

A further ranking title should be mentioned. The 'rekh-nisut', 'king's acquaintance' is important, especially in the Eleventh and Twelfth Dynasties.[7] As a sole ranking title, it announced a high position at the royal court, just below the titles already discussed. 'King's acquaintance' could also appear at the end of the above mentioned titles. Interestingly, the highest officials such as the vizier or the 'treasurer' avoided this label; this can be seen from the Old Kingdom when there is no vizier with that title. The title was obviously seen as important for some people, but not relevant for the highest officials.

In the late Middle Kingdom 'king's acquaintance' became a function title for people working in the administration of the treasurer at the royal palace. In these cases the title appears directly in front of the name of the title-holder.

Ranking titles were already used in the Old Kingdom to denote a high position of an official at the royal court. At the end of the Old Kingdom, and especially in the First Intermediate Period, they lost their importance. At certain places, almost everybody who had an inscribed monument boasted of being a 'member of the elite' or 'foremost of action'. This is best seen on the stelae found at Naga ed-Deir. These stelae are often of rather poor quality and the function titles of the people they commemorate are often low, but they claim many of these high titles. At other places the titles were still confined to a limited number of people. This did not change until the reign of Mentuhotep II, who restricted the ranking titles to a small number of people, to the highest managers of the Egyptian court and state.[8]

Other titles and biographical phrases

Other titles borne by officials might indicate a certain honour, refer to certain events in their lives, or express certain responsibilities. One example is 'overseer of all royal works in the whole country'. In the Middle Kingdom, the title appears within title strings and rarely directly in front of the name of the title-holder. It also appears with different variations, such as 'overseer of all royal works in the whole country' or just 'overseer of all works'.[9] These are two reasons for thinking that this is not a function title, but rather a phrase announcing an event in the life of the official. Most officials with this title had high function titles such as vizier, 'overseer of the gateway' or 'treasurer'.

Many titles and biographical phrases are centred on the king. The king was the heart of Egyptian society. He was in many respects perceived as the centre of the Egyptian universe. This is clearly expressed in many biographical phrases which might provide a clue to the position of officials relating to the king and also to other officials. 'Who filled the heart of the king'[10] is a popular biographical phrase, as are 'foremost in position in the palace',[11] 'the one in the heart of his lord' and 'the one in the heart of the king',[12] each providing a good idea of this element within the title strings of some officials. Egyptian society has been described as a 'court society'.[13] Every step of a higher official's career, at least in inscriptions, is related to the favour of the king. However, although the king is an important part of biographical phrases in the texts of high state officials, the king is only one part of the self-presentation of officials.

In the Eleventh and Twelfth Dynasties there seems to have been a clear distance between officials and the king. In the Old Kingdom, king's sons became high officials. Many viziers of the Fourth Dynasty were part of the royal family. High officials were also married to kings' daughters. The royal family and the circle of the people around the king were basically one big family. For the Middle Kingdom, before the Thirteenth Dynasty, nothing like that is attested. The king's daughters were most likely not married to commoners, not even to the highest state officials. Or at least there is so far no evidence for it. The sons of the kings did not become high state officials. The Twelfth Dynasty king's son Ameny appears in an inscription on a mission for the king. However, he does not have any administrative title and it has been argued that he was the crown prince. A similar case is the king's son Amenemhat-ankh, known from a number of monuments. He bears religious titles not often otherwise attested. He is the only well-known king's son of the Twelfth Dynasty and obviously had a special status. He was certainly not part of the regular administration, as his unique titles indicate.[14] This changed only in the Thirteenth Dynasty and Second Intermediate Period, when there is evidence that at least some kings were closely related to officials. It might be assumed that many of the short-reigned kings of this period came from families of officials.

1. Historical Background

Sources

The sources providing information on the high officials are essential for understanding the limits and potential of current research. There are several different types of sources for officials of the Middle Kingdom.

Stelae

The highest number of Middle Kingdom stelae was found in Abydos. This town was one of the most significant religious centres of the period. Many of those who could afford to do so built a chapel there in order to be symbolically close to Osiris, god of the underworld, and to the offerings made for him. There is good evidence for some mysteries or dramatic plays being performed at the town and there was always much building work going on at the main temple.

About 2,000 stelae have been found at Abydos, giving the impression that these represent a good average of the people belonging to the ruling class who could afford to set up a stela. However, many officials well known from other places are simply missing. So who were the people putting up stelae at Abydos? Perhaps the most logical explanation is that these were officials working, at least for a short time, in or near the town. Thus we have many stelae of 'treasurers' and their staff, because they were involved in local building projects. Many viziers are missing, certainly because they were not occupied on such projects. The Abydos stelae are therefore an important source, but only for a certain selection of people.

The information given by stelae changed over time. In the Eleventh Dynasty and under Amenemhat I, people, especially lower officials, appear on monuments often without any titles at all. At the same time, there are some biographical inscriptions and other officials often have long title strings. The people depicted on stelae are mainly the owner of the stela, his family and his servants. Under Senusret I till about Senusret III, there are still many biographical inscriptions.

In the late Middle Kingdom biographical inscriptions became rare. The only longer texts frequently found are hymns to Osiris or other deities of the Underworld.[15] Title strings in this period and for the Second Intermediate Period are much shorter, but the titles themselves become more precise. The range of people depicted on stelae changed. There are still many stelae that show the family of the stela owner and his servants, but on other stelae groups of people working together are shown. Clearly people at a certain place connected by work commissioned stelae. These stelae are an especially important source for the relationships between officials.

The dating of stelae is a problem, in that only a small number bear the name of a king. For the Twelfth Dynasty before the reign of Senusret II, it is possible to group several of them together based on their having similar patterns, as well as sharing stylistic and iconographical features.[16] Some of the stelae belonging to each group are datable and therefore the other stelae in these groups can also be at least roughly dated. For the late Middle Kingdom several other groups have so far been identified, but most cannot as yet be dated more precisely. This is especially problematic as the custom of placing a royal name on a stela stopped almost completely.

Tombs

The tombs of Middle Kingdom officials are not yet well known. Most Middle Kingdom cemeteries are badly researched and often much destroyed. The exceptions are several provincial rock-cut tombs, often entirely decorated and therefore providing valuable information on the life of these local officials. Several of these tombs have long biographical inscriptions.

The evidence from the tombs of high court officials provides a more balanced picture of the people in the administration. Important officials working only at the palace, who normally did not go on missions, would not appear on stelae found in Abydos, but had their tombs at the royal residence. Tombs of many state officials are indeed known from the Eleventh and early Twelfth Dynasties at Thebes. There are those of the viziers Dagi and Ipi, the 'treasurers' Khety and Meketre, the 'stewards' Henenu and Buau, the 'overseer of sealers' Meru, and the 'overseer of troops' Antef. For the not so well excavated and published cemeteries of the Twelfth Dynasty the picture is more broken, but there is still a range of officials attested, providing at least an idea of their importance, especially if the tomb sizes are compared. The few surviving remains indicate that at least some tombs were decorated with biographical inscriptions. This would be a first class historical source, but most of these inscriptions are now lost. So far few tombs are known for the Second Intermediate Period, perhaps because they were no longer monumental structures and so more vulnerable to destruction.

There was more space in tombs for placing titles and title strings, and we are therefore often confronted with a much higher number of titles and title strings for these tomb owners. Sometimes it is a problem even to see the function title as different titles appear in front of the tomb owner. However, these cases are rare and concentrated in the early Middle Kingdom, when titles and title strings are often still very much in the Old Kingdom tradition.

Scarabs

One major source of information for Thirteenth Dynasty officials is the corpus of scarab seals. In most cases they provide only the titles and names of officials. Any identification with officials known from other monuments must therefore be made with some reservation, especially if they have a common name and title. However, it is alarming how many officials are only known from seals. For the mid-Thirteenth Dynasty they seem to provide a full picture of the court; for other periods, when scarabs were not so common, this is not the case. For the periods when seals were rarer, a high number of officials are almost certainly missing, confirmed by recent excavations at Dahshur where many newly discovered tombs belong to officials not known from other sources.

So far, the earliest securely datable scarab with the name and titles of an official belongs to the 'foremost of action, overseer of the Northerners and leader of the king's acquaintances' Antef.[17] His title combination is unique and it is therefore almost certain that an Antef with identical titles, known from a stela, refers to the same person. The stela bears the name of a king Senusret, without providing a second royal name. At first glance it might seem an open question which Senusret the stela belongs to.[18] However, royal name scarab seals appear at the end of the Twelfth Dynasty under Senusret III[19] and it seems likely that private name scarabs appear at about the same time. Senusret therefore most likely refers to Senusret III. Interestingly, the scarab of Antef belongs in many ways to a type normally assigned to the Thirteenth Dynasty, thus demonstrating the problems researchers are facing when attempting to date scarabs.[20] In the Twelfth Dynasty scarabs with names and titles are rare. In the Thirteenth Dynasty they became more common and are more often stylised, although they are often still nicely crafted. The scarab of Antef mentioned above dates under Senusret III, although it is of a style previously thought to belong to the Thirteenth Dynasty (the crucial point seems to be its back type; 'back type 6' dates to the Thirteenth Dynasty), indicating that this type started much earlier than was formerly thought. Other private name scarabs dated by their style ('back type 3') to the Twelfth Dynasty and belonging to the highest officials include a lapis lazuli scarab from tomb E.108 at Abydos of the 'master of the secrets of the king's domain, royal sealer' and 'treasurer' Hor[21] and another one of the 'member of the elite, foremost of action, royal sealer, sole friend, overseer of the police, leader of all kilts in greatness' Senusret.[22] The latter scarab is made of a green and yellow speckled stone, obviously some special material confirming the impression that the name and title scarabs of the Twelfth Dynasty were regarded as something special. The Twelfth Dynasty dating of both scarabs is confirmed by the inclusion of biographical phrases on the scarabs, which are only rarely found on other monuments after this period.

Another option for dating scarabs is the epithet 'wehem ankh' – 'repeating life', which sometimes appears after a name on objects of the Thirteenth Dynasty and later periods. A third option for dating scarabs and monuments of high officials in general is the writing of 'Lower Egyptian king' in the title 'royal sealer'. This writing provides a rough guide for the scarabs of the mid Second Intermediate Period. The full

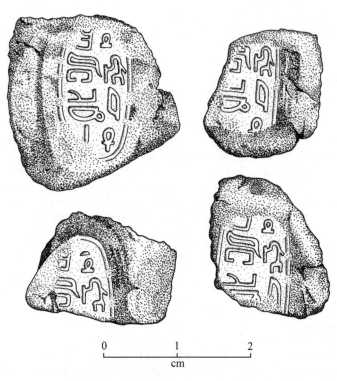

0   1   2
cm

3. Seal impressions of the 'royal sealer' and 'high steward' Aki, found at Nubt (Naqada). Seal impressions with names and titles were found at most late Middle Kingdom settlement sites and indicate that sealing goods and documents was an important administrative task. The recording of seal impressions by drawing and photography is always a problem. They are small, often broken and in many cases the signs are not clearly visible. In this example, Aki has the epithet *wehem-ankh* – 'repeating life'. However, the sign for *wehem* is barely legible.

translation of the title in question is 'sealer of the Lower Egyptian king'. In the early Middle Kingdom 'Lower Egyptian king' is always written with a bee. In the Thirteenth Dynasty, the writing with a red crown appears. This is the only writing used for the title for the rest of the Second Intermediate Period. Following this observation, the officials with the title 'royal sealer', exactly the group of people under research, can be dated into two groups. On seals, the writing seems to have changed under Sobekhotep IV. The officials with the bee on their seals date to the early Thirteenth Dynasty, those with the red crown to the second half of that Dynasty and later, although there are some single pieces showing the red crown which are perhaps datable under Neferhotep I or slightly earlier.[23]

1. Historical Background

Rock inscriptions

Expeditions to quarries, military missions or other missions to rocky regions often left inscriptions in the area they were sent to. They were either carved on the rocks or even placed on stelae. These inscriptions provide valuable information on the organisation of the expeditions and the people involved. A high percentage of the inscriptions are precisely dated with a king's name and often even with a year date. The type of inscription changed within the Middle Kingdom. In the early Middle Kingdom, descriptions of the expedition are most common. They often include many biographical phrases and a date. In the late Middle Kingdom, this type of inscription became less common. Now, just the list of family members of the main person in charge and of the expedition members appears; dates are rare. This reflects the situation known from other stelae of the same period. Prosopographical data are becoming richer, narrative texts are less common. Few rock inscriptions can be dated after the late Thirteenth Dynasty and Second Intermediate Period. This reflects the decline of royal expeditions in these periods.

Other objects

Names of officials appear on a number of different objects. They range from coffins, statues and weights to vessels. Most of these objects bear just the title and the name. If it is possible to date the official, the inscriptions are often important for providing a date of the object itself. One example of a common object with a unique inscription is a staff found in the burial of Senebni bearing a dedication of his king. It bears a short formula 'given in honour by the king to the royal sealer, overseer of marshland dwellers Senebni' and it bears the king's name Sewahenre.[24] A highly exceptional object is the bronze finial of a ship's mast, mentioning an otherwise unknown vizier Qemeni. [25]

2

The Vizier, 'Prime Minister' of Egypt

In almost all periods of Egyptian history the vizier was the highest office at the royal court. Some of the most famous Egyptian men held this position, such as Mereruka of the Old Kingdom and Rekhmire or Ramose in the New Kingdom. They are well known from their decorated mastabas at Saqqara or Theban tomb chapels. The word 'vizier' is of Persian origin and denotes the most important minister next to the ruler in several Islamic countries. In nineteenth-century Egyptology it was taken from there and refers in Egyptological literature to an official with the title 'tjaty'. Although they may have had responsibilities similar to those of Persian viziers, it should always kept in mind that 'vizier' is a translation of a specific word with a specific meaning in another culture and time. Another possible translation of the word 'tjaty' would be 'prime minister' or 'premier'. However, since it is hard to provide an exact translation of 'tjaty' it seems wise to continue to use 'vizier'.

The office of the vizier dates back to the Old Kingdom. The first secure example of a person with the title is Menka, dating to the Second Dynasty and attested on several inscriptions of vessels found re-used in the pyramid complex of the Third Dynasty king Djoser.[1] In the Fourth Dynasty there appears a sequence of title-holders, indicating that the office became regular. At this time they often had the title 'overseer of all royal works' and were therefore most likely the main organisers of the royal pyramid buildings. From their families it is clear that they were closely related to the king, some were sons of kings or married to a king's daughter. In the later Old Kingdom this changed a bit, but it seems clear from the sources that many of them still had close ties to the king and were still the main builders of the pyramids. Especially from the Sixth Dynasty there are many title-holders known, making it possible that there was more than one vizier at a given time.[2] The office is not well attested in the First Intermediate Period in the North of Egypt, but it seems likely that it was still important and it is just that the sources are missing, for there are indications that the administration in the North went on without a major break.

The Antef kings of the early Eleventh Dynasty organised their court like that of a private estate. They therefore had no vizier in their administration; at least no vizier is so far attested for these kings. With the unification of the country under Mentuhotep II, the king also reorganised the royal court and introduced several offices, already known from the royal court of the Old Kingdom. The most important new office taken over from the Old Kingdom was that of the vizier.

Duties and functions

The functions of the vizier are better known than those of many other officials. In several New Kingdom tombs of viziers there is a text describing his daily tasks, known in Egyptology as the 'Duties of the Vizier'. The dating of the composition is disputed, but there are reasons to assume that it was composed at the end of the Middle Kingdom, reflecting the situation at that time.[3] According to this text, the vizier was the main person in charge of the whole palace administration, who also oversaw the civil and provincial administration. He was also the main judge of Egypt. The vizier was responsible for right procedures in the offices and would punish in case of wrongdoing. To the vizier were reported the closing and opening of certain 'enclosures', which were sealed. He received notice of everybody entering and leaving the palace complex. In the same way officials responsible for the security of the palace reported to him. He met with the 'treasurer' and both officials exchanged reports about their own affairs. Together, they opened the 'Gold House', which is the Egyptian description of the royal workshops.[4]

The vizier was the head of the provincial administration. In the tomb of the New Kingdom vizier Rekhmire local officials are depicted bringing revenues of some kind, often described in modern literature as taxes. Several place names are mentioned, some of them, like Wahsut (south Abydos), are of Middle Kingdom towns, no longer important in the New Kingdom, indicating that this list is a copy of a late Middle Kingdom original, reflecting the situation in that period. It further confirms the impression that many legal texts relating to the vizier in the New Kingdom tombs were originally composed in the late Middle Kingdom. In the 'Duties of the Vizier' it is also mentioned that he appoints certain local officials. In the early Middle Kingdom several governors of Khemenu (Hermopolis in Middle Egypt) received the vizier's title and gained with it special responsibilities for organising the provinces (see p. 112).

Although the 'Duties of the Vizier' gives us a good idea of what viziers actually did, other sources need to be consulted as well in order to gain a fuller picture. There was an institution translated as 'office of the vizier', which appears in several texts of the Middle and New Kingdom. This office is related to several places. On seals appears the 'office of the vizier of the southern town'[5] and the 'office of the vizier of the head of the South',[6] both obviously referring to such an office in Thebes. Other seals refer to an office in the Fayum region once mentioned as being in Hotep-Senusret, the ancient name of the pyramid town at Lahun.[7] It may seem strange that this office is not yet attested for Itj-tawy, the Middle Kingdom capital, but as the main office at the capital it may have had no special qualification and been known simply as 'the office of the vizier'.

The physical remains of such an office have not yet been found or identified. This comes as no great surprise as Thebes and Itj-tawy have not yet been excavated. Hotep-Senusret has been quite well unearthed. However, there are almost no structures which could be identified as offices or administrative buildings. They might be destroyed, or situated in the part of the town not yet excavated. However, another option is that this 'office' was in the house of the vizier itself, and was the main reception room of a vizier's house, similar to the 'diwan' in the Islamic Period.[8] On the other hand the 'office of the vizier' is listed in a papyrus as head office for the palace,[9] making it more likely that it was located in the palace, although where is uncertain.[10]

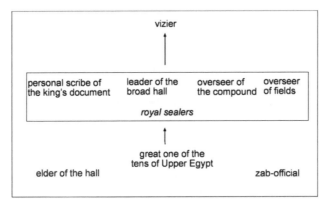

4. Hierarchy under the vizier.

For the Middle Kingdom it is possible to reconstruct several careers of viziers, and certain career patterns are visible. This is important as it is possible to see from which part of the administration officials were appointed to the position of a vizier. This is also helpful for establishing command hierarchies, thus providing further evidence for the administration under the vizier and his tasks.

In the early Middle Kingdom there are three viziers closely connected with the 'treasurer'. Bebi had that office before becoming vizier;

Montuhotep and Siese had both titles and were perhaps 'treasurers' honoured with the vizier's title but not carrying out the vizier's full functions. A similar situation is visible for certain local governors of the early Middle Kingdom. The 'treasurer' was the second most important official at the royal court and it seems that in the case of Montuhotep and Siese the two most powerful titles were united in one person. In the case of the local governors it shows the importance of the vizier in the provincial administration.

In the late Twelfth and Thirteenth Dynasties there is no longer any secure evidence for the close connection between 'treasurer' and vizier (however, compare Sobekemhat on p. 31). This might indicate that in the late Middle Kingdom the branches of administration were much more clear-cut than before. There was the vizier branch on one side, and that of the 'treasurer' on the other. There are few indications of officials crossing in their career from one branch to the other, while there is plenty of evidence for officials making careers within one of these branches. Indeed other offices closely connected to the vizier were the 'personal scribe of the king's document', the 'overseer of fields', the 'leader of the broad hall' and the 'overseer of the compound'. All these offices seem to have strong links to scribal offices, work organisation and legal matters at the palace. They all had the ranking title 'royal sealer'. Under these officials were, in the late Middle Kingdom, the zab-official, the 'elder of the hall' and the 'great one of the tens of Upper Egypt', people obviously also closely connected to the vizier and his administration. The real meaning and function of these titles remains largely obscure. However, these people seem to be involved in legal matters and related to the palace, perhaps acting as representatives of the vizier in different tasks throughout the whole country. They rarely bear ranking titles and were therefore clearly under the other officials mentioned in rank.

Viziers on special missions

The different tasks of the viziers are also reflected in their titles, in the depictions in their tombs and in texts relating to them found in almost all parts of the country. Investigating these sources it should be made clear that it is unlikely that the Egyptian administration had a legal code in which the tasks and duties of all officials were fixed. The 'Duties of the Vizier' may be an exception, but this is perhaps not a legal document, rather a glorification of the office. The function of titles certainly changed over time. It is therefore problematic to compare documents from different periods, even if they refer to the same title. Furthermore, many biographical inscriptions mention special events in the life of an official. These may not reflect their usual assignment but something exceptional, and could therefore give a false impression to a modern researcher.

2. The Vizier, 'Prime Minister' of Egypt

The Eleventh Dynasty vizier Dagi had a huge tomb at Thebes. It is so far the only vizier's tomb with some scenes from this period which are published. Of the several wall paintings which were preserved when recorded in the early twentieth century, today only few remains are still visible. On one wall Dagi is shown standing with his wife in front of workmen in the treasury, indicating that he had some responsibility over this institution. This is especially remarkable as no later vizier was involved in the treasury. This responsibility is also reflected by Dagi's title 'overseer of the double treasury'.[11]

The viziers Amenemhat under Mentuhotep IV and Antefiqer under Senusret I appear in several expedition and military inscriptions. After these reigns and until the Thirteenth Dynasty, no vizier was involved in any military campaign or expedition, or at least this is not reported in our sources. This might demonstrate a shift in function. It will be seen that this also applies to other high officials. Obviously in the early Middle Kingdom people close to the king were sent on important missions. The king wanted only people he could trust on such operations. Later, not so high officials were chosen, presumably because the administration was established and the king could rely on it.

Remarkably little is known about special missions and tasks of viziers for the rest of the Twelfth and the Thirteenth Dynasty. There are several rock inscriptions of the vizier Ameny at Aswan, the vizier Neferkare Iymeru placed a statue into the sanctuary of Heqaib on Elephantine indicating that he worked in that region and visited the place. The vizier Senusret, who served under Senusret I, travelled to Koptos, and this mission is mentioned in one of the tombs at Beni Hasan. Viziers are well attested at Abydos, although not so well as the 'treasurers' who most likely went there for building projects, while viziers are not so much involved or in charge of these. One exception might be the building of pyramids, and it is therefore no surprise that there was a vizier's office at Lahun, a place from which the building of Amenemhat III's pyramid at Hawara and most likely the pyramid complex of Senusret II was organised.

Titles of viziers

Unlike many others, the functional title of the vizier consisted of not only one, but a combination of titles. The core element was certainly 'tjaty', vizier, but it is rare that the title appears alone. The most common title combined with vizier was 'overseer of the city'.[12] This is certainly not an expression for 'mayor', as 'mayor' (hati-a) is a title in its own right. In fact, at the end of the Old Kingdom 'overseer of the city' was introduced as a title for viziers and it seems that it represents the responsibility of the vizier for the administration of the pyramid town, and perhaps in this context the organisation of building the pyramid.

Later it seems that the title become a traditional part of the vizier's titles, especially as in the Eleventh Dynasty and the Second Intermediate Period no pyramid towns are attested, and there is no evidence that viziers were in charge of the pyramid towns of the Twelfth Dynasty, although the office is well attested at Lahun. The same traditional inclusions of old titles seem to apply to the other elements of the vizier's titulary. The titles 'zab-official'[13] and 'belonging to the curtain' (tatiti)[14] are known from the First Dynasty. Their real significance is still under discussion, but one has the impression that in the Middle Kingdom they were used mainly for traditional reasons.

While there are only a few examples in which 'overseer of the city' does not appear in the titles of the vizier, the other titles were used on monuments only sporadically and often dropped in shorter inscriptions. The last important title of a vizier is 'overseer of the six great houses'.[15] Again this dates back to the Old Kingdom, and it is often translated 'overseer of the six law courts'. However, there is not much evidence that there were law courts in ancient Egypt. The title might rather symbolically express some responsibility over six important administrative units, which also dealt with legal matters. In the Middle Kingdom the title is not restricted to viziers, but also sporadically used by other officials.

Ranking titles were important for announcing the high position of an official at the royal court. This is also true for the viziers. However, in this context it should be pointed out that they do not appear often with the vizier. While there were several 'treasurers' and 'stewards' in the country, there was only one vizier. He was not forced to announce his important status at the royal court with ranking titles. Nevertheless, when they appear, the vizier always bears the highest title. Interestingly, the title 'royal sealer' does not appear often, and the title 'king's acquaintance' never appears.

Besides these titles, typical for a vizier, they could bear many others, most often expressions and biographical phrases also known from other court officials. Dagi, for example, was 'leader of all kilts'[16] and 'setem-priest'.[17] These are ritual titles connected with king, perhaps deriving from officials especially responsible for the royal kilt. Whether this still applies for the Middle Kingdom is not really known. Dagi was also 'mouth of Nekhen'.[18] Nekhen is the Egyptian name of Hieraconpolis, the city of the royal god Horus in Upper Egypt. These titles are old, dating back to the Old Kingdom, but their function and meaning are totally obscure.

The vizier is often called the highest judge of Egypt. However, officials on different levels often had titles indicating their juridical functions. The most common of these titles is perhaps 'priest of Maat'. Maat was the goddess and personification of justice. An official with this title therefore most likely had some responsibility in this area. No temple of

Maat is known in the Middle Kingdom, so the priestly title was probably symbolic. Service for Maat was service for justice. Another even more symbolic title was 'master of the secret in hearing alone', indicating some kind of special power in juridical matters not for public cases, but perhaps for those of a more private nature involving affairs of the king. Finally, there are several titles in the Old Kingdom often connected with juridical functions. This is basically assumed because they appear in a context of other juridical titles. To these belong 'pillar of the leopardskin' and 'staff of the rekhyt people'.

A formal juridical system did not exist in the Middle Kingdom. There were no people acting solely as judges. Instead, juridical functions were performed in different ways. In towns and villages a group of people was formed when needed, often called 'qenbet'. They decided together about troubled cases. Most likely there was no legal code, nor were laws written down. The 'qenbet' judged according to tradition. At work places and outside the close environment of communities, the situation was most likely slightly different. Here the highest person in charge would judge in cases of trouble within his people. The best example of the latter practice is the story of the Eloquent Peasant. Some injustice was done to the peasant and in order to have things put right he went to the 'high steward'. The 'high steward' was normally an official more concerned with estates of the king and agricultural products of the palace. However, in the case of this story the 'high steward' was the owner or administrator of the lands on which the peasant was badly treated. As holder of these lands the 'high steward' was therefore responsible for everything that happened on them, including all possible juridical disputes.

On expeditions it was the leader who acted as judge of the people, so many 'overseers of troops' have juridical titles.

The staff of the vizier

It is not easy to reconstruct the staff of people around and under the vizier. Most of the title-holders known from the sources relating to the vizier's staff belong to the late Middle Kingdom, after the time of Senusret II. This leaves a gap in our sources for the early Middle Kingdom. However, for both the early and the late Middle Kingdom we know of the 'scribe of the vizier'.[19] His main task was not being literally the scribe of the vizier, but working at different places around the country for the vizier as his deputy, since they appear in most sources as independently acting officials. The 'chamberlain of the vizier's office'[20] is not so well attested, and little can be said about his duties, but he was obviously in some way in charge of the organisation of the vizier's office. The 'keeper of items, with right of entry' sat in formal meetings next to the vizier, on his left side.[21] This official is mentioned in the 'Duties of the Vizier'. Another official appearing in

21

connection with the vizier is the 'great one of the tens of Upper Egypt'. This title is one of the most common in the late Middle Kingdom, but it is hard to be sure of its specific function. It might denote some kind of status rather than a special task. High officials with ranking titles also came under the vizier in the hierarchy, though it might be disputed whether they should be called 'staff'. However, it is possible to argue that the administration of fields, via the 'overseer of fields' and the scribal officials, via the 'scribe of the king's document' were under him. In general terms it must be said that the people working with the vizier must have changed from occasion to occasion. For an expedition he must have chosen certain people who normally were not directly under his command. The same can be seen with Antefiqer, who was responsible tor a building project and for this was in charge of 'stewards', officials normally not directly connected with a vizier.

One or two viziers?

In the New Kingdom there were two viziers operating at the same time, one in charge of Upper Egypt, the other in charge of Lower Egypt. It is uncertain and disputed whether the same situation applied in the Middle Kingdom, especially the late Middle Kingdom when the administration was reorganised on almost all levels. There are several indications that the office was already divided, although none of these are really conclusive.

In the early Middle Kingdom there are several governors at Khemenu with the titles of the vizier. Basically there are three opinions about them in research. Some scholars see them as titulary viziers, having the vizier's title just for reasons of honour, others see them as regular viziers, while recently it has been argued that they were regular viziers but with local functions.[22] From the middle of the Twelfth Dynasty there is no further evidence for two viziers.

New data are known from the late Middle Kingdom. At the town now called Lahun, in ancient times called Hotep-senusret, near the pyramid of Senusret II, many fragments of papyri were found. On one of them appears a list of wooden statues once placed in the pyramid temple of Senusret II. The list names the wood, the title of the statue owner and perhaps his name. The names are all destroyed, but some of the titles have survived. Interestingly in this context, the list starts with two statues of viziers.[23] It could be argued that both were in charge at about the same time. However, it could also be argued that they belonged to two successive viziers or even that they were two statues of the same vizier. A stela found at Abydos reports that the Thirteenth Dynasty vizier Ankhu came from the South to oversee building work at Abydos. Ankhu was therefore at Thebes, or at least south of Abydos, and it has been argued that his main office was there. However, it is possible to argue

2. The Vizier, 'Prime Minister' of Egypt

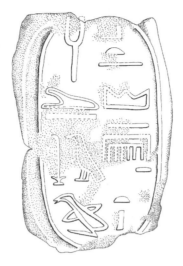

5. Seal impression found at Lahun, mentioning an office of the vizier for the Fayum. The text reads: 'Deliveries (?) of the Fayum, office of the vizier'.

that he was simply on a mission and on his way back to the North. The 'Duties of the Vizier' also clearly refers to two viziers and was most likely composed in the late Middle Kingdom.[24] However, there is always the option that it was 'updated' at least for certain points. Another hint is the distribution of objects relating to single viziers. Thirteenth Dynasty objects with the name of viziers were all found in Upper Egypt, giving the impression that this was their power base. The exceptions are some scarab seals of viziers found in Lisht. None of these viziers is known from other sources. They might be Lower Egyptian viziers. However, at the moment it is not possible to decide whether there were one or two viziers in the late Middle Kingdom. For each of the arguments given, others could be provided to challenge the evidence.

The vizier's attire

The vizier is one of the few Egyptian officials with special attire, a long garment covering the chest with a string or necklace around the neck. However, this developed only in the Twelfth Dynasty. There are few preserved depictions of viziers, so the development of their attire is hard to follow. On a relief found in the mortuary temple of Mentuhotep II at Deir el-Bahari, the vizier Bebi of the Eleventh Dynasty is shown in a short kilt, no different to depictions of other officials of the period (see Fig. 8). The vizier Dagi appears in his tomb at least twice in a long kilt

23

leaving his breast free. Around his neck he wears a long string with an object at the lower end, perhaps showing a cylinder seal. It has been argued for good reasons that this is the oldest depiction of the vizier's attire. In later representations, the cylinder seal would disappear under the dress of the vizier and just the necklace is still visible.[25] However, in the tomb of the 'overseer of troops' Antef was found a small fragment showing exactly this kind of cylinder seal in a necklace.[26] The fragment may belong to the figure of the tomb owner. It therefore seems that two officials under Mentuhotep II were shown with a long necklace and a cylinder seal: the vizier Dagi and Antef. It is possible to argue that the fragment does not belong to the tomb of Antef, or that a vizier was depicted in his tomb. However, there is so far no example of a tomb decoration of the Middle Kingdom depicting a colleague or an official of higher status than the tomb owner.[27]

There is no secure depiction of a vizier in service in the reign of Amenemhat I. There may be some local governors with the title of a vizier, but their exact position as vizier is disputable. Antefiqer is datable under Senusret I, and he is shown in the tomb of his wife or mother Senet at Thebes. Once he is hunting, and once he is standing partly dressed in a leopard skin. Beside him is depicted 'his beloved wife, the priestess of Hathor, Zatzasobek'.[28] There is nothing special about his dress in these depictions, which seem to relate not to his office as the vizier, but to the occasion on which he is depicted.

The next vizier known from a depiction is Senusret. He is shown twice on a stela now in the Louvre dated at the beginning of the reign of Amenemhat II. Here he has again some kind of long necklace, the lower end disappearing under his kilt which leaves the whole chest free. This is the earliest representation of a vizier in special attire.

There are two or three statues dating to the Twelfth Dynasty known showing an official with the same band or necklace around his shoulder, obviously representing viziers, although the inscriptions on these stat-

6. Bust of an early Twelfth Dynasty vizier.

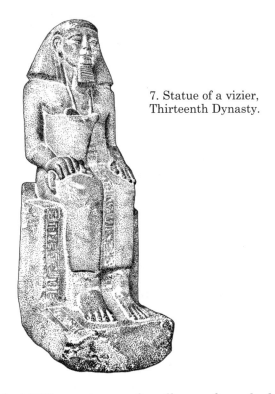

7. Statue of a vizier,
Thirteenth Dynasty.

ues are now lost.[29] The next examples all come from the late Twelfth or
even early Thirteenth Dynasty. Zamont is shown on a stela now in Cairo
(see Fig. 16 on p. 37) with a long kilt covering his legs and going up to
the belly. Under the long kilt there is a pleated short one. Again he has
some kind of necklace whose lower end disappears under the kilt.
Senusret-ankh is shown on a small stela now in Florence. He has a long
kilt, leaving much of the breast free, but there are again two strings visible and the kilt is a little bit higher. The next depictions of viziers are
known from the Thirteenth Dynasty, when Ankhu was in charge. There
is the statue of Ankhu's father, whose name on the statue is not preserved, and there are two statues of viziers close in style which were reinscribed in the Third Intermediate Period. One of them most likely
depicts Ankhu. In these statues the kilt is again higher. There is still a
necklace which now appears almost like straps of the long kilt. Later
this becomes the canonical way of depicting a vizier.

All depictions of viziers in relief and as statues belong to the period
from Sobekhotep II to about the reign of king Ibiau. No picture or statue of a Second Intermediate Period vizier is known, although the office
itself is still attested. The exception is a stela of the period found at Edfu
showing an Old Kingdom official, Isi, who was worshipped in later times

25

as a local deity. Although he was not vizier in his lifetime, he bears that title in later inscriptions. On this stela he is even depicted and shown with the vizier's attire. The partly destroyed text says: '... vizier Isi, the protector'.

History of the office holders

The first person in the Middle Kingdom with the titles of a vizier was most likely Bebi. He appears on a relief found in the mortuary temple of king Mentuhotep II in Deir el-Bahari (Fig. 8). This temple was once decorated with reliefs, including many pictures of people at the royal court. Bebi is not yet identified for sure on any other monument. However, there is a good chance that he is identical with the 'treasurer' Bebi, known from a stela. Before unification, the 'treasurer' was the most important official at the royal court. It therefore seems more than likely that with the unification and the introduction of the vizier, the most important official was appointed to the new office.[30]

A little more is known about Dagi, who seems to have followed Bebi as vizier at the end of the reign of Mentuhotep II. First in his career he held the important position of 'overseer of the gateway'. With this title he also appears on reliefs in the temple of king Mentuhotep II at Deir el-Bahari. In this position, he also seems to have prepared a rock-cut tomb not far from the mortuary palace of the king. His sarcophagus, decorated with religious texts and pictures, was found there. On this monument he appears with that title. It is not known when he was appointed vizier, but it was still in the reign of Mentuhotep II as he is depicted with the new title in the funerary temple of the king. With the promotion his tomb was extended and decorated. It had wall paintings, while other parts were decorated with fine reliefs, now only preserved in small fragments. All paintings name Dagi with the titles of a vizier, showing that the tomb's decoration was executed while he was already vizier.[31] His successor is not known for sure.

At about the same time there are several governors in the provinces with the title of vizier. In Egyptology there is no general agreement whether they hold the office as formal viziers at the capital or bear the title for honorific reasons.[32] Perhaps they had some local responsibilities similar to those of a vizier (p. 56).

Amenemhat is the most famous vizier of the Eleventh Dynasty, perhaps the most famous of the whole Middle Kingdom. He served king Mentuhotep IV at the end of the Eleventh Dynasty and is so far only known from several Wadi Hammamat rock inscriptions.

My majesty cause the coming of the member of the elite, the overseer of the town, vizier, overseer of all works, who fills the heard of the king, Amenemhat together with soldiers, 10,000 men of the

8. Relief showing the vizier Bebi.

southern nomes of Upper Egypt ... for bringing a great, pure block
from this mountain ... for (making) a coffin

Another inscription is dated to year 2 of Mentuhotep IV's reign and mentions his first Sed-festival. This inscription reports a miracle. A gazelle
appeared before the expedition and gave birth on a rock which turned
out to be perfect for the lid of the sarcophagus. In celebration of the
appearance of the gazelle it was sacrificed as an offering to Min.

Amenemhat as vizier is known only from rock inscriptions, but it has
always been assumed that he became king shortly afterwards; he
reigned over Egypt for about 30 years as Amenemhat (I). The viziers
under this king are a big problem. There is no vizier who can be placed
for certain in his time. Ipi was buried in a big rock-cut tomb at Thebes
and his name appears on the sarcophagus in the tomb chamber. Stylistic
considerations might place him at the beginning of the reign, but there
is no vizier known for the following years. The gap might be filled with
some governors in the provinces with the vizier's title, but as has
already been stated this remains problematic. In general there are not
many Abydos stelae securely datable under this king and the tombs of
high officials are mostly missing, making it possible that several viziers
are simply missing from the sources.

Antefiqer held the office of vizier in the last years of Amenemhat I and
the first part of the following reign. With him we are confronted with an
embarrassing wealth of sources. They demonstrate that with more information, new and more complex problems arrive. For most Middle
Kingdom officials there is simply a dating problem, but not with
Antefiqer. He is one of the best attested viziers of the Middle Kingdom.

He is known from the tomb of a woman called Senet in Thebes, from his own tomb in Lisht, from several rock inscriptions and from copies of letters found on papyri in a tomb at Naga ed-Deir in Upper Egypt. His origins are not recorded. His mother is called Senet. The name and position of his father are disputed and basically unknown. In the tomb of Senet, just mentioned, the figure of a man is overpainted and it has been assumed that this was his father. Next to this erased figure appears several times 'his beloved wife' Senet. A woman called Zatzasobek ('Daughter of the son of Sobek'), a 'priestess of Hathor', appears next to the preserved figure of Antefiqer in this tomb. Is it possible that the father, the husband of Senet, fell into dishonour and his figure was overpainted, while Antefiqer, the husband of Zatzasobek, did not suffer this fate and his figure was left intact? The case has been much debated. Recently it has been argued that in the scene of the journey to Abydos preserved on the south wall of the corridor in the chapel, the figure of Antefiqer is once preserved and once deleted. In comparison to other journeys to Abydos the same people appear, making it likely that the preserved and destroyed figures are of the same person.[33] This would weaken the argument that two officials are depicted in the tomb, one who was deleted and one whose figure was left. Only one person was shown in the tomb next to Senet, whose figure was rather inconsistently erased. It would mean that the one official shown was the vizier Antefiqer, born of Senet and with two wives: another Senet and Zatzasobek. That the wife and mother of Antefiqer had the same name is no problem. Senet is one of the most common female names of the early Middle Kingdom. However, the case is much more complicated, since the figure in the Abydos journey belongs to an area of the wall where great parts are destroyed, not just the figure of the unknown person as in other parts of the tomb. The person in the boat on the Abydos journey might not have been destroyed deliberately but simply have gone missing with this part of the wall. In the tomb of Senet, the name of the father is not preserved, but may appear on an 'execration text' as Antefiqer. 'Execration texts' were used in rituals and bear the names of enemies. The objects with these names were smashed, hoping that the destruction of the text would also hurt or kill the people named. This relates well to the overpainting of a figure in the tomb of Antefiqer at Thebes. At least one member of the family obviously fell into dishonour.

Antefiqer represents one of the few cases in the Middle Kingdom in which power struggles at the royal court are visible. Power struggles and intrigues at the royal palace, and most likely also at provincial courts, must have been common. Such events are not recorded in official inscriptions, where the court and the king appear in almost perfect harmony. Power struggles are visible only under certain circumstances. The Sixth Dynasty official Uni reports in his biographical inscription found at Abydos that he was involved in a court case against a queen. The text is very discreet and does not mention any details, not even the name of the queen, but provides evidence that everything was not as perfect as it often appears. More direct is the Teaching of Amenemhat, which dates to the Middle Kingdom. Here an attack on the king is described. It has been debated whether the king survived the attack or was killed. However, the important point in this context is that even in a literary composition, with a document certainly of a more official character than comparable modern compositions, such an event is mentioned. It remains unknown what happened to the father of Antefiqer, if he was the one who fell into dishonour. In the tomb of Antefiqer at Lisht there are no signs that his name was erased, although it is possible to argue that the whole tomb, and not just single inscriptions, was destroyed.

In the tomb of Senet, Antefiqer also bears the title 'foster-child of the king', indicating that he grew up at the royal court, perhaps close to Amenemhat I. His name might indicate that he was born in the Eleventh Dynasty, as Antef was the name of several kings of that Dynasty. Antefiqer means 'Antef, the excellent one'. There is some evidence for the enterprises of Antefiqer. Possibly the oldest documents mentioning him are several rock inscriptions found in Lower Nubia. One of them refers to the 'overseer of boats' Redies and says: 'Coming to Lower Nubia on behalf of the overseer of the city, vizier, zab-official, the one belonging to the curtain Antefiqer'. The vizier was obviously involved in military actions in Lower Nubia. A second inscription confirms this impression. It reports the fighting of another Antefiqer against Nubians and even states that the vizier was at this place. The dating of these inscriptions is disputed. They are both undated. At least one of them mentions a ship called Sehetepibre (the throne name of Amenemhat I). This might indicate that the inscriptions date to that king's reign, perhaps to his last years, although it is also possible that a ship with that name was in use even later. Most of the inscriptions found there date to the time of the co-regency between Amenemhat I and Senusret I, making it most likely that the inscriptions of Antefiqer also belong to around that period.

The next inscriptions of Antefiqer were found on the Red Sea coast and report an expedition to Punt:

His majesty (Senusret I) ordered to the member of the elite, foremost of action, overseer of the city, vizier, overseer of the six great houses Antefiqer, that he should build these ships on the dockyard of Koptos to travel to the mine of Punt in order to reach in peace and to come back in peace ... He (Antefiqer) finished his task very magnificently, as it was ordered to him by the majesty of the palace. See, the reporter Ameny, son of Mentuhotep was on the coast of the sea for building these ships together with the magistrate of the head of the South of Thinis. There were with him the soldiers on the coast of the sea ... the troops together with the reporter.

Antefiqer appears as the sender of three letters found on a papyrus in a tomb at Naga ed-Deir. They are written to the 'stewards of the palace in Thinis' and are about building work (on a dockyard?) in this region. They are dated to a year 17 (reading of the year not certain). The last datable inscription comes from the Wadi el Hudi and is dated to a year 20 (+ x; exact number not preserved). It reports the coming of an 'assistant treasurer' with the name Weni, who came under the charge of Antefiqer. Weni came here to collect amethyst, the main raw material found at the Wadi el-Hudi. Amethyst is a violet stone, often used for jewellery.

Antefiqer was most likely buried in his mastaba next to the pyramid of Amenemhat I at Lisht. The building is not well preserved but was once decorated with reliefs, there were remains of a false door and a statue was found.

The viziers after Antefiqer are not well known, the succession of these people remains often unclear, and the identification of several people with the same name creates further problems. It is possible that there was a vizier Antef in charge, but his inscriptions are hard to read and the titles are not well preserved, making it possible either that he is not a vizier or that he is Antefiqer. The famous 'treasurer' Mentuhotep, in office under Senusret I (see p. 56), appears on one stela with the titles of a vizier. It remains an open question whether he was in office for just a short period or bears the title as an honour without having the function of a vizier.

At the end of the reign of Senusret I a certain Senusret was in office. An inscription in a tomb at Beni Hasan reports that he was on a mission to Koptos. In the Louvre there is an Abydos stela showing him twice. It is an impressive monument again demonstrating the power of these officials. It is dated to year 8 of Amenemhat II. Senusret was buried at Lisht, where he had a big tomb. It was decorated with high quality reliefs and with a biographical inscription, found only in small fragments. The successor of Senusret might be a certain Ameny, mentioned on the annals stone of king Amenemhat II found at Memphis. The placing of a statue in a temple for Amenemhat II is mentioned. Nothing more is known about him. For the following years till the reign of Senusret III it is at the moment impossible to establish any reliable sequence of title-holders. There might have been another Ameny in charge, but his position is uncertain and the person mentioned on an offering table might be identical with Ameny known from the annals stone. The 'treasurer' Siese (see p. 57) also held the title of vizier, but his main function was that of 'treasurer' and there are doubts whether he was really a vizier in charge. To this period might also belong a certain Amenemhat-ankh, known only from fragments of a false door (Fig. 9).

9. Fragment of a false door belonging to the vizier Amenemhat-ankh.

The viziers under Senusret III are better attested. Sobekemhat had a big mastaba next to the pyramid of Senusret III at Dahshur. On the fragment of an offering table he appears as 'treasurer' (Fig. 10), indicating that he was promoted from that office to the position of the vizier. Although the publication of his mastaba is quite short by modern standards, it provides a good idea of a tomb of a high court official in the second half of the Twelfth Dynasty. The mastaba was placed north of the pyramid of Senusret III. It was the first in a row of three big mastabas, at least two of them belonging to viziers. The mastaba of Sobekemhat was built of mud bricks and measured about 14 m long and 9 m wide. The shaft leading to the burial chamber was found on the western side of the mastaba. From the shaft there was a small passageway leading to the burial apartments. The passageway was vaulted. The chamber at the end of it was small and its walls were covered with fine limestone blocks (Fig. 11). There was an undecorated sarcophagus and a stone canopic box next to it. The sarcophagus and canopic chest were found placed under the floor of the chamber, so that there were in effect two chambers one above the other. It remains uncertain whether this is the burial chamber of Sobekemhat or perhaps of his wife and his own burial was overlooked by the excavators. In the remains of the mastaba were found several limestone slabs providing us with the name and titles of Sobekemhat. The fragments of the already mentioned offering table record his title of 'treasurer'. Fragments of other inscriptions obviously once covered the outside of the mastaba. There is no indication that the inside was decorated or even had rooms. The published fragments (Fig. 12) most often show rows of titles: 'member of the elite', 'foremost of

31

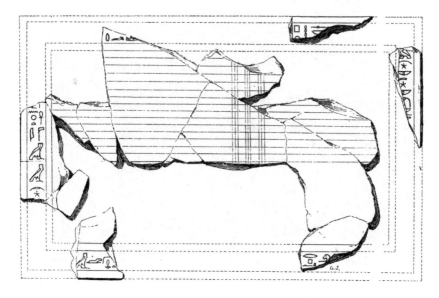

10. Offering table of Sobekemhat, where he appears as 'treasurer'.

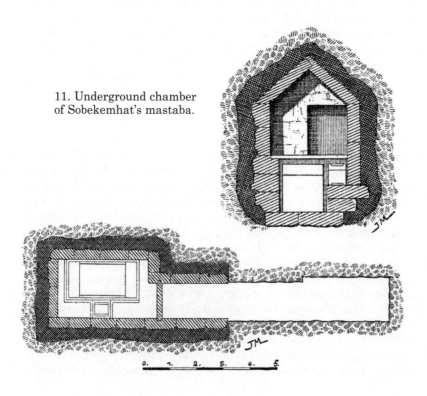

11. Underground chamber of Sobekemhat's mastaba.

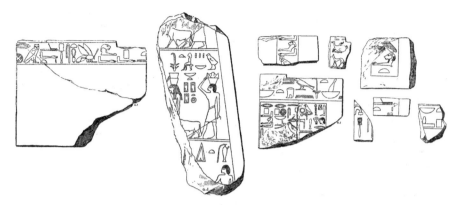

12. Reliefs from the mastaba of Sobekemhat, providing vizier's titles.

action', royal sealer', 'sole friend', 'overseer of the city', or: 'member of the elite', 'foremost of action', 'mouth of Buto', 'chief lector priest'. On only one fragment are figures visible. There are three rows of offering bearers. The latter fragment belonged to the corner of the mastaba. It shows that the walls of it were not straight but built at a certain angle. From other excavated mastabas it can be assumed that the front was adorned with two offering niches, one in the north, one in the south. The offering table may come from one of the niches.

Next to the mastaba of Sobekemhat, there was one for Nebit. It is a monument of the same scale. Nebit was most likely the successor of Sobekemhat, perhaps in the middle or at the end of the reign of Senusret III. Not much is known about him. The reliefs on his mastaba were found heavily destroyed. However, one wall survived well as it had already fallen down in ancient times and was covered by sand. Stone looters searching for building material missed these blocks. This wall shows mainly bands of inscriptions finely carved into the limestone.[34]

Khnumhotep was the last vizier at the end of the reign of Senusret III or perhaps already under Amenemhat III, when both kings ruled together. He was the son of the mayor of Menat-Khufu (a town near to Beni Hasan in Middle Egypt) and was a young man appointed to the royal court. He went on an expedition to the Red Sea, where at the Wadi Gasus a stela mentioning his operation was found. Another important point in his career was his involvement in a mission to Byblos, the sea port on the coast of Lebanon where cedar wood was traded. He finally became 'high steward' at the royal court and after that vizier.[35] He may have received the latter office late in his career and only for a short time. On his canopic chest found in his tomb he is still 'high steward'. The inscription in his tomb mentioning the title 'vizier' is rather carelessly executed, while the one mentioning 'high steward' is finely carved. This might indicate that the vizier title was a later addition to an already

13. Two examples of inscriptions found at the mastaba of Nebit. The relief is of the highest quality known from Ancient Egypt. The text on the left reads: 'member of the elite, foremost of action, overseer of the city, the one belonging to the curtain'.

existing decoration. However, the tomb has recently been re-excavated and new research may shed more light on this question.

For the remaining part of the reign of Amenemhat III and the following early Thirteenth Dynasty, several viziers are known, but most of them only as names. Khety is mentioned in a dated (year 29) papyrus found at Lahun and was perhaps involved in building work of the king's funerary temple at Hawara. A vizier Khety is also known from a New Kingdom reference in the tomb of the vizier Rekhmire, about 400 years later. As the name Khety is quite common, it remains uncertain whether both documents refer to the same person. However, this example makes us again aware that people well known from our sources were not automatically the most influential or important individuals in their times. Khety belongs to the least known viziers of the Middle Kingdom but was obviously still well known in the New Kingdom.

Ameny is known from three rock inscriptions found at Aswan and the Shat er-Rigal. The inscriptions provide good evidence for his family. He

2. The Vizier, 'Prime Minister' of Egypt

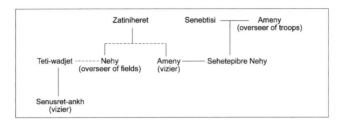

14. Family tree of the viziers Ameny and Senusret-ankh. The reconstruction is highly hypothetical. It rests on two unproven assumptions, that the Zatiniheret, mother of Nehy, is the same woman as the Zatiniheret, mother of Ameny, and that Nehy is the father of Senusret-ankh.

was the son of a woman called Zatiniheret ('daughter of Onuris'). His wife was Sehetepibre Nehy, the daughter of the 'great overseer of troops' Ameny. The sons of the vizier all had lower administrative positions, such as 'great one of the tens of Upper Egypt', or 'scribe of the town'. Through his mother it may be possible to connect Ameny with some further high officials. The mother of the 'overseer of fields' Nehy is also called Zatiniheret. So it is possible that the vizier Ameny and Nehy were brothers. Furthermore, the latter appears in inscriptions together with the official Senusret-ankh who later became vizier. Is it possible that Nehy was the father of Senusret-ankh or related in some other way? This relationship connects the vizier Senusret-ankh with the vizier Ameny (Fig. 14).[36]

For the vizier Senusret-ankh, datable perhaps at the end of the Twelfth or the beginning of the Thirteenth Dynasty, it is again possible to reconstruct a career. None of his monuments is connected with a royal name, so that it seems impossible to place him under a specific king. In rock inscriptions found in the Aswan region he appears as 'personal scribe of the king's document'. In other rock inscriptions he is appointed 'overseer of the fields'. From there he must have become vizier, the title which he holds on a statue found at Ugarit in Syria and on a stela. The stela was set up by 'his steward' and is of rather low quality (Fig. 15). The statue shows him together with his wife Henutsen and his daughter Zatamun. A short phrase mentions that 'it was given to him the gold of praises in front of the courtiers'. We do not hear for what reason he received that honour. The offering formula on the statue refers to Ptah-Sokar suggesting that it may have originally come from Memphis. However, Ptah-Sokar also appears on many objects found at Abydos, Esna and other places from Upper Egypt, so the attribution to Memphis remains speculation. It seems unlikely that the vizier ever visited Ugarit. Such state visits are rarely attested for the ancient world. The statue was perhaps taken from a temple or even his tomb sometime after his death and traded to that city.

15. Stela showing the vizier Senusret-ankh, his wife Henutsen and his daughter Zatamun. The vizier is shown in an early version of the vizier's costume with the necklace and the long garment, not yet going up to the chest. The stela was set up not by the vizier but by 'his steward'. This explains the rather low quality of work-manship.

Qemeni belongs perhaps to about the same period. He appears in a short inscription on a ship mast finial made of bronze. This is a highly exceptional object; sadly its original findspot is not known. Zamont appears on two stelae, one recording members of his family which includes a 'royal sealer' and 'priest of Amun'. Zamont is perhaps identical to a zab-official known from some rock inscriptions found at Lower Nubia which report military missions at the beginning of the reign of Amenemhat III. He is perhaps the founder of the vizier's family in which the office was held for at least three generations. This means that he was a young man, perhaps not much older than in his mid twenties, at the beginning of Amenemhat's III reign, in his ninth year, the year date given. Assuming that he became a father at this time, his son Ankhu, who later became vizier, was about 55 years old when he became that official under Sobekhotep II and Khendjer. This seems possible, although a son did not automatically follow his father and there are viziers in office between Zamont and Ankhu who do not come from the same family.[37]

36

16. The figure of Zamont on his
stela in Cairo.

17. Statue of the vizier Ameny.

The viziers of the early Thirteenth Dynasty are little known. Khenmes served under king Sekhemkare, a statue mentions the vizier and the king. The name and function title of his son are not known, but he was 'royal sealer' showing again some concentration of highest positions within one family. His wife was perhaps a woman called Senebtisi. Other viziers such as Hori, Minhotep, Ameny (Fig. 17) and Iuy are basically only names for us.

Next to Antefiqer, the Thirteenth Dynasty vizier Ankhu, just mentioned, is perhaps the most famous official of the Middle Kingdom. He is known from a number of impressive monuments indicating that he probably remained in office for longer. His mother was the 'lady of the house' Henutpu, who was herself daughter of a 'royal sealer' and 'priest of Amun', obviously a high position in the Amun temple at Thebes (see p. 98).[38] The wife of Ankhu was Mereryt. Not much is known about her. They both had a daughter called Senebhenas. She was married to the 'royal sealer' and 'overseer of the royal production place' Wepwawethotep, who himself came from an important family. One of their members was the 'king's wife' Iy. Both families were therefore related to the king's family. The most important document mentioning Ankhu is a papyrus found at Thebes and known as Papyrus Boulaq 18. It is an administrative document relating to the Theban palace. The papyrus is dated under king Amenemhat Sobekhotep II, although the name of the king is not well preserved and there has been some doubt about its reading.[39] Ankhu appears several times in this document bearing the titles 'overseer of the city, vizier' and sometime additionally 'overseer of the six great houses'. In the lists where Ankhu appears, he is always the first person mentioned, heading the other officials.

After Ankhu his sons Resseneb and Iymeru seem to have been in office. They are not attested on many monuments, although they appear together with their father on a stela.[40] Besides this reference, only Iymeru is known from another monument, a small statue now in Turin. These two sons were perhaps in charge for only a short time.

Neferkare Iymeru was the vizier under king Sobekhotep IV. His father was a 'royal sealer' and 'leader of the broad hall' with the name Iymeru. Neferkare Iymeru had a double name. Neferkare is the throne name of Pepy II, the last important ruler of the Old Kingdom. The name is not common in the Middle Kingdom but appears several times for people living in the Memphite region and involved in the mortuary cult of Pepy II.[41] This might indicate that Neferkare Iymeru was born in Memphis. The vizier Neferkare Iymeru is mainly known from monuments found at Thebes in the temple of Amun-Re. On an almost life-size statue he reports the building of a 'house of million years', a temple for the king's cult. He also reports the building of a canal. This statue, as well as another one without provenance, mentions the name of Sobekhotep IV and therefore provides good dating. The vizier seems to

18. Statue ensemble found in the Amun temple of Karnak, most likely of Ankhu (*right*); the statue was reinscribed in the Third Intermediate Period and none of the original inscriptions were left. The identification is based on another statue showing Ankhu's father (*left*) made by Ankhu, who also placed there a statue of his mother Henutpu (*centre*).

have received a higher status after he died. In a Memphite tomb of the Ramesside period a vizier Iymeru is depicted under other important people of the past. As Neferkare Iymeru is the most important one with people of this name and the list seems to include some locals, it is possible that Neferkare Iymeru is the vizier mentioned in the tomb.

The viziers after Neferkare Iymeru are a problem. Basically it is not yet possible to establish a sequence, as it seems likely that there are still many gaps in the sources. This impression is confirmed by the fact that several viziers of the period are attested only once. However, Ibiau is known from several sources. There are some discussions about him and his family, which was reconstructed by Labib Habachi. The vizier Ibiau himself is known for sure only from two stelae and a statue of his son, 'the leader of the broad hall' and later 'overseer of fields', Senebhenaf, who states that he was the son of a vizier Ibiau. From a stela dated under king Ibiau and a statue found on Elephantine is known a 'royal sealer' and 'overseer of the compound' with an identical name. It has been proposed that he was identical with a vizier of the same name.[42] This seems possible, but it should be understood that there are other high state officials at the same high level as the 'overseer of the compound' with the name Ibiau, dating to about the same time. The burial of the 'royal sealer' and 'overseer of fields' Ibiau was found at Thebes. The titles and name were found on fragments of a coffin. A scribal palette of a 'royal sealer' and 'leader of the broad hall' is known and belongs to another person with that name, dating to about the same time (see Fig. 41 on p. 92). For all these titles it is known that they were closely connected with the vizier and it seems possible that these people were appointed to that office. It is even possible that all these people were one and the same person with the different titles representing steps of his career. The coffin might have been produced before he was appointed vizier.

According to the reconstruction of the family by Habachi, the son of Ibiau, the 'overseer of fields' and 'leader of the broad hall' Senebhenaf, also became vizier. There is indeed a vizier Senebhenaf attested on a coffin of a queen called Mentuhotep,[43] wife of a little known king Djehuty. The vizier Senebhenaf is the father of the queen. However, the connection between the 'the leader of the broad hall' Senebhenaf and the vizier of the same name is again nothing more than a guess. This reconstruction of the family of two viziers is therefore speculative: possible but not proven. Interestingly, this case was used several times to date king Djehuty and queen Mentuhotep two generations, 40 to 60 years, after king Ibiau.[44] Needless to say, that is a dangerous enterprise. Even given the fact that all the people involved were identical, the counting of generations is problematic. Ibiau might have become vizier in the reign of Ibiau, who was on the throne for about ten years, followed by the 23-year reign of Merneferre Iy. The vizier Senebhenaf might have been at an advanced stage of his career when his daughter reached marriageable age, maybe just fifteen; he could well have become vizier as special promotion when his daughter married a king. The dating of king Djehuty based on this evidence is insecure. His position in the sequence of kings remains uncertain, floating within the late Middle Kingdom and Second Intermediate Period. The whole case offers a perfect example of how Egyptian sources are used to construct evidence which basically does not exist.

The next family of viziers is a little better attested, but also quite problematic. This family is mainly known from a monument known as the 'stèle juridique' found at Karnak, and from inscriptions at Elkab, in the far South of Egypt, where some of the important family members had their tombs.[45] The monument and the viziers mentioned belong basically to the Second Intermediate Period, when Egypt was divided into several parts with Thebes as the capital in the South. A typical feature of the administration of this time seems to be the close connection of provincial courts to the king's court at Thebes. The king was obviously concerned about maintaining his power and appointed influential locals as important officials at the royal court. A certain Iy was 'mayor of Elkab' around the middle of the Thirteenth Dynasty. From this position he was appointed vizier in year 1 of king Merhetepre Ini, one of the last rulers of the Thirteenth Dynasty, perhaps already at a time when Egypt was fallen apart and the power centre moved to the South, as can be seen from the involvement of locals coming from the South into the central government. The vizier Iy was married to a 'king's daughter' Reditnes. The date of the appointment, in the first year of the king's reign, is interesting and seems to throw some light on the practice of appointments at the royal court, at least at the very end of the Middle Kingdom/beginning of the Second Intermediate Period. Obviously king Merhetepre chose new people and did not take older officials already in power in the previous reign. It is not known whether the 'king's daughter' Reditnes, wife of vizier Iy, was related to Merhetepre, but it seems likely. Iy had a son named Iymeru, who was first 'mayor of Elkab' and later became vizier, as his father was. The mayors of Elkab were evidently powerful people in the Second Intermediate Period, playing an important part at the royal court and able to place at least two viziers next to the king. On the 'stèle juridique' just mentioned, a third vizier appears. His name is Sobeknakht. This name is also well known for several mayors of Elkab and one wonders whether Sobeknakht belonged to the same family of mayors.

Not many other viziers can be securely dated to the Second Intermediate Period. One called Amenemhat is attested by his burial in Thebes, but he is hard to date. The same or another Amenemhat appears on a papyrus found on Elephantine. He is also hard to date and it remains uncertain whether both people with that common name are identical. Viziers in the Second Intermediate Period are so far known only from the Theban kingdom in Upper Egypt, better known as the Sixteenth Dynasty. None are certain in the Seventeenth Dynasty, but this might be just a gap in our sources. They are not known from the region of Hyksos rule.

41

3

The 'Treasurer' or 'Chancellor'

As far back as the tombs of the Old Kingdom a lower official appears with the title 'overseer of the sealed things', more simply translated 'treasurer'.[1] People with this title are shown in tomb chapels of important officials carrying furniture, oil and other goods belonging to the main tomb owner. The 'overseer of the sealed things' was not an important official in the state administration. He was responsible for the private belongings of a high official. Unlike the 'stewards' also shown in these tombs, there are no tombs of 'treasurers' known, demonstrating that they did not have the resources for a decorated tomb chapel. These officials are not yet attested in the household of Old Kingdom kings and are known only from the private sector of household organisation.

The situation changed slightly at the end of the Old Kingdom and in the First Intermediate Period, when some of these people seem to have received more power and higher positions in the household of high state officials. At least one 'treasurer', named Sehu, seems to be attested at the royal court at Heracleopolis in the First Intermediate Period. 'Treasurers' were also found at the local courts in the provinces. These provincial courts were organised like the private household of an official at the royal court. In this context, it seems most likely that there was also one 'treasurer' at the local court at Thebes. However, these 'treasurers' at Thebes first appear in our sources only when Thebes was already the capital of a small kingdom in Upper Egypt. Two of them are known by name. Tjetji is datable with certainty under Antef II and Antef III, and Bebi in the years before the unification of the country under Mentuhotep II. Tjetji is mainly known from his stela which bears a long biographical inscription providing important information about his person and the office of a 'treasurer'. The stela is one of the most important sources for this office.

From the number and quality of their monuments it is certain that in the Middle Kingdom 'treasurers' were the most significant officials after the vizier. It is even possible to argue that they were more important than viziers, as the number and quality of their monuments seem to be higher than those of the latter.[2] However, such observations should be made with great caution. The 'treasurers' were often involved in organising building works at Abydos. The stelae set up in Abydos are one of our major sources for Middle Kingdom officials. Thus an official who worked often in Abydos is highly visible to us. On the other hand, an official who did not work at Abydos, and was not involved in sending expeditions to other places, might have been much more significant, but his monuments have a much higher chance of not surviving, especially as we do not know many of the tombs of the Middle Kingdom courtiers.

It must be noted that it is not always certain whether the 'treasurer' was part of a mission. The Thirteenth Dynasty 'treasurer' Senebsumai is known from many stelae found at Abydos. All these stelae were set up by his officials; none of those mentioning him was set up by Senebsumai as 'treasurer' himself, giving the impression that although he sent his staff to Abydos, he was never present at the site. The same impression is given by a rock inscription mentioning the 'treasurer' Senebi, found on the island of Sehel. The inscription mentions the family of king Neferhotep I, Senebi and the 'king's acquaintance' Nebankh. Senebi is not known from any other monument at Sehel or in this region, but Nebankh left several rock inscriptions and placed stelae into the chapel of Heqaib on nearby Elephantine. The impression here is that Nebankh visited the region and placed many inscriptions there, in some of which important people are mentioned such as the king's family, the king and his chief, Senebi.

For the tasks and duties of the 'treasurer', three main sources are important. There is the aforementioned biography of Tjetji, so far the only known long biographical text of a 'treasurer'; there are their titles; and there are many stelae especially of the late Middle Kingdom showing their staff, or at least some of them. Further evidence comes from officials with the word 'treasurer' as part of their title, such as 'scribe of the treasurer' or the 'deputy treasurer'.

The important biography of Tjetji gives some of the most direct information on the title:[3]

> ... the treasurer, the one who carries the head of the head, the revered one, Tjetji says: I was a beloved one of his lord, his honoured one every day. I spent a great lifetime in years under the majesty of the lord of Horus Wah-ankh, the dual king, son of Ra Antef, when this land was from Elephantine to Tjeni (near Abydos) under his control as I was his servant and his true liegeman. He made me great, he advanced my position, he took me into his confidence in his palace of privacy. The sealed things were in my hand under my seal, the selected things from all good things brought to the majesty of my lord from Upper Egypt and Lower Egypt, consisting of every thing that gives pleasure, and of the produce of this

entire land, because of the fear of him throughout this land and
that was ever being brought to the majesty of my lord by the hand
of the chieftains of the desert because of the fear of him throughout
the hill countries.

Here again, as in the tomb depictions of the Old Kingdom, the 'treasurer' was in charge of the more private property of a person, in this case of
the king. He controlled the revenues coming to the palace from all
around the country, including raw materials. These were not so much
food and agricultural products, but often objects which we would call
'treasures'. As we can see from other sources, the agricultural products
were under the charge of the 'high steward'. In this context it has to be
remembered that in Ancient Egypt other materials than in our culture
were regarded as precious, one of which was linen. It is therefore no surprise that the name and title of the 'treasurer' Khety, dating under
Mentuhotep II, were found on linen in tombs of queens.[4] Obviously it
was the treasury of the palace which supplied the burials of these
women and Khety was in charge of the treasury. In this context it is also
interesting that Meketre is shown in the mortuary temple of
Mentuhotep II with a broad collar, an object we would be more likely to
consider today as 'treasure'.

'Treasurers' found in expedition inscriptions were sometimes in
charge of supplying building materials for the king and collecting 'raw
materials'. The 'treasurer' Sobekhotep is mentioned in an inscription
dated to the reign of Senusret I. Merykau appears in an inscription from
the Eastern desert. However, as already mentioned, it might be doubted whether they were really part of these expeditions or just the highest
officials sending them. The 'treasurer', as controller of the raw materials
of the palace, was obviously also in charge of royal building projects.
Mentuhotep was the main person organising the construction of the
Amun temple at Karnak under Senusret I, and a 'treasurer' perhaps
called Senankh (his name is not clearly readable in the copy of the
inscription published) supervised the digging of a canal for Senusret III
in the Aswan region. Also in the reign of Senusret III, Iykhernofret
arranged the Osiris mysteries at Abydos and one wonders whether he
was also in charge of building the huge tomb of the king at Abydos
South.

From the late Middle Kingdom Abydos stelae and representations of
working staff (p. 130), it becomes clear that the 'treasurer' was in charge
of the palace as an economic unit, responsible for incoming goods and
their production. Under the 'treasurer' was the 'overseer of the storerooms', and there were several people in charge of 'units', perhaps some
kind of storage or production places for certain types of food and other
items.[5] The 'treasurer' was much involved in sealing goods. It therefore
comes as no surprise that the 'treasurer' is the official with the highest

number of known seals. From Senebsumai, in office under Sobekhotep II to about Neferhotep I, there are more than 30 seals and seal impressions known. Even more impressive is the number of seals belonging to the 'treasurer' Har: more than 100 are known. This is the highest number of seals known from an Egyptian official of any period. Har is attested only on his seals and there are so far no other monuments where he appears, making him hard to date.

The titles of the 'treasurers'

'Treasurers' were some of the most important officials of the Middle Kingdom and had therefore the most important ranking titles. On a seal Meketre is called simply 'member of the elite', a title which, when it appears alone, denotes someone in the highest position in the administration. In the Thirteenth Dynasty most officials around the king were just called 'royal sealer' and never 'sole friend'. Here, the 'treasurer' was an exception. On many monuments he was 'royal sealer' and 'sole friend', indicating a higher status than the other officials. Two 'treasurers' had the title 'member of the elite at the chapel of Geb'. It has been assumed that this relates to the Sed-festival of the king. The Sed-festival was a celebration of kingship and being part of it must have been a great honour. In the late Middle Kingdom many 'treasurers' are called 'member of the elite' and 'foremost of action'. In this period these titles appear in general rather rarely in the title strings of other officials, giving 'treasurers' with these titles a special status. From these titles alone it seems clear that the 'treasurer' in the late Middle Kingdom and Second Intermediate Period was one of the most important officials at the royal court.[6]

Two of the common titles for 'treasurers' are 'overseer of the two houses of silver' and 'overseer of the two houses of gold', obviously indicating that the title-holder was responsible for a treasury, as 'white house', or even better, 'house of silver' is best translated as 'treasury'. In the Middle Kingdom the title was not a function title as in the Old and New Kingdoms. It never appears in front of the name of an official but in the long title strings of highest state officials and was more something like a biographical phrase.

The staff of the 'treasurer'

Our sources preserve the names and titles of many of the people who worked with and under the 'treasurer'. Directly alongside or under the 'treasurer' there was the 'deputy treasurer'.[7] The office is well attested. Some of the 'deputy treasurers' even had high ranking titles demonstrating their important position. Several of their monuments are quite impressive, such as the stela of Sehetepibre from Abydos (Plate 5). They

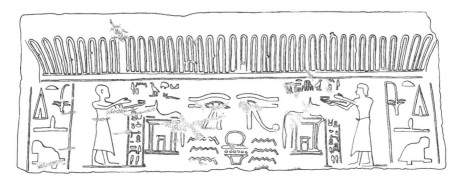

19. Lintel (limestone) of the 'deputy treasurer' Ameny-seneb, Thirteenth Dynasty.

seem to have basically the same function as the 'treasurer'. It is unknown whether they were directly responsible to him, or were put in charge next to him, perhaps just for a short time or for a single mission, but equipped with the same power. This view is supported by the fact that some 'deputy treasurers' had a further function title, announcing that 'deputy treasurer' was given only on a special mission. Ameny-seneb was also 'high steward'; Sehetepibre, just mentioned, was also 'overseer of the royal production place'.[8]

Other people belonging to the staff of the 'treasurer' are the 'scribe of the treasurer', the 'great scribe of the treasurer', the 'chamberlain of the treasurer's bureau' and the '(great) chamberlain of the treasurer'. These titles are easy to identify as belonging to the 'treasurer's' staff as they have the word 'treasurer' as part of the title. Other members of his staff have titles without explicit reference to the 'treasurer', but we can identify them because they appear on monuments close to a 'treasurer'. The most important title is the 'overseer of the storerooms', already mentioned; he is evidently the person in charge of the storerooms and magazines in the palace. Several 'overseers of the storerooms' are shown on stelae next to a 'treasurer'. There is even one case where both officials were buried close to one another (p. 129). Another official working under and very closely with the 'treasurer' in the late Middle Kingdom was the 'king's acquaintance', again often shown next to him and sometimes even as more important. The 'king's acquaintance' seems to have undertaken missions all around the country for the 'treasurer'.

The history of the office

The first 'treasurer' at the royal court, after unification in the Eleventh Dynasty, was a certain Khety, known from a remarkable number of monuments. He is often shown close to the king, underlining his importance. Perhaps the earliest attestations are his title and name written

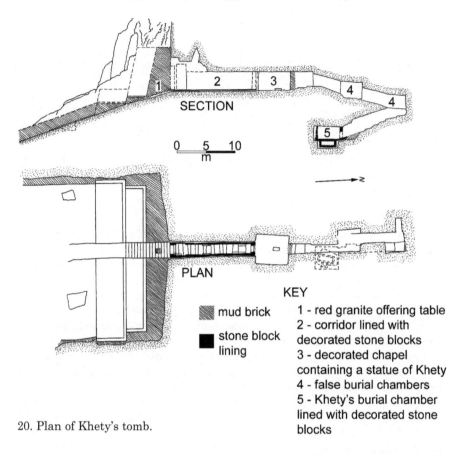

SECTION

0 5 10
m

PLAN

KEY

mud brick

stone block lining

1 - red granite offering table
2 - corridor lined with decorated stone blocks
3 - decorated chapel containing a statue of Khety
4 - false burial chambers
5 - Khety's burial chamber lined with decorated stone blocks

20. Plan of Khety's tomb.

on linen, found in the tomb of the queens Ashait and Henhenet,[9] datable perhaps shortly before the unification of Egypt.[10] Khety seems to have been involved in the Sed-festival of Mentuhotep II shown at Shat er-Regal before the king, who wears the Sed-festival dress. Other people depicted here are a mysterious person called Antef and the king's mother Iah. On other monuments Khety has the title 'god's father' perhaps indicating some family ties with the royal family. One can only guess about this family relationship. One option is that he was the father of the king's wife Tem, not shown on the relief at Shat er-Regal, or that he was related to one of the minor queens or to the king's mother. Another option is that he was the teacher of the king's children (compare p. 148). Khety is mentioned in the mortuary temple of the king and appears several times on reliefs there, perhaps once again involved in the Sed-festival. Khety was in office till around year 39 of Mentuhotep II.

The most important monument of Khety is his tomb (Figs 20-1) carved into the rocks next to the temple of the king at Deir el-Bahari. It

3. The 'Treasurer' or 'Chancellor'

(a) Offering bearer.

(b) Head.

(c) Single soldier.

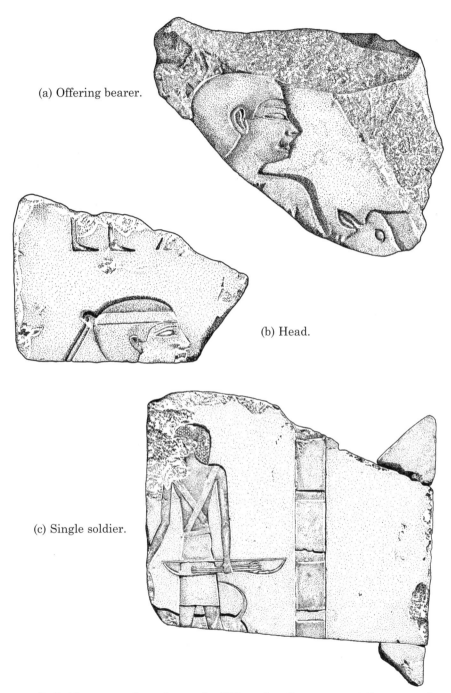

21. Relief fragments from the tomb of Khety (continues on next three pages).

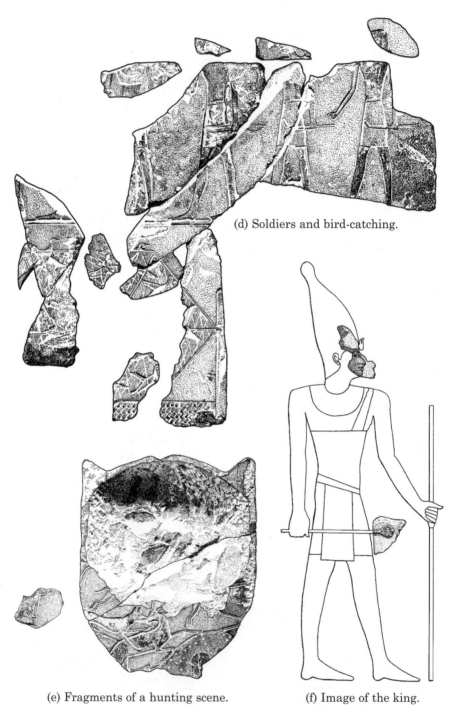

(d) Soldiers and bird-catching.

(e) Fragments of a hunting scene.

(f) Image of the king.

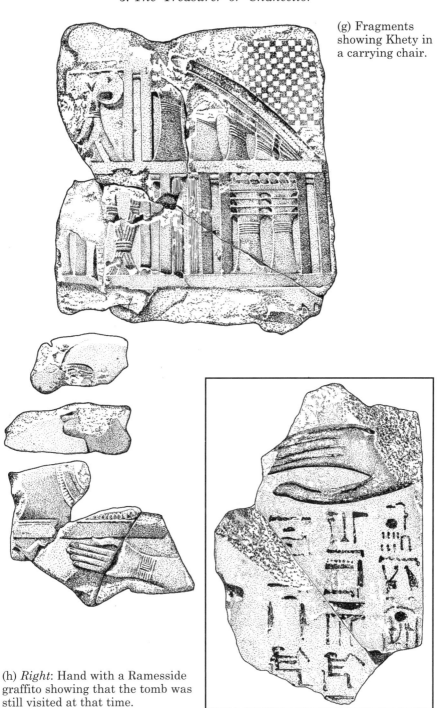

(g) Fragments showing Khety in a carrying chair.

(h) *Right*: Hand with a Ramesside graffito showing that the tomb was still visited at that time.

51

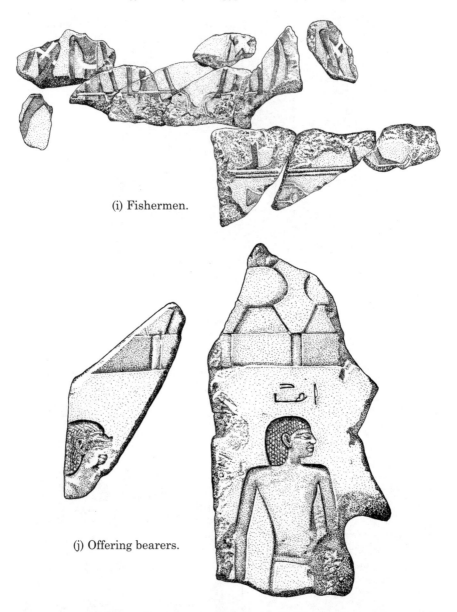

(i) Fishermen.

(j) Offering bearers.

was excavated and found already badly destroyed, but the remains show that it was certainly one of the most impressive private monuments of its day. In front of the tomb was a big courtyard, which was on the slope of the hill. At the entrance of the tomb a granite offering table inscribed with the name of Khety was also found. At the top were stairs leading to a corridor almost 15 m long which was paved and clad with fine lime-

stone incised with scenes, sadly preserved only in many small fragments. It is one of the first, if not the first, tomb of an official in ancient
Egypt which had a depiction of the king. Other scenes show bowmen and
friezes of objects, which are otherwise more commonly found on coffins.
There are scenes of hunting in the desert and in the marshes and scenes
showing funerary rituals. In or after the New Kingdom the blocks with
the fine reliefs were recycled to make stone vessels. The inner cult
chapel was painted in a rather simple style, perhaps by an artist not of
the highest calibre.[11] The burial chamber was found looted but also
paved with limestone slabs which were painted with friezes of objects,
again typical of coffins but also well known from other burial chambers
of the late Old Kingdom to the early Middle Kingdom. The sarcophagus
of Khety was sunk into the floor of the burial chamber. Not much survived of the original tomb equipment, although fragments of a fine wood-
en statue may be of Khety.

Meketre followed Khety in the office of 'treasurer' at the royal court.
He is well known for his tomb and also seems to have played an important part in the king's Sed-festival, as indicated by his title: 'member of
the elite at the chapel of Geb'. Meketre is one of the most famous officials of the Middle Kingdom. In his tomb was found an undisturbed

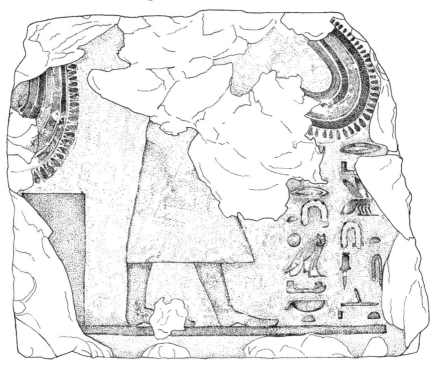

22. Meketre, relief fragment from the mortuary temple of Mentuhotep II.

chamber containing wooden models which are some of the most beautiful examples of their kind so far excavated in Egypt. Most depict workshops, offering bearers and boats. All these types of wooden models are
well known from other tombs of the early Middle Kingdom. Rather
exceptional are two models of houses, both showing the garden of an official's residence; another exceptional scene shows Meketre sitting under
a canopy counting cattle in front of him.

What else is known about him? Meketre appears in our sources for the
first time in a short rock inscription at the Shat er-Rigal, in the South of
Egypt. Here he bears the relatively low title of 'sealer'. This particular
inscription is not dated, but there are many inscriptions, some naming
king Mentuhotep II and dated under year 39, indicating, but not proving, that the king and his court were here on some kind of unknown mission in that year. The 'treasurer' Khety appears in the inscription of the
king and was obviously in office at that time. In another inscription,
found at Aswan, dated to year 41, Meketre appears together with the
'overseer of sealers' Meru and was perhaps part of a military campaign
against Lower Nubia.[12] The next inscriptions of Meketre were found in
the mortuary temple of Mentuhotep II at Deir el Bahari. Meketre's
name and titles appear on several fragments. In the meantime he was
appointed to the post of 'treasurer'. These depictions must date to the
very end of the reign of Mentuhotep II. Meketre's career under the following kings is guesswork. At some point he must have been appointed
to the position of 'high steward', a title preserved in his tomb. A life-size
statue names him simply as Meket; unfortunately the function title on
the statue is partly destroyed and only 'in the whole country' survives.
This could be restored as 'high steward in the whole country', but also as
'treasurer in the whole country'. Meketre received one of the most splen-
did tombs in the Theban necropolis of the Eleventh Dynasty.[13]

In recent years the dating of the end of Meketre's career has been
debated. The tomb's excavator, Herbert Winlock, placed him under
Seankhkare Mentuhotep III because the tomb was built next to a huge
but unfinished royal tomb which was originally assigned to that king.
However, the royal tomb is not connected with any royal name and more
recently, for various reasons, it has been assigned to Amenemhat I. The
problem seems to be unresolved.[14] In any case, Meketre became 'high
steward' at the end of his career, although whether he had this title
simultaneously with that of the 'treasurer' or as a new appointment
while there was a new 'treasurer' remains unknown.

Perhaps a certain Antef followed Meketre in office. He was buried in
the same tomb complex as Meketre with a burial chamber almost identical in size. Besides this not much is known about him, and it might
even be doubted that he was a 'treasurer' at the royal court.[15]

In year 7 of Amenemhat I there is another 'treasurer' attested. Ipi is
known mainly from the fragments of his coffin and from a rock inscrip-

tion found in the North of Egypt. His inscription is placed close to an inscription of Amenemhat I which is dated to that year, so it is likely that both inscriptions were carved at about the same time. A further hint in favour of that early date comes from the titles of Ipi. He is called 'steward' and 'treasurer' on his coffin. This title combination is similar to that of Meketre who is 'high steward' and 'treasurer'. For the following years the succession of 'treasurers' is uncertain. There was perhaps another Khety in office because a statue and an offering table mentioning a 'treasurer' Khety have been dated stylistically to the reign of Amenemhat I. However, the dating of these monuments is far from certain and the objects might belong to the Khety just mentioned. Another candidate for the office under that king is Nakht, buried at Asyut. He is in general hard to date. He might be a provincial 'treasurer', although he bears the title 'royal sealer'.[16]

Rehuerdjersen is known from his mastaba found next to the pyramid of Amenemhat I at Lisht and from a stela datable on stylistic grounds under Amenemhat II. His dating seems problematic. The pyramid of Amenemhat I was finished late in his reign or even after the king's death. Tombs around his pyramid can be expected only under Senusret I or even later, but there might be exceptions. Perhaps Rehuerdjersen can be placed into the last years of Amenemhat I or the first years of Senusret I, or, following the style of his stela, to Amenemhat II.

Sobekhotep appears in an expedition inscription found at Hatnub, in the alabaster quarries in Middle Egypt. The inscription mentions year 22 of Senusret I. Nothing else is known about him. His successor was one of the most famous 'treasurers' of the Twelfth Dynasty, Mentuhotep, who was perhaps born in the Eleventh Dynasty, as his name might indicate. There are an amazing number of monuments belonging to him. A series of statues shows him sitting on the ground with a papyrus in his hands. They were placed in the Amun-Re temple of Karnak. On these statues he bears the title 'overseer of all royal works' several times, indicating that he was the main person in charge of the rebuilding of that temple, as can also be concluded from the find spot of the statues. A stela found at Abydos which contains a long list of titles and many biographical phrases also reveals that he was in charge of rebuilding the Abydos temple for Senusret I. This king is known to have rebuilt many temples in Egypt. From the titles of Mentuhotep and his involvement in the building work at Karnak and Abydos one might infer that he was one of the main architects of several of these temples. However, he was certainly not involved in the temple building at Heliopolis, as has sometimes been argued. From there, a copy of an inscription is preserved mentioning an unnamed 'overseer of the double treasury', a common title for 'treasurers', but in the Middle Kingdom not a function title. The function title and the name of the official in charge are not given. The inscription is dated to the beginning of the reign of Senusret I when

Mentuhotep was not yet 'treasurer'.[17] It remains an open question whether the person mentioned in the building inscription is a real official or a fictional one, a prototype of an official.

Mentuhotep was buried at Lisht in a huge mastaba with its own causeway. Its chapel was found much destroyed, but was once adorned with reliefs. The building was about 14 x 29 m in area. Inscribed column fragments were found showing that the building had once a court. There are fragments of six life-size statues showing Mentuhotep as scribe. The mastaba was placed within an enclosure. On its south side were rooms or even living quarters for the funerary priests. The underground burial chamber was reached by a shaft. Two sarcophagi were found, one smashed and the other made of granite and certainly once used to contain Mentuhotep's body. It is uncertain how long Mentuhotep stayed in office, but there is no evidence that he was still in charge under Amenemhat II. In Abydos, as already mentioned, several parts of an offering chapel were found belonging to Mentuhotep. These are parts of a false door and a stela inscribed on all sides. The long list of titles on the stela starts with that of vizier. Mentuhotep is called vizier on no other monument, and his place in the succession of viziers is therefore problematic.

The fact that Mentuhotep also bears the titles of a vizier on one monument might need further discussion, as there are other similar cases, such as the 'treasurer' Siese and some governors buried at Deir el-Bersheh. All these people have a regular function title, but also occasionally bear the titles of a vizier. There are two opinions in Egyptology about this point. Some Egyptologists just regard them as normal viziers, bearing two function titles at the same time, while others call them 'honorary viziers'.[18] In general, the evidence seems clear. Almost all officials discussed in this volume bear their function title in inscriptions directly in front of the name. There are few exceptions. These are indeed mainly the governors and 'treasurers' just mentioned. Scholars who regard them as regular viziers do not try to explain this fact. Furthermore, the vizier's titles of Mentuhotep are slightly different to those of the other viziers, as he is not 'overseer of the city' as are almost all Middle Kingdom viziers in office. It needs to be explained why some viziers, also known with another and more prominent function title, chose to be called vizier and did not place this, the highest title, in a prominent, regular position on their monument. It might be assumed that they undertook certain tasks and had the powers of a vizier perhaps just for a time to reflect these responsibilities. For the governors at Deir el-Bersheh, it has been assumed that they were indeed local viziers.[19]

The 'treasurer' Merykau is also not clearly datable; he appears on a stela with the name of Amenemhat II, found in the Eastern desert. Finally, Siese ('son of Isis'), perhaps datable under the same king, had a huge tomb at Dahshur next to the pyramid of the king. Siese is possibly also known from several monuments before he became 'treasurer'. On a stela in the British Museum he appears as 'chamberlain' and 'overseer of Upper and Lower Egypt', obviously a man at the royal court in charge of the administration of the whole country. On other monuments he is 'high steward', apparently appointed from one to the other position. In his tomb he is finally a 'treasurer', but also called vizier. This seems to be a similar case to that of Mentuhotep. It is uncertain whether Siese was vizier in charge, or an important 'treasurer' with the titles of a vizier for reasons of honour, or provided with that title to give him some special responsibilities. His tomb was excavated a long time ago and only briefly published, so that the architecture remains basically unknown. The tomb chamber is decorated with long religious texts. In the above-ground chapel four slabs were found with his image and titles (Plate 2). The reliefs are among the most remarkable of the Middle Kingdom, showing Siese as an older man, almost like a portrait. On only three of the four slabs is he called vizier. Was he appointed vizier after the first relief was finished, before the others were made?

The order of Merykau and Siese is unknown. Neither is attested on a monument with a year dating. Siese was buried at Dahshur and belongs perhaps to the second part of the reign of Amenemhat II. Merykau is attested only once. His name sounds like a 'court name', almost like a royal name, given to a person as a second name after he became an important official. One wonders whether he is identical with one other 'treasurer' known under a different name. Double naming was common in Middle Kingdom Egypt, and several times there is evidence that one person is known by one name on one monument and a second one on another.[20]

There is no 'treasurer' who can be securely placed under Senusret II. Given his short reign of about eight years, this is no great surprise. However, several of them are datable under Senusret III. Sobekemhat had this office before becoming vizier (p. 31) and was perhaps in office early in the reign; Senankh built a canal at Sehel in year 8 and appears there in a rock inscription mentioning him, the king and the digging of the canal (Fig. 23).

Iykhernofret, who served under Senusret III at the end of his nineteen years of (sole) reign, arranged the mysteries of Osiris in Abydos and belongs to the better attested officials of the Middle Kingdom. There are quite a lot of stelae known for him. Only one, now in Berlin, reports in detail some events in his life, including the mysteries of Osiris. However, although there is little biographical information on the stelae, they do provide a number of important details about the 'treasurer' and his staff. The origin of Iykhernofret, as so often for high state officials, is not clear. His mother was a certain Zatkhons ('daughter of Khons'). His father and his wife are not yet attested. The stelae of Iykhernofret were set up in his chapel at Abydos. This is the first big Middle Kingdom group of ste-

23. Inscription on the island of Sehel near Aswan mentioning the opening of a canal under Senusret III. On the left, behind the king and Satet, appears the 'royal sealer, sole friend, leader of works in the whole country, treasurer Senankh'. The main inscription reads: 'Year 8 of the majesty of the double king Khakaure, may he live: order to make a new canal, whose name is Beautiful are the Ways of Khakaure, eternally. This [was made] after his majesty went South to overthrow the wretched Nubians. Length of this canal 150 cubits, breadth: 20 cubits, depth: 15 cubits ...'.

lae from Abydos relating to a 'treasurer'; the other groups belong to the Thirteenth Dynasty 'treasurers' Senebsumai and Senebi. On these stelae are shown lower officials working for and with them. Here, for the first time, it becomes clear how much the 'treasurer' was in charge of the economic part of the palace. On the stelae of Iykhernofret appear the 'overseer of the storerooms' Aaptah and the 'king's acquaintance' Minhotep, who also bore the title 'assistant of the treasurer'. People bearing titles in other sources are also connected with the 'treasurer'.

From the biographical part of his large stela, now in Berlin, we know that Iykhernofret was brought up at the royal court and was a foster child of the king. When he was 26 he became 'friend' of the king, perhaps receiving ranking titles. The main part of the text deals with the work of Iykhernofret at Abydos. The king ordered that the official should travel south to Abydos, in the Thinite nome, to make an image of his father Osiris-Khontyamentiu with gold and electron which the king had brought from Nubia, and clothe the god, as well as making images of other gods. Finally Iykhernofret conducted the procession of Wepwawet, which seems to have been a ritual performance including repulsing attackers of the neshmet-bark, and he arranged the Great Procession of Osiris at Abydos.[21]

The large number of stelae set up for Iykhernofret and his staff at Abydos is obviously connected with his work at that place. Outside Abydos he is not so far securely attested. The activity of Iykhernofret at Abydos correlates well with the activities of Senusret III there. The king had a great tomb cut into the desert cliff at Abydos South, with its own valley temple. Alongside this he founded the town Wahsut, which functioned as the place where the king's cult was organised, and also as a local administrative centre. The stelae of Iykhernofret are dated by kings' names to the end of Senusret III's reign and the early years of Amenemhat III.

As with most other officials, there are few 'treasurers' that can be reliably dated from the reign of Amenemhat III to about Sobekhotep II in the Thirteenth Dynasty. Many names and objects of 'treasurers' are preserved, but it is impossible to put them in a sequence. Several were called Ameny, one of whom is known from a huge sarcophagus found at Tanis, but originally coming from Hawara, the location of Amenemhat III's pyramid. Herfu has his name on several scarab seals and a wonderful weight made of green schist. He is perhaps also known from a statue, although his name is partly destroyed. Seneb appears on a nicely crafted stela, Ameny-seneb on a seal impression found in Nubia and on a relief from Abydos. Khentykhetyemsaf is known from a statue and appears on a stela found at Harageh.

The sources become richer with the 'treasurer' Senebsumai, perhaps the most influential official of the Thirteenth Dynasty. He is known from a wide range of monuments, indicating a long time in office. He was in

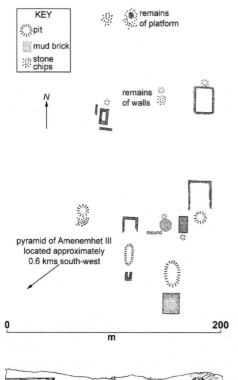

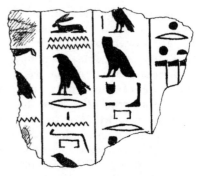

24. The mastabas of high officials at Hawara: the mastaba field was heavily reused in later periods. The mastabas found belong to the largest of the Middle Kingdom. Few of them can be assigned to a certain official. This is one reason why we know little about the court of Amenemhat III. *Left*: sketch plan of the mastaba field; *above*: block with pyramid texts from this field mentioning a 'high steward' whose name is lost; *middle left*: limestone fragment bearing the titles 'sole friend, overseer of all [royal] works' found in the Fayum but originally perhaps from one of the mastabas; *below*: sarcophagus of the 'treasurer' Ameny, found at Tanis but most likely from here; the inscription mentions 'Osiris, count in the middle of the Fayum'.

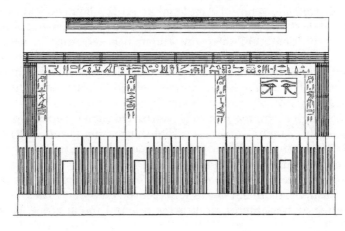

25. Bronze statue of the 'treasurer' Senebsumai, most likely from Hawara and placed in the temple there.

26. Inscription with titles of Senebsumai, copied by Mariette at Dahshur, most likely from the tomb of the treasurer.

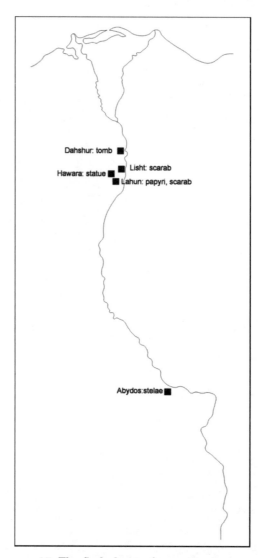

27. The find-places of monuments
belonging to Senebsumai.

charge from about the reign of Sobekhotep II perhaps until that of
Neferhotep I. While a 'treasurer' such as Iykhernofret left many stelae,
it is important to note that they all come from Abydos and might have
been put in place over a short period. He is well known to us, but might
nevertheless have been just an average 'treasurer' in a line of more
important title-holders who did not work at Abydos and are therefore
less well attested.

3. The 'Treasurer' or 'Chancellor'

In contrast, Senebsumai appears on a wide range of documents. There is evidence for his tomb, seal impressions were found at Abydos, accounts where found at Lahun and he has the highest number of stelae set up for an official at Abydos. However, although there are many sources relating to Senebsumai, little is known about him. His social background remains mysterious. His father was a certain Wepwawethotep, known only from the filiation and never mentioned with a title. Senebsumai appears first on some monuments as 'high steward' – not as 'treasurer' – and it is in this position that he mentions his father. From 'high steward' he was appointed 'treasurer'. More than thirty of his scarab seals are known, making him the best attested person on seals and seal impressions of the late Middle Kingdom. He appears on papyrus fragments found at Lahun which mention the delivery of fish, perhaps destined for the royal residence at Lisht. From Hawara comes a bronze statue inscribed with his titles and name. The statue was found in the 1960s and sold on the art market. The context of this remarkable find remains unknown. However, the statue was found with another depicting the 'high steward' Senusret, perhaps dating to the beginning of the Thirteenth Dynasty, as well as other unnamed officials and royal statues. These statues may have been dedicated to the mortuary temple of Amenemhat III, and may belong to different times within the late Middle Kingdom.

Of some importance is a fragment of an inscription found at Dahshur (Fig. 26). This is inscribed with the name and titles of Senebsumai and includes coffin texts. It seems highly likely that the fragment comes from his tomb at Dahshur, either from the mastaba or the burial chamber of his tomb, and shows that he was buried in a substantial tomb. It is unlikely that the fragment formed part of a coffin, since at this time they were often inscribed with mutilated hieroglyphs (in which animals are shown without legs), whereas the signs on the fragment are unmutilated. Few tombs of Thirteenth Dynasty officials are known and this fragment provides good evidence that Dahshur still functioned as the burial place of officials of that period. The most important sources for Senebsumai are his stelae from Abydos. They strongly indicate that he was involved in some projects at Abydos on which occasions he and his staff placed stelae in an offering chapel. These stelae do not mention the mission in which these people were involved. From other inscriptions two projects are known which seem to date to the period when Senebsumai was in office. Under king Khendjer the Osiris temple originally built under Senusret I was renovated, and under Neferhotep I the king renewed the image of the god. At the moment it is not possible to decide in which of these projects Senebsumai was involved. Another option might be that he was involved in building a royal tomb at Abydos, as new research indicates that several Thirteenth Dynasty funerary monuments were constructed near the tomb of Senusret III.

28. Coffin fragments of the 'royal sealer, sole friend, treasurer' Amenhotep.

Senebi followed Senebsumai in the office. He was the son of the 'soldier of the town regiment', a leading military official on a middle command level. Senebi started his career as 'king's acquaintance' and was later promoted to the post of 'treasurer'. He is named in rock inscriptions found at Aswan in connection with the family of king Neferhotep I. Later he is mentioned in connection with the 'king's acquaintance' Rehuankh, who himself is well datable under Sobekhotep IV, indicating that Senebi might have been in office under that king too. Senebi is also known from a number of stelae found in Abydos, again demonstrating some involvement in building works at this site.

In the following years the succession of 'treasurers' remains unknown. They are mostly known from their scarab seals, which just tell us their names. At present it seems impossible to place them in any order or under a specific king. One exception is Amenhotep, attested on several seals (Fig. 29) but also known from his burial next to the pyramid of Amenemhat II at Dahshur. Here he re-used a Twelfth Dynasty tomb and was placed close to a queen called Keminub. From other sources we know that some queens of the Thirteenth Dynasty were related to families of high officials, and one wonders in that case whether Amenhotep and Keminub were father and daughter or brother and sister. In the tomb of Amenhotep were found fragments of an inscribed coffin (Fig. 28),

29. Scarabs of the 'royal sealer, sole friend, treasurer' Amenhotep.

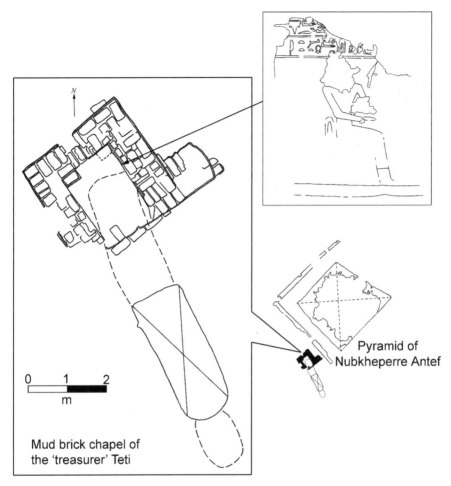

30. The tomb of Teti (*left*); wall painting showing Teti sitting (*top right*); the tomb in relation to the pyramid of king Nubkheperre Antef (*below right*).

today preserved only in the form of late nineteenth-century copies made by the excavators. The style of his scarabs indicates that he might belong to the late Thirteenth Dynasty, perhaps under Wahibre Ibiau or Merneferre Iy.

For the Second Intermediate Period too little is known of the 'treasurers'. Teti was in office at the end of the Seventeenth Dynasty under Nubkheperre Antef. He had a small tomb next to the pyramid complex of his king (Fig. 30). This is so far the only tomb of a high court official of the Second Intermediate Period whose chapel and burial chamber are well recorded and preserved. His mud brick chapel is small; externally it measures only 2.5 x 2.5 m, and on the inside just 1 x 1 m. The inside walls still show remains of paintings, including traces of the king's name: Nubkheperre. Teti is shown sitting in front of offerings (the latter not preserved). His titles are given above his figure: 'member of the elite', 'foremost of action', 'royal sealer', 'sole friend', the 'treasurer' Teti. In front of the chapel was the shaft leading to his burial chamber, already heavily looted when found and re-used in later times.[22] Nothing more is known about Teti, but his titles and his tomb demonstrate the strong position of the 'treasurer' even in the Seventeenth Dynasty, as he was buried directly next to the king. Neshi was 'treasurer' under Kamose at the very end of the Second Intermediate Period and is shown on the famous stela where the king reports his battle against the Hyksos.

In the Second Intermediate Period the picture is different for the Delta, the kingdom of the Hyksos rulers, and for other most likely foreign dynasties ruling from the North. Here many 'treasurers' are known from scarab seals. Indeed they are the only well attested officials of that dynasty. The outstanding example is the 'treasurer' Har, known from more than 100 seals (Fig. 31). It has been proposed that he served under king Maaibre Sheshi, also known only from scarabs – indeed he is the king with the highest number of seals dating to the Second Intermediate Period. Another 'treasurer' well known from many seals is Periemhezut. A certain Aperbaal appears on an offering stand and on a door jamb. The offering stand also bears the name of the Hyksos king Apophis. As in Thebes, there is evidently a close connection between the 'treasurer' and the king here. Under the Hyksos no vizier is attested. It has been argued that the 'treasurer' took over the duties of the vizier. This may be partly true, but another explanation might lie in the functions of the vizier, who had a strong link to the scribal offices. These may not have been so important under the Hyksos. A further explanation is perhaps that the administration of the Hyksos was very much simplified in comparison to that of the Middle Kingdom. They just took over the office of the 'treasurer' because this was the official they knew from the Egyptian administration when they traded with the Egyptians.

31. Two scarabs of the 'treasurer' Har.

Plate 1. Deir el-Bahari, Tombs of Eleventh Dynasty court officials. There is an open courtyard on the slope of the hill and at the back the entrance to the cult chapel.

Plate 2. One of the four reliefs found in the mastaba of Siese at Dahshur.

Plate 3. Stela of the vizier Zamont.

Plate 4. Statue of the 'treasurer' Khentykhetyemsaef.

Plate 5. Stela of the 'deputy treasurer' Sehetepibre. The names of Amenemhat III are in the roundel.

Plate 6. Scarab of the 'steward' Senebtifi; scarabs are one of the most important sources for names and titles.

Plate 7. Statue (two views) of the
'high steward' Nebsekhut; Thirteenth
Dynasty.

Plate 8. Fragment (full view and view
of the head) of a life-size statue, most
likely of an official of very high status
(Thirteenth Dynasty, Karnak, Khons
temple). The statues of the highest
court officials are among the finest
works of art.

4

Other Important Officials

The vizier and the 'treasurer' were the two most important officials at the royal court in the Middle Kingdom and also in the Second Intermediate Period. Under these two officials were other significant people, also bearing high ranking titles. This group of high officials was never large, perhaps never more than about ten people at any one time. In the Eleventh and Twelfth Dynasties the group of men around the king, those with the highest ranking titles, seems not to have been consistent. There was the vizier, the 'treasurer', the 'high steward' and the 'overseer of troops'. Other officials with ranking titles are only sporadically attested. It is not possible at present to establish a line of 'scribes of the royal documents' or of 'overseers of the gateway'. Is this evidence of a gap in our sources? In other words, were these officials always at the royal court and honoured with ranking titles and the sources are simply missing? Or were they just not there, such that the gap in title-holders reflects a reality? If the latter is the case, this would mean that there were 'overseers of the gateway' with ranking titles only at certain times at the royal court, while under other kings they were not rewarded with these titles. We do not know; the sources are for the moment just too fragmentary.

The picture for the late Middle Kingdom and especially for the Thirteenth Dynasty is clearer. Although there are certainly many people missing, there seems to have been a sequence of certain officials with ranking titles. However, any conclusion regarding a difference from the early Middle Kingdom must be made with great caution. The better picture for the later Middle Kingdom might be the result of a wider range of available sources, for instance scarabs with name and titles and Abydos stelae, more common at this time.

It is not easy to gain a picture of the hierarchy of the highest officials and one wonders whether there was even some kind of chain of command. However, there are two sources listing the highest officials in a certain order and they may give us a preliminary clue. In Papyrus Boulaq 18, the administrative document relating to the Theban palace dating to the Thirteenth Dynasty, several lists of officials appear. The highest state officials with ranking titles head these listings. At the top of one list was the vizier, followed by the 'overseer of troops', the 'overseer of fields', and finally the 'personal scribe of the king's documents'.

Another list places the 'high steward' below the 'overseer of troops', and the 'mouth of Nekhen' before the 'personal scribe of the king's documents'. Another source for putting the officials in order is a list of statues placed in a temple at Lahun. The list is heavily destroyed, but starts with the statues of two viziers, five 'royal sealers' whose function titles are lost, a 'royal sealer, who is in ...', an 'overseer of sealers' and finally a 'scribe of the king's documents'.[1] Another source is the use of the highest ranking titles. While in the early Twelfth Dynasty, 'member of the elite' and 'foremost of action' were regularly used for highest state officials, these titles were only sporadically given in the Thirteenth Dynasty, and 'royal sealer' became the common and sole ranking title. From that it seems clear that after the vizier and 'treasurer', the 'high steward' and 'overseer of sealers' were the most important officials. These officials appear at least sometimes with the highest ranking titles 'member of the elite' and 'foremost of action'. For all others these highest ranking titles are only sporadically attested.

Careers in the late Middle Kingdom became more fixed and it is possible to separate categories of officials on stelae and through the careers of the high officials into two groups. There are the officials more closely connected to the vizier and there are those more closely connected to the 'treasurer'. These groups are clearly visible in the careers of these officials. Promotions are visible only within these groups and these officials often appear together on stelae while rarely on the monuments of those of the other group. Here, then, two sides of the palace administration are visible. The vizier was the head of the branch responsible for the scribal offices, for the organisation of workforces, for royal projects and perhaps for provincial administration. The 'treasurer' was the head of the economic part of the palace. He was the overseer of officials involved in food production and of certain working and storage places. These two groups of officials differ not only in the career paths they followed, but also in the way they are attested on monuments. From the administration of the 'treasurer', many more seals are known. Senebsumai is known from more than 30 seals. The 'treasurer' Har is known from more than 100. Viziers are only sporadically attested on seals. The same is true for the officials working under them. The 'high steward', the 'overseer of sealers' and the 'overseer of marshland dwellers' are often known from more than one seal. They belonged to the administration of the 'treasurer'. In contrast, the 'leader of the broad hall' and the 'personal scribe of the king's document' are most often known from only a single seal, if at all. Obviously, sealing in general and sealing goods were important in the administration under the 'treasurer', but not essential for the administration under the vizier. People of the 'treasurer's' administration seem to have used the seal of the 'treasurer' to send sealed commodities all over the country. The administration under the vizier also used seals, but more likely just for sealing documents.

4. Other Important Officials

The officials under the 'treasurer' are also better attested on stelae from Abydos. Taking other sites into consideration too, it can still be said that more monuments are known for them. At first glance, this might point to a higher position for these people. However, there is another explanation for this. The officials around the 'treasurer' were more involved in building projects and collecting raw materials from all over the country. On their missions, especially to Abydos, they left many monuments and inscriptions. In contrast, the 'leader of the broad hall' or the 'personal scribe of the king's document', both under the vizier, perhaps most often worked only at the royal palace. They were important and powerful people. They might have had important tombs and placed important statues and other monuments in the temples of the capital, but these are now gone, leaving fewer traces and giving the false impression of these officials having been less important.

This division of the palace in two parts is not only visible for the higher officials, but also for the officials on a lower level. The 'king's acquaintance' worked closely with the 'treasurer'. Several of them are known on stelae depicted in front of the 'treasurer'. For some 'treasurers' and 'high stewards', their career from a 'king's acquaintance' to their final post is known. On the other hand, the 'great one of the tens of Upper Egypt', the 'elder of the hall' and 'mouth of Nekhen', common late Middle Kingdom titles, are always connected with the vizier, rarely with a 'treasurer'.

The following survey of other important high officials is separated into two parts: the officials under the 'treasurer' and those under the vizier.

Officials under the 'treasurer'

The 'high steward'

Certainly the third important man at the Middle Kingdom royal court was the 'high steward'. More than 60 holders of this title are known, making this the best attested court official with ranking titles. Not many biographical inscriptions of 'high stewards' are known. Their tasks have to be reconstructed from their title strings and from the evidence of 'stewards' of the Old and New Kingdoms.

The 'steward', or 'overseer of the house' is known from the Fourth Dynasty. In Old Kingdom tombs 'stewards' are shown in the front row of the lower officials under the tomb owner. They are often depicted as scribes or bringing cattle. 'Stewards' in the Old Kingdom are known only from the households of higher officials, where they managed the estates and household. They never appear in the administration directly under the king. This changed only in the First Intermediate Period. The kings of the Eleventh Dynasty started as local governors, as officials, and therefore had a 'steward' in charge of their estate. At some point these governors became kings. Their office was not dropped from the administration, but became a high state function. Here a similar development as for the 'treasurer' is visible, who was also at first only in charge of the private belongings of an official or governor, but became a high ranking official with the founding of a new state.

In the Eleventh Dynasty the office was most often just called 'steward', distinguished from other 'stewards' only by the ranking titles. However, Henenu, the first 'steward' under Mentuhotep II, called himself 'steward in the entire land'. In the Twelfth Dynasty the title was finally transformed to 'high steward in the entire land', while the same people on other monuments were still called simply 'steward' or 'high steward'. The extension 'in the entire land' was dropped under Amenemhat II, and from then on they appear as only 'high steward' in our sources.

The other titles of 'high stewards', most likely relating to their main functions, include 'overseer of the double granary', 'overseer of what the sky and the earth created' and 'overseer of the horned, hoofed, feathered and scaled animals'.[2] These titles indicate, as already found with Old Kingdom 'stewards', a strong connection with agrarian products. 'High stewards' in the early Middle Kingdom were also expedition leaders. This is similar to the viziers of the same period, also known as expedition leaders. Evidently, in the early Middle Kingdom the king chose officials close to him for important expeditions, while these were later led by lesser officials. However, unlike the vizier Antefiqer (p. 29), they never led military campaigns.

From this evidence it can be concluded that the 'high steward' was the administrator of the domains of the country, basically responsible for the fields and the cattle which were important for providing the palace and its people with food. The 'high steward' seems to have been directly under the 'treasurer'. While the 'treasurer' managed all the goods in the palace and the raw materials not used as food, the 'high steward' was especially responsible for all agricultural matters outside the palace.

In the late Twelfth and the Thirteenth Dynasty there were, at least sometimes, several 'high stewards' in charge. The best evidence for this is a stela now in Leyden (no. 34), dating under Neferhotep I, showing three 'high stewards' sitting next to each other. Furthermore, from the first years of the reign of Amenemhat III and from the reigns of Neferhotep I and Sobekhotep IV there are so many 'high stewards' known that it seems most likely that at least some of them were contemporary. Otherwise it must be assumed that each was in office for just a year or even less.

Like all highest officials, the 'high steward' could have other important functions at the royal court. Hor under Senusret I was also 'overseer of the gateway'. Kheperkare was 'overlord of the whole country' and Khentykhetywer bears on one statue, now in Rome, many important religious titles indicating that he was the main religious person at the royal court. In the Thirteenth Dynasty many of the 'high stewards' were called 'the one who followed the king',[3] giving evidence of a close connection to the king. Others were 'the one circulating commissions',[4] and a few were known as 'the one in the chamber'.[5] Some of these attachments to the title are also well known from the 'overseers of sealers', providing evidence for the close working relationship of these two officials. The most famous 'high steward' of the Middle Kingdom is perhaps Rensi, who appears in the story of the 'Eloquent peasant'. The narrative takes place at the end of the First Intermediate Period but was written in the Twelfth Dynasty. In this story the 'high steward' appears as some kind of judge, giving the impression that this was one of his main tasks. However, as the 'high steward' was in charge of estates, all juridical matters relating to that estate would presumably be put under his charge (compare p. 21).

The history of the 'high steward'

There are two 'high stewards' known from the Eleventh Dynasty after the unification. Henenu is perhaps the first of these two. He did not have the exact title 'high steward', but was a 'steward' with all important ranking titles announcing his important position at the royal court. He had a large rock-cut tomb in Thebes, adorned with several stelae which were inscribed with long biographical texts. The stelae were found smashed and the texts are therefore fragmentary. His tomb dates under Mentuhotep II, as can be seen from inscriptions found there. In year 8 of Mentuhotep III Henenu appears in a rock inscription in the Wadi Hammamat, reporting an expedition to Punt. The other 'high steward' (called 'steward in the entire land') is Buau, basically known only from his finely painted coffin found in a simple shaft tomb. The coffin bears two names, Mentuhotep and Buau. It is uncertain whether these were two different names of Buau or whether the coffin was re-used by a person called Mentuhotep. The latter name is found only on the coffin's outside. Buau is not well datable. The tomb, found in the nineteenth century, contained next to the coffin some wooden models typical of burials of this period. He may belong to the end of the Dynasty and was perhaps in office for only a short period, not having time to prepare his own monumental tomb.

At the beginning of the Twelfth Dynasty Meketre, better known as 'treasurer', and Ipi, also known as 'treasurer', were in charge. There are no further 'high stewards' who date securely to the reign of Amenemhat

I. However, some 'high stewards' basically known only by name might date under that king, such as Sobeknakht who appears on a block found next to the pyramid of the king at Lisht and a statue of him found at Thebes. His exact placement remains uncertain, but the findspot of the statue might indicate that he still belongs to a time when Amenemhat I was ruling from there. Gemniemhat had a tomb at Saqqara, but is again hard to date. Dates from the end of the First Intermediate Period to the reign of Amenemhat I have been proposed.[6] In contrast, the 'high stewards' under Senusret I are well known and sometimes even well datable. Hor appears on three stelae, evidently once forming parts of his offering chapel in Abydos. The largest one of these is now in the Louvre, on which he is shown in front of an offering table, accompanied by inscriptions which record most of his titles, such as 'high steward in the entire land, priest of Maat, mouth of Nekhen, overseer of the horned, hoofed, feathered and scaled animals'. The stela was the main one in the chapel and is also dated by the name of king Senusret I in his ninth year.[7] The other two stelae were most likely arranged next to the larger central one. They show on one side Hor and in front of him servants and family members. Here he is just called 'steward' not 'high steward', but bears ranking titles announcing his high position. It seems unlikely that the monuments were carved at different stages of his career. 'Steward' and 'high steward' in combination with ranking titles were in the early Middle Kingdom more likely regarded as the same title, one being the shorter version, the other the fuller form. The names and titles of the people depicted on these stelae are interesting as they tell us much of the organisation of private households. Depicted on one of the stelae are what are clearly the servants of Hor.[8] There is an 'overseer of store-rooms', a 'treasurer', a 'builder' and a 'sealer'. On the other stela the family of Hor is shown, including his sons and daughters and further relatives. Interestingly, there appears a 'steward' of the 'high steward' Hor between the family members. Perhaps he was regarded as special; certainly he administered the private estates of Hor.[9] Hor is also known from a stela found in the Wadi el-Hudi. This is a region where amethyst was found. Nakht built at the pyramid of the king and is known from a life-size statue found in his tomb chapel at Lisht.

Two other 'high stewards' under Senusret I both have the name Antef. One of them, the son of a woman called Zatamun, is known from several high quality Abydos stelae. The other Antef, born to a woman called Zatuser, is known only from a statue. And there is perhaps Zanofret, known from a statue and a stela. Not much can be said about them. Kheperkare (compare p. 96) is known from three stelae, each of them produced at a different stage of his career. He appears in our sources first as 'steward' with the ranking title 'king's acquaintance'. On another stela he is 'member of the elite, foremost of action, chamberlain' and 'overseer of all royal works'. There is a short biographical text reporting that he, Kheperkare, dug a canal in the Thinite nome. On the stela appears the name of king Amenemhat II, providing a welcome dating of this event. The last object belonging to him is a massive (164 cm high) well carved stela in the shape of a false door. Here he is 'high steward in the entire land', but also has an exceptional list of important titles, such as 'beloved god's father' and 'overlord of the whole country'. The title 'beloved god's father' might indicate some connection with the king, either via family relations or as a teacher of the king's children. The name of this official, Kheperkare, is remarkable. Kheperkare is the throne name of king Senusret I. This is not exceptional, as there are sometimes people named after a ruler. However, in this case the name is even provided with the royal cartouche. Interestingly, the name is written without a cartouche on the stela where the name of the reigning king Amenemhat II appears in a cartouche.[10]

32. Relief fragments found at Lahun, most likely belonging to the tomb of the 'high steward' Antefiqer.

33. Inscriptions found on statues from Dahshur, both belonging to 'high stewards'. The statues themselves were not published. *Above*: inscription of the 'high steward Sobekemhat, begotten of Zatwerut'. *Left*: inscription of Nesmont.

The 'high stewards' of the following reigns up to the Thirteenth Dynasty are less well known. Their titles and monuments often indicate that they held considerable power, but in most cases it is hard to gain a clearer picture. Antefiqer was 'scribe of the king's document' before becoming 'high steward'. This first title is found on a statue excavated at Lisht. He had a tomb at Lahun and might therefore date under Senusret II or shortly after. The two findspots of monuments for Antefiqer might indicate that the two title-holders, though having the same mother's name, are not identical. The tomb at Lahun has yet to be positively identified, but blocks with his name (Fig. 32) and a wonderful statue of him were found there, obviously coming from his tomb. On the statue he is 'high steward'. The function title on the blocks is lost. Khnumhotep has already been mentioned, as he later became vizier (p.

33). Sobekemhat and Nesmont are basically known only from their statues, found at Dahshur (Fig. 33). One wonders whether Sobekemhat is identical with the 'treasurer' and vizier of the same name buried at Dahshur next to the pyramid of Senusret III (p. 31). Khentykhetywer is attested on two stelae and two statues, all from his chapel at Abydos. One of the statues is inscribed with a remarkable list of religious titles. He was evidently some kind of high priest in many important cults of that time.

Several 'high stewards' can be dated to the beginning of Amenemhat III's reign. Meketankhu is known from an Abydos stela (Fig. 34) and a rock inscription dated to year 4 of this king. Senmeri appears in the Semnah despatches, administrative documents relating to the Nubian fortress of Semnah. Senebef is also securely datable under this king and appears on a stela found at the Red Sea and on a papyrus fragment. Ameny-seneb might be identical to the 'deputy treasurer' of the same name attested under Amenemhat III. Other 'high stewards' of the late Twelfth and early Thirteenth Dynasties are hard to date; for us they are most often simply names known from their remarkable monuments, such the realistic statue of Gebu, and those of Ptahwer or Senusret. The latter owned a fine bronze statue, now in a private collection, and some other objects.

Another example of a 'high steward' known only from a statue, now in the Egyptian Museum, Cairo, is Nebsekhut (Plate 7). The statue shows the official sitting on the ground. His face is that of an elderly man. Statues of officials depicted as old and far removed from all conventional beauty are known from many periods of Egyptian history. The most famous examples are Hemiunu and Ankhkhaef, who were viziers in the Fourth Dynasty. In the late Twelfth Dynasty in particular, the king's portrait also changed. However, Egyptian art most often depicted an ideal type of person, never, or at least not very often, something we would regard as a true portrait. So why did some kings of the late Twelfth Dynasty and many officials choose to be portrayed as old men? One answer is perhaps to be found in the demography of ancient Egypt and pre-modern societies in general. Not many people reached old age. Most, if they did not die in childhood, were lucky to survive their twenties. People in their forties, fifties or even sixties were rare, perhaps just a few per cent of the whole population. People who became old must have been very proud of that. Obviously, they might have suffered several illnesses, best described in the introduction of the 'Teaching of Ptahhotep': 'Old age has struck, age has descended, feebleness has come, weakness is here again.' These statues and reliefs showing officials in their advanced age may therefore be a statement that the people depicted had reached a certain age, had survived many others, and had come closer to the ancient Egyptian's ideal age of 110. On the other hand, in the late Middle Kingdom, after Senusret II and up to the middle of the

75

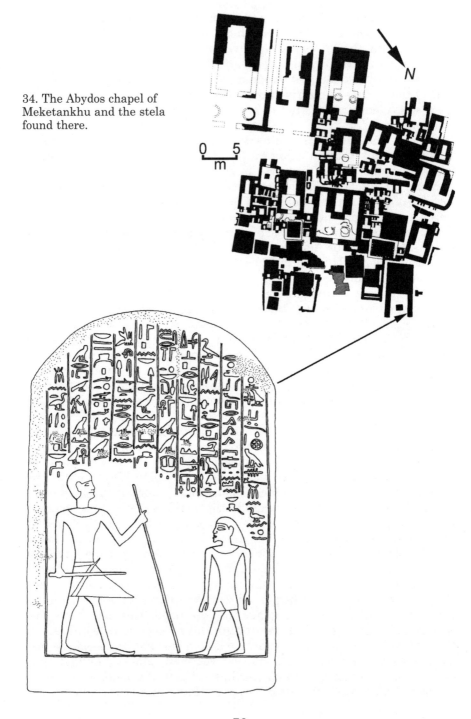

34. The Abydos chapel of Meketankhu and the stela found there.

Thirteenth Dynasty, kings were very often shown as old men and one could argue that officials simply followed their ruler's model, perhaps without reflecting on the original meaning of this type of depiction. There were, however, always images produced showing idealised youth-fulness,[11] which shows that the image of an old man was chosen for a purpose. The image of an old, perhaps wise and wealthy, official in the late Middle Kingdom was therefore partly influenced by royal portrai-ture, but was obviously also the result of that official's individual deci-sion. In the Old Kingdom and in the first half of the Twelfth Dynasty, the image represented the desire to be seen as a wise man who was able to survive others and reach old age.

With the reign of Sobekhotep II we reach firmer ground for establish-ing an order of 'high stewards'. Aabni appears in the famous Papyrus Boulaq 18 and is therefore datable under Sobekhotep II. He is also known from other objects. There is a stela in the Cairo Museum naming several other officials, including a 'pure-priest of Sakhmet', a title of healers often found on expeditions into the desert. The stela is of some importance for chronological reasons, as it provides a fixed point for the 'treasurer' Senebsumai. On the stela appears the 'chamberlain of the Djed-bau'[12] Neni, who appears on another stela, where in turn a certain Nebirut is depicted, a well known official under Senebsumai.[13] The name of Aabni also appears on a weight, and on a stone slab found at Abydos. Nothing more is known about his family or career.

Two of the best known officials of the Thirteenth Dynasty were 'high stewards' and are datable shortly after the officials mentioned above. Titi appears on several monuments, including seals, stelae and statues. Although these monuments tell us little about his private life, they pres-ent one of the longest careers of the Middle Kingdom. He started his career as a simple 'cupbearer', was promoted to the position of a 'cham-berlain of the inner palace', then 'overseer of sealers' and finally 'high steward'. He lived in the first part of the Thirteenth Dynasty and was perhaps 'high steward' under Neferhotep I. As 'cupbearer' he was a mid-dle official in the administration of food production and storage at the royal palace. Out of context, the title may sound lowly, but it was most likely already a relatively elevated administrative post, organising labour and being in charge of other people. The 'chamberlain of the inner palace' was one of the main persons responsible for the food supply of the palace, organising deliveries and distribution to the palace officials. The function of the 'overseer of sealers' is not yet known for sure, but was most likely also connected with food production or the production sector in general at the royal palace. With this position he received the impor-tant ranking titles 'member of the elite, foremost of action' and 'royal sealer'. He also became 'the one who follows the king'. The last stage of his career was finally as 'high steward'. Although Titi is known from quite a large number of objects, in the end little is known about him. His parents are a certain Min-aa ('Min, the great' or perhaps better 'Min is great') and the 'lady of the house' Nitnub. His wife is not yet known for sure, nor do we know any of his children. Most of his monuments show him with colleagues or alone, but never with his family.

The best known 'high steward' of the Thirteenth Dynasty is Nebankh. He was in office after Titi, although there are problems in arranging a succession of title-holders for this time, especially because there is clear evidence that several of them were in office at the same time.[14] Nebankh was the son of the simple 'steward' Sobekhotep and of the 'lady of the house' Hapyu. Nebankh started his career as 'king's acquaintance' and is known in this position from a number of rock inscriptions found in the region of Aswan. Here he appears together with the family of king Neferhotep I, undoubtedly having been sent on a mission in that region for the king. As 'high steward' he appears on monuments datable under Sobekhotep IV and was perhaps promoted when the king came to the throne. Nebankh is known with this new title from an inscription in the Wadi el-Hudi and one in the hard stone quarry region of the Wadi Hammamat. The Wadi el-Hudi was the place where amethyst was mined. Nebankh was clearly leading or at least involved in royal expeditions to these regions. He appears on a number of his own monuments. There is part of a statue providing a long list of titles, such as 'master of the secret of heaven and earth' and 'guardian of silver and gold'. There are fragments of a lintel perhaps from his tomb at Abydos and there is a stela which bears a hymn to Osiris-Khontyamentiu. One stela, also found at Abydos, was set up by the 'singer' Tjeniaa and inscribed with a short song, this time for Nebankh himself. An important monument mentioning the 'high steward' is the stela of the queen Nubkhaes, now in the Louvre. This lists the family of the queen including Nebankh, who was her uncle. Nebankh's brother was the 'scribe of the vizier' Dedusobek, father of the queen. Another important member of the family was Sobekemsaf, known from several monuments. He was 'overseer of the double granary' and later 'reporter'. On the stela, Nebankh is described finally by the additional phrase, 'the one who follows the king', which also appears on his few seals. One last, exceptional object belonging to Nebankh is his heart scarab (Fig. 35), made of dark green jasper. This finely crafted object, just 3.1 cm high, has a human face and is inscribed on the underside with a spell known as 'Book of the Dead' chapter 30b. It is the earliest dated example of that spell. The text reads:

> The high steward Nebankh, he says: heart of my mother, heart of my mother, my foreheart of my forms, do not stand against me as witness, do not stand against me, do not oppose me in the tribunal, do not incline against me in the presence of the keeper of the scales, you are my ka in my body, Khnum who lets my limbs be well, may you come to the good place, which will be prepared there, make not

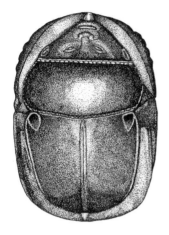

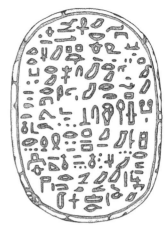

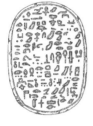

35. The heart scarab of Nebankh, enlarged and original size (3.1 cm high).

foul my name at the court which sets people in the right standing, it would be good for us, and good for him who hears, a pleasure for him who judges, do not be false beside the god, see your character is your eternity.

Other 'high stewards' of about this time are Nehy, Zasatet, Senebikhered and Res, all kown from a number of monuments, mostly stelae and scarabs. The relationship between them is unknown. They all had ranking titles, but it remains unclear whether they were in office at about the same time or followed one another. The 'high stewards' after Nebankh are less well known. One of them, perhaps in office shortly after, is Rehuankh. He is mainly known as 'king's acquaintance' under Neferhotep I and Sobekhotep IV and seems to have belonged to the entourage of the 'treasurer' Senebi (p. 64). He also went on a mission with Nebankh to the Wadi el-Hudi, but after that disappears from our records. However, there are seals of an 'overseer of sealers' Rehuankh and a statue of a 'high steward' with the same name. The close connection of these three titles is well known, so it seems possible that all these monuments belong to the same person. To about the same period under or shortly after Sobekhotep IV also belongs the official Amenemhat-seneb Nemtyemweskhet.[15] He is not securely datable, but must belong to about this period. He had a chapel in Abydos. On one of the stelae there is also shown the 'overseer of sealers' Aki, who later also became 'high steward'. The chapel of Nemtyemweskhet was equipped with a model sarcophagus which contained a decorated model coffin and a figure inside, obviously representing Nemtyemweskhet. Finally, he is known from several seals. Further title-holders of the second half of the Thirteenth Dynasty are again mainly known only from their seals. From the writing of the title 'royal sealer' with the red crown on seals, more typical of the second part of the Thirteenth Dynasty, the following people might date to that time: Antef, Wenen, Mentuweser, Nemtyhotep, Renefemib, Redienptah, Sobekhotepwer and Sobekhotepmerytef.

The office of the 'high steward' is not well attested in the Second Intermediate Period. However, there is the canopic box of the 'high steward' Khonsmes, belonging on stylistic grounds to that period, and a certain Neferhotep appears in the tomb of Sobeknakht at Elkab, at least providing evidence for the existence of that office.

'Overseer of sealers'

Under or even alongside the 'high steward' was the 'overseer of sealers'. In the late Middle Kingdom the two seem to have worked closely together. In the Thirteenth Dynasty these two state officials were the only two to bear the additional titles or title extensions 'who follows the king' and 'the one in the chamber'. There are about eight 'overseers of sealers' in the Thirteenth Dynasty who went on to be appointed 'high steward', further indicating the close relationship between the two titles. However, the function of the 'overseer of sealers' is rather obscure. As the literal translation implies, he was presumably responsible for lower-status 'sealers'. As he was, at least in the late Middle Kingdom, closely related to the 'high steward', it might be argued that he was particularly in charge of the workforce and the storage/sealing of products in the palace, while the 'high steward' was responsible for agricultural products and their delivery to the residence.[16]

'Overseers of sealers' are attested from the Eleventh Dynasty. The first known title-holder is Khety, who appears in a dated inscription (year 41) under king Mentuhotep II. The inscription reads: 'coming north (from) Wawat of the royal sealer, sole friend Khety, born of Zatre'.[17] Wawat is the Egyptian word for Lower Nubia. The inscription might indicate that Khety was in charge of all or part of a military expedition to the southern neighbour of Egypt. This does not mean that 'overseer of sealers' was a military title, but indicates that Khety was a high

36. Stela of Emhat, dated to year nine of Senusret I. He was 'overseer of sealers' and 'keeper of the diadem in adorning the king'. The latter title indicates that Emhat was responsible for the crowns and dress of the king.

official at the royal court, entrusted by the king with an important mission. The inscription also mentions the 'sealer' Meketre. This is the first time that this famous 'treasurer' appears in our sources (p. 53), obviously working under Khety. Meru is attested slightly later under Mentuhotep II. He had a tomb at Thebes and is known from a large stela mentioning him and his family. The stela is dated to year 46 under the king and might come from his tomb, but Abydos has also been proposed. A rock inscription is known from the Shat er-Rigal, where he appears with the title 'overseer of the foreign lands'. This again may indicate some involvement in military actions against Lower Nubia.

It is not possible to establish a clear line of title-holders for the following (Twelfth) Dynasty. A certain Sokarhotep might date under Amenemhat I and was buried at Helwan, opposite Memphis. Emhat dates to the beginning of the reign of Senusret I and is known only from his finely crafted stela (Fig. 36). For the rest of the Twelfth Dynasty the 'overseers of the sealers' almost disappear from our sources at the royal court. Better known are the title-holders of the Thirteenth Dynasty. As already mentioned, many of them, such as Ankef, Nehy, Rehuankh and Titi, were promoted later in their careers to the post of 'high steward'. Herunefer was in office under the 'treasurer' Senebsumai (p. 63). He appears on several monuments, such as a stela, a rock inscription and a statue. Neteriemmer started his career in the household of the 'king's acquaintance' Senebi, who later became 'treasurer'. Under Senebi as 'treasurer' Neteriemmer finally became 'overseer of sealers'. Senebi, upon receiving his own high position, appointed lower officials to other more important posts.

Iahnefer is the only 'overseer of sealers' attested for certain in the Seventeenth Dynasty. He is shown on a stela found at Abydos directly behind king Nubkheperre Antef. He had in addition to his function title the rank of a 'royal sealer' and the title 'who follows the king'. These are the typical titles of an 'overseer of sealers' at the royal court in the late Middle Kingdom. The titles of Iahnefer demonstrate perfectly how patterns of the administration or at least title strings carried on till the end of the Second Intermediate Period. The 'overseer of sealers' was still important in the Eighteenth Dynasty.

'Overseer of the marshland dwellers'

The 'overseer of the marshland dwellers' is another official working in the economic part of the palace under the 'treasurer'. His function is obscure.[18] 'Marshland dweller' is a term relating to people living at the edge of cultivation. They were not always farmers, but seem to have lived by hunting and gathering in the marshes. The 'overseer of marshland dwellers' was therefore possibly an official in charge of these people and responsible for exploiting their products and bringing them to the palace.

The earliest known title-holder is Ameny, who dates to the end of the reign of Senusret I and under Amenemhat II. He appears in a rock inscription and on the annals stone of Amenemhat II found at Memphis, where it is stated that a statue of him was placed in the mortuary temple of a king. Another attestation of the title from about the same time appears in the famous 'Story of Sinuhe', where it is said that the 'overseer of marsh-land dwellers of the palace' had come to guide Sinuhe on his way home after he had just returned from Palestine. Almost no other title-holders are known with certainty for the rest of the Twelfth Dynasty.

The title is better attested in the Thirteenth Dynasty. Many title-holders are known only from their seals and some stelae. Ibi appears on two stelae, one belonging to the famous 'treasurer' Senebi (p. 64), show-ing that Ibi dates from Neferhotep I to about Sobekhotep IV. The other shows his family, including his wife Nefernay and three sons, all with a similar name to their father. One is called Ibiwer (Ibi the elder), one, like his father, simply Ibi, and one Ibiiyadj. The 'overseer of marshland dwellers' Senebni is datable by a king's name and belongs to the end of the Thirteenth Dynasty or the Sixteenth Dynasty. His tomb, containing his well preserved coffin and canopic chest as well as those of his wife, was found at the end of the nineteenth century. The objects were not found dur-ing a controlled excavation and were sold to different collections. On his own coffin, now in Cairo, and his canopic box, now in Moscow, he is called simply 'king's acquaintance'. To this tomb group also belongs an inscribed staff. Here Senebni appears as 'overseer of the marshland dwellers' and 'royal sealer'. The staff also bears a dedication of king Sewahenre, who is himself at present not datable to a particular dynasty. Obviously Senebni was promoted from one position to the other (compare p. 141).

Officials under the vizier

Under the vizier were the officials responsible for the scribal offices, the provincial administration and legal matters, but not so much involved in organising the economic aspects of the palace.

'Scribe of the king's document'

The 'scribe of the king's document' or, as he was called in the late Middle Kingdom, the 'personal scribe of the king's document' is attested, although not well, throughout the Middle Kingdom. The task of this per-son seems clear from the translation of the title: he wrote the king's let-ters and official documents. He was perhaps also the head of the scribal offices at the palace, although this is not clear from the sources. The first title-holder at the royal court is Iai, dating under Mentuhotep II. Not much is known about him and his tomb is as yet unidentified. However, he appears in inscriptions in the mortuary temple of the king and in rock inscriptions at Shat er-Rigal. In the rock inscriptions he also bears the titles 'royal sealer' and 'sole friend', indicating his high position. The next known title-holder is known only from one stela, which bears a biographical text providing detailed information on his career.

> I was born in the time of the majesty of the king Sehetepibre (Amenemhat I) when he departed in peace, I was a child when I knotted the head band in front of his majesty ... Kheperkare (Senusret I). His majesty appointed me as the scribe of the prison of hearing. He praised me therefore very much; His majesty appointed me as the scribe of the tema (unknown word), his majesty praised me therefore very much. His majesty appointed me as the counter of grain in Upper and Lower Egypt. He praised me therefore very much. His majesty appointed me as the scribe of the great compound. He praised me therefore. His majesty appointed me as scribe of the royal tablet and overseer of the works in the whole country ... the scribe of the royal document Zamont.[19]

At all stages of his career Zamont had titles where writing was important. All his promotions were made by the king and his good relationship with the ruler is always stressed.

Another 'scribe of the king's document' of the Twelfth Dynasty was Antefiqer, perhaps in office under Amenemhat II or Senusret II. He was promoted to the position of a 'high steward'. This is a career path unknown from the late Middle Kingdom, as the 'high steward' belonged to the branch of the administration that came under the 'treasurer'. However, Antefiqer dates to the early Middle Kingdom when the two branches of palace administration were most likely not yet fixed.

The title-holders of the Thirteenth Dynasty are a little better known. Senebtifi Ptahemsaf appears on a stela and is known from a well preserved statue, now in the British Museum. Iuy is mentioned in Papyrus Boulaq 18, the Theban administrative document belonging to the palace. Iymeru is known from a stela showing his whole family. His wife was the 'king's sister' Senebsimai, demonstrating a link to the king's house. This link is also known for Nebsun, who belonged to the wider family of the 'high steward' Nebankh and whose niece was the queen Nubkhaes. He dates shortly after Sobekhotep IV. From the last two examples, one gains the impression that the kings of this period chose men for this office who were already well known from their family background.

4. Other Important Officials

'Overseer of the compound'

The 'overseer of the compound' is especially well attested in the Thirteenth Dynasty. The 'compound' or 'enclosure', or as it is more often called, the 'great compound', was an institution for collecting people who had to work for the state. It is not fully clear whether their labour was some form of punishment or whether this work was some kind of corvée, which would mean that people needed for different state projects were collected for these purposes by the 'great compound'. The 'overseer of the compound' was obviously the highest official organising this workforce. Perhaps there were several of these institutions in the country and he was the main person in charge of them all, while the 'scribe of the great compound' seems to have been the official in charge of one of them, most likely the 'great compound' in Thebes. In the Thirteenth Dynasty the 'overseer of the compound' seems to have possessed considerable power. There are indications that several of them were directly appointed to the position of vizier, demonstrating their close link to that official. There is Ibiau, often identified with a vizier of the same name. However, the name Ibiau is quite common in the late Middle Kingdom and so the identification remains hypothetical. A clearer case is the 'overseer of the

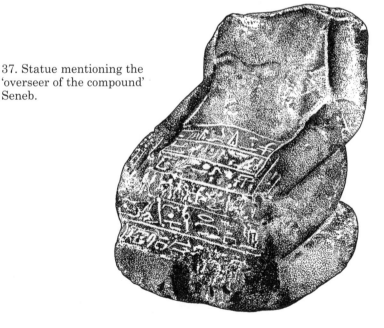

37. Statue mentioning the 'overseer of the compound' Seneb.

compound' with the double name Sobekaa Bebi. A person with exactly this double name is known as vizier. Both individuals are known only from seals. Sobekaa Bebi most likely dates to the Thirteenth Dynasty. The close connection of the office to the vizier also seems indicated by the family relationships of the 'overseer of the compound'. One of them was the father of the Thirteenth Dynasty vizier Ameny, while another was the brother of a vizier.

As has already been noted, in general the officials under the vizier did not have many seals. However, the 'overseers of the compound' are an exception. Many of them are known only from seals, indicating that sealing was an important part of their office.

'Overseer of fields'

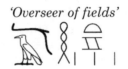

The title 'overseer of fields' itself goes back to the Old Kingdom and is first found in the provincial administration. At the end of the Old Kingdom two viziers also hold the title, indicating already for this period a close link with that office. This close connection is still visible in the Middle Kingdom. Senusret-ankh was 'overseer of fields' and was appointed vizier. A similar career is perhaps visible for the 'overseer of fields' Senebhenaef, although the connection is only via a common name and should be made with great caution. The close association between this office and the vizier's is also visible via family relationships. The vizier Ibiau was the father of the 'overseer of fields' Senebhenaef, while the father of the 'overseer of fields' Zahathor was 'scribe of the vizier'.

The function of these officials is not clear, but a papyrus found at Harageh indicates that they were responsible for measuring the land, perhaps after the Nile flood.[20] They were responsible for the land registers and worked closely with the institutions involved in recording information regarding agricultural land. Thus another connection to scribal offices is visible. At the beginning of his career, Senusret-ankh was 'personal scribe of the king's document' before becoming 'overseer of fields'.

Officials with this title but without ranking titles are also well known from the provincial administration. They sometimes had religious titles. On a local level there is an indication that for the 'overseer of fields' religious and secular administration were not fully separated. The most famous case is the 'first overseer of priests' and 'overseer of fields' Horemkhauef at Hieraconpolis. He was certainly the main priest of his establishment, but was also responsible for the fields and land, which at least here were under the charge of the temple administration.[21]

An 'overseer of fields' with ranking titles is known at the royal court

38. Two blocks from the tomb of the 'overseer of fields' Ankhu.

from the time of Senusret I or Amenemhat II. The first known title-holder with ranking titles was Imhotep, known from his mastaba at Lisht, which had a decorated tomb chamber. Imhotep had several important titles, including 'overseer of works'. The title indicates that he was involved in important building works, perhaps even in building the pyramid for Senusret I or Amenemhat II. Mentuhotep is known only from a statue that is hard to date, but he may belong to the Twelfth Dynasty.

Ankhu is known from a number of objects. He started his career as 'reporter' and is attested in rock inscriptions near Aswan with this title. In a biographical inscription once decorating his tomb he states that he was scribe at a temple of Senusret III. The inscription does not mention his function as 'reporter' (Fig. 38). One wonders whether the identification of the 'reporter' and 'overseer of fields' is correct, although they both have a mother with the same name. It seems possible that the scribal title relating to Senusret III may have been a prestigious position worth mentioning in a biographical inscription, but in reality not an important administrative position, while 'reporter' was his real function title. Another option is that 'reporter' is the function title Ankhu was given specifically for his mission to the Aswan region. As 'overseer of fields' Ankhu had the highest ranking titles 'member of the elite', 'foremost of action' and 'royal sealer'. These high titles are not common at the end of the Twelfth Dynasty and indicate special royal favour. Looking at the family of Ankhu this royal favour is indeed visible. His mother was called Merestekh. On earlier monuments she appears without titles, while later she suddenly has the titles 'member of the elite' and 'king's sister'. Obviously her brother became king and must have been one of the first rulers of the Thirteenth Dynasty. The high ranking titles of Ankhu were found only on monuments on which his mother also appears with her titles relating to the king. These high titles were obviously a special honour given by the king to a close relative.

Several other 'overseers of fields' are known from the late Middle Kingdom, but they are most often just names for us. However, the families of several of them are known, providing some insight into the social structure at the highest court level. One example is Amenemhat, attested on a stela formerly in Liverpool but destroyed in World War II.[22] He was the son of a 'lady of the house' Hapyu. His father is so far unknown. His wife was the 'lady of the house' Hebegeget. Three sons are mentioned on the stela and they are all officials connected with the administration under the vizier. There is the 'scribe of the great compound' Dedusobek, the 'great one of the tens of Upper Egypt' Mentuhotep, and the 'scribe of the seal of the unit of the head of the South' Dedusobek Renefseneb. The latter was born to a woman with the unusual name Shenethetepankh Henut, who was perhaps a second wife of Amenemhat or related in another way to the family. However, all the male members of Amenemhat's family had important administrative titles, albeit not on the same high level as Amenemhat; none had ranking titles. The stela itself was produced by a workshop on Elephantine; its find-place is unknown as it is only recorded that it was bought in the first half of the nineteenth century in Egypt. A similar case is the family of the 'royal sealer' and 'overseer of fields' Dedetu, who is known from two stelae (Fig. 39). His father came from a high, but not the highest, social background and was 'great one of the tens of Upper Egypt'. Two of his brothers were 'zab-official' and 'mouth of Nekhen', positions slightly under that of their father. Only Dedetu received a high court position with a ranking title. He was married to a woman with the title 'member of the elite' Hatshepsut. Her title indicates that she was a relative of the royal family (see p. 162). One wonders whether a member of her family suddenly became king and this presently unknown king promoted members of his wider family, like Dedetu, to the highest court positions. This is only a guess, but seems one option. The sons of Dedetu had high titles such as 'elder of the hall' or 'guardian', but not the highest positions at the royal court.

There are several 'overseers of fields' mentioned on stelae or rock inscriptions around Aswan and Elephantine, obviously left there by those on missions in that region. The Ankhu discussed above as 'overseer of fields' is attested there by a statue. Another example is Zahathor, also known from a stela made by the same workshop as the one of Amenemhat, mentioned earlier, and certainly close to it in date. The stela of Zahathor was found in the sanctuary of Heqaib on Elephantine. His brother was the 'great one of Upper Egypt' Ameny. His father was

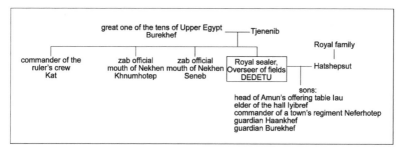

39. Family of the 'overseer of fields' Dedetu.

the 'scribe of the vizier' Amenaa.[23] These are again titles closely related to the vizier. Kheperka is known from a statue now in Turin, Italy. Here his parents are mentioned. His father was the 'steward of the production-place'[24] Sobekemmer, his mother, whose name is hard to read, was perhaps called Tjenet. The statue of Kheperka is dedicated by a king, whose name is sadly much too destroyed to be read, but is most likely a ruler of the early Thirteenth Dynasty. In all these examples, as with most Middle Kingdom officials, it is again apparent that there was no father to son succession in office.

'Overseers of fields' are still well attested in the Second Intermediate Period; two are known from their Theban burials. The name and titles of a certain Ibiau appear on coffin fragments, and the name of Redienamun appears on a gilded canopic chest. The tomb of Redienamun (Fig. 40) is so far the only fully published tomb of a high official dating to the Second Intermediate Period. Although his tomb had been looted, the finds from it give a fair impression of a burial of that time. Redienamun was buried in a shaft tomb with two chambers. One of the chambers had a groove at the bottom for a box coffin and canopic chest. They were both made of wood and already totally decayed when found. Only inlays and the imprint of the wood in the ground provided a guideline. They show that the burial equipment included a canopic chest adorned with gold foil, inscribed and providing the name and titles of Redienamun. The gold foil was found in fragments but it was possible to put it together. Its position on the canopic chest remains pure speculation. There are no other canopic chests known with such gold foil. Inside the canopic box were the four canopic jars, made of clay and well preserved. The stoppers were of human shape and once made of wood; only the gilded ears are preserved. Other finds in the tomb are some pottery vessels and pieces of jewellery, a single partly gilded bead most likely from a necklace, and a scarab. There are gold foil fragments of a rishi coffin (anthropoid form with feathered decoration), which had presumably served as the inner coffin. The burial shows the essential elements of a burial at the top of Egyptian society in the Second Intermediate Period. These

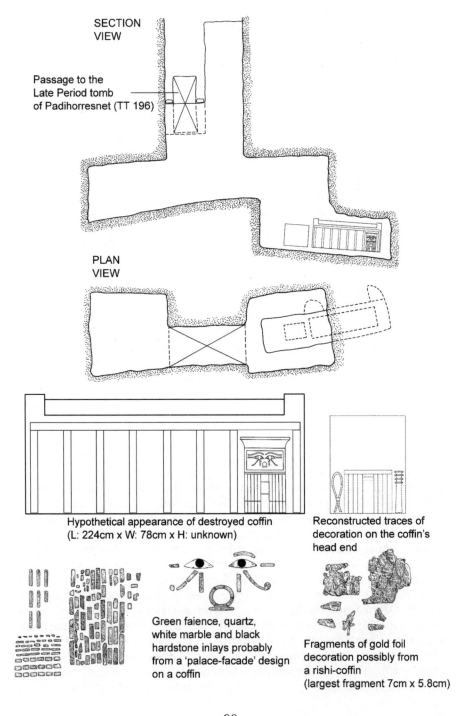

SECTION
VIEW

Passage to the
Late Period tomb
of Padihorresnet (TT 196)

PLAN
VIEW

Hypothetical appearance of destroyed coffin
(L: 224cm x W: 78cm x H: unknown)

Reconstructed traces of
decoration on the coffin's
head end

Green faience, quartz,
white marble and black
hardstone inlays probably
from a 'palace-facade' design
on a coffin

Fragments of gold foil
decoration possibly from
a rishi-coffin
(largest fragment 7cm x 5.8cm)

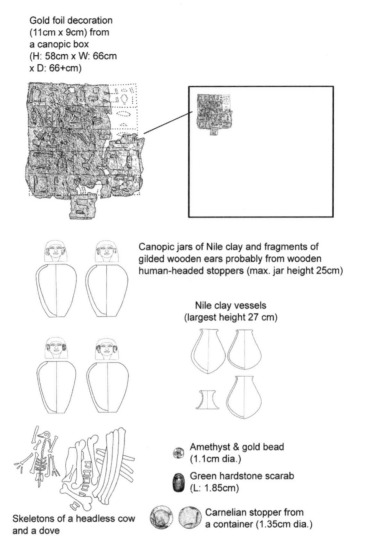

Gold foil decoration (11cm x 9cm) from a canopic box (H: 58cm x W: 66cm x D: 66+cm)

Canopic jars of Nile clay and fragments of gilded wooden ears probably from wooden human-headed stoppers (max. jar height 25cm)

Nile clay vessels (largest height 27 cm)

Amethyst & gold bead (1.1cm dia.)

Green hardstone scarab (L: 1.85cm)

Skeletons of a headless cow and a dove

Carnelian stopper from a container (1.35cm dia.)

40. *Opposite and above*: the tomb and tomb equipment of the 'overseer of fields' Redienamun.

include two coffins – an outer box coffin and an inner anthropoid one, in this case a rishi coffin – and a canopic chest with canopic jars. The mummy of Redienamun was most likely adorned with jewellery. An essential part of the tomb equipment was also pottery vessels, serving perhaps as symbolic containers for the eternal food supply. Finally, there is Nebiryrau, dating to about the same time. He appears on a stela also found at Thebes, which most likely came from his tomb.

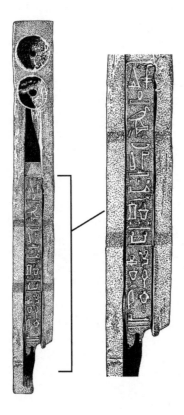

41. Scribal palette of the 'royal sealer' and 'leader of the broad hall' Ibiau (Thirteenth to Seventeenth Dynasty). On the palette there is a short offering formula invoking 'Thoth, lord of the god's word' and asking for incense and oil.

'Leader of the broad hall'

The 'leader of the broad hall' is another important official directly under the vizier. People with this title are known from the Old Kingdom, where the title often appears in a juridical context, and sometimes in the title strings of viziers.[25] In the early Middle Kingdom it is attested so far only once, in the tomb of the vizier Antefiqer at Lisht. One has the impression that Antefiqer just copied a title string of the Old Kingdom, as is often the case in early Middle Kingdom contexts.

'Leader of the broad hall' became a regular office at the royal court connected with the ranking title 'royal sealer' only in the late Middle Kingdom. However, it is not well attested and all the officials of the Middle Kingdom seem to date to the Thirteenth Dynasty. In the Thirteenth Dynasty officials had only short title strings. Only a few biographical inscriptions on stelae are preserved. Information on the

42. Stela of the 'leader of the broad hall' Khons.

duties of this official therefore remains limited and any statement regarding his function must be speculative.[26] One of the best attested title-holders is Renseneb, dating to the Thirteenth Dynasty and known from several impressive stelae. Before becoming 'leader of the broad hall', he was 'great one of the Tens of Upper Egypt' and 'commander of the ruler's crew'. The latter is a military title, and perhaps his career from a military position to high office indicates that the 'leader of the broad hall' had the core task of providing security in the palace. Khons is known from his burial at Abydos. On a large stela found there he is shown sitting in front of an offering table. On another stela he bears the titles 'royal sealer' and 'overseer of the royal production place', most likely a position he had before becoming 'leader of the broad hall'. In this case a connection with the economic parts of the administration is visible.

Khons is mainly known from two stelae found in a tomb at Abydos (Fig. 42). Few tombs of highest officials dating to the Thirteenth Dynasty are known. Three of them were found at Dahshur,[27] which was obviously the main cemetery for court officials of the late Middle Kingdom. However, other officials were perhaps buried at Abydos. The case of Nebankh has already been mentioned (p. 78). Another case is Khons. His tomb complex was already heavily looted when found and consisted of several shafts placed side by side. At the bottom of each shaft was a small chamber, one presumably belonging to Khons himself, the others perhaps for members of his family. This is one of the few known Thirteenth Dynasty burials of a high official.

'Overseer of the gateway'

The title 'overseer of the gateway'[28] is already known from the late Old Kingdom. In this period it is best attested at the provincial courts, not the royal residence. It is therefore one of the titles which entered the royal court in the Middle Kingdom via the provincial administration of the First Intermediate Period. The first known title-holders of the Middle Kingdom are all officials who later rose to higher positions. The earliest is Dagi, known with this title from his sarcophagus and from inscriptions in the mortuary temple of king Mentuhotep II at Deir el-Bahari. He later became vizier (p. 26). There is no successor known until much later. The next official at the royal court is the 'high steward' Hor (p. 72) under Senusret I. He bears the title on two monuments, once as one of several titles in connection with the 'high steward', indicating that 'overseer of the gateway' was a minor office for him and not his main function title. In the middle of the Twelfth Dynasty there are three title-holders, all attested on important monuments, thus indicating that the office had become very influential at the royal court. Ipi had a tomb at Lisht, a statue of him was found on Elephantine, and a stela is known from Abydos. On the statue found on Elephantine, an inscription states that 'the affairs of the Two Lands were reported to him'. He bears the highest ranking titles and was 'controller of the king's acquaintances'.[29] The tomb at Lisht is of some interesst as it is of a new type. It is only partly preserved, but the chapel had two rooms decorated with reliefs and paintings. It seems to have had a wide entrance, perhaps once even

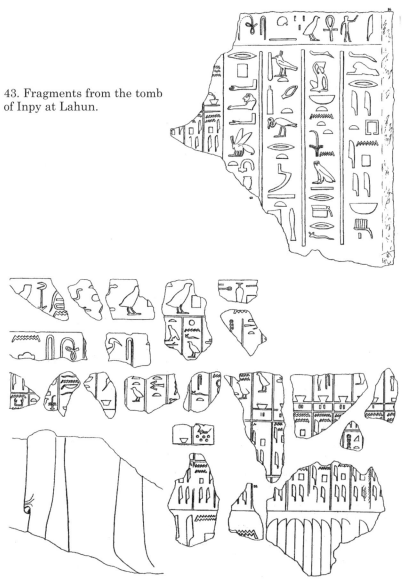

43. Fragments from the tomb
of Inpy at Lahun.

adorned with columns. The complex is surrounded by a wall and is more
like to a temple than a mastaba. Similar tombs are common at Lisht and
Saqqara, and seem to be the prototype for the New Kingdom temple
tombs. Khentykhetywer is known from a stela dated to year 28 under
Amenemhat II recording the safe return of an expedition to Punt. He
had a tomb at Dahshur, from which at least one fragment of an inscription with his name was found. Inpy had an impressive tomb at Lahun

(Fig. 43) consisting of a mastaba and a decorated chapel arranged like a rock-cut tomb. The tomb chamber was found at the end of a shaft under the mastaba. His titles include 'overseer of all royal works in the whole country', clearly indicating that he was responsible for important royal building works. Very little is known about the 'overseers of the gateway' in the late Twelfth and Thirteenth Dynasties. Basically, so far only two people for that period with ranking titles are attested on seals. These seals at least provide evidence that the title was still part of the royal court in the late Middle Kingdom.

The function of these officials remains highly enigmatic and rests on the meaning of the term here translated as 'gateway', which was perhaps the entrance part of the palace. In other cultures it is often the place where the law was pronounced – that is, in effect, 'published'. From the few biographical phrases of these officials it seems clear that they did not administer commodities, as the 'treasurer' or 'high steward' did, but were more involved in the organisation of specific sectors of the palace.[30]

Other officials

There are several titles that are just occasionally combined with ranking titles. Obviously these officials had received special status and some kind of promotion to the highest circle of people around the king. One promotion is clearly visible in Papyrus Boulaq 18. Here, as one of many officials appearing in the record, is the 'mouth of Nekhen' Titi. He is listed once as the first official after members of the royal family, while at another time in a similar list he appears further down, and finally in another list he appears as just one of eight officials listed. In yet another long list of officials he appears suddenly in the group of the highest officials with the ranking title 'royal sealer', behind the 'overseer of fields' and before the 'personal scribe of the king's document'. He was evidently appointed in the meantime to a higher position; however the reason for that promotion remains unknown.

A possible reason for one promotion is visible in the case of Kheperkare (compare p. 73), who is known from three stelae, on each of which he is given a different function title. Once he appears as a simple 'steward', but already with the ranking title 'king's acquaintance'. This demonstrates that he was most likely a 'steward' working in the palace administration. On another stela, now in Cairo, he had the function title 'chamberlain'.[31] On the same monument he also has the title 'overseer of all royal works' and the ranking titles 'member of the elite' and 'foremost of action'. He reports the building of a canal in the Thinite nome on a stela dated under Amenemhat II. The impression is that he received these highest ranking titles because of his building works. The function title 'chamberlain' is rarely connected with the highest ranking titles, making Kheperkare a special case.

Finally, there are several instances of certain titles connected with ranking titles. At present it is hard to decide whether these title-holders at the royal court were regularly promoted to the highest circle around the king, or whether it is just that these people were promoted more often, but still not on a regular basis. One example is the 'reporter'.[32] Three of these are known, all dating to the first half of the Twelfth Dynasty. The 'great one of the tens of Upper Egypt'[33] is another example. It is one of the most common titles in the late Middle Kingdom. Some of its holders also bear ranking titles.

High priests

In the Old and early Middle Kingdoms there were no high court officials exclusively acting as high priests of a god or at a temple. This is in stark contrast to the New Kingdom, when the high priests at Thebes, Memphis, Heliopolis and other important places were leading figures on the political scene. In the Middle Kingdom, only the high priest of Ptah, who had the title 'great one of the leader of craftsmen',[34] was of some importance. At least one of them, Senusret-ankh, was buried at Lisht close to the pyramid of Senusret I, thus indicating his close ties to the royal court. He also had high ranking titles, supporting the impression that he was a high court official. His mastaba is a huge complex with an underground burial chamber decorated with long religious texts. However, an important point is that his high priest title appears as one under many other titles. Senusret-ankh was an important official with religious titles, but it is almost impossible to pinpoint his main function. There are other monuments belonging to high priests which indicate their high status at the royal court. There is, for example, an impressive group statue showing a grandfather, father and son, all three with the titles of a high priest of Ptah. Senebuy was high priest of Ptah in the Thirteenth Dynasty. He is known only from one modest stela which shows him and 'his beloved wife, the "one adorning the king" Nubemhab'. Of special importance is the short inscription on the stela: 'member of the elite, foremost of action, one whose coming is awaited in the god's house, on the day of the rising of Sothis, the great one of the leaders of craftsmen for the Lord of all, great priest for his god, the lector priest Senebuy'. This passage may imply that the duties of the high priest of Ptah also included observing the rising of Sothis. Senebuy bears several titles including the highest ranking titles, underlining his high position. Of these, the title 'great (or greatest) priest of his god' is of special interest. In the Twelfth Dynasty there were several priestly titles, such as 'pure-priest' or just 'priest' (literally: 'servant of a god'). The title 'great pure priest' appears at that time. Clearly there was a new interest in expressing, and perhaps creating, a hierarchical order for priestly titles.

In the late Middle Kingdom several other important cults received a leader who could be called 'high priest'. The title 'great one of the seers' is known from the Old Kingdom. It is connected with the cult of Re and Atum at Heliopolis. In the Old and Middle Kingdoms it is often found in the title strings of officials with other important functions, such as the 'high steward' Khentykhetywer, who bears the title as one of many religious titles on one of his statues. There is no sign that it was of special importance for him. This changed in the late Middle Kingdom, when several officials had as their main function title 'great one of the seers'. The only other title they bear is 'royal sealer', indicating their close connection to the royal court or at least their high social status. Not much is known about these priests; in most cases only their names and titles are preserved on monuments.

A little more is known about the first high priests of Amun. They did not have a special title but were called simply 'priest of Amun'. However, there are several of these priests known with the ranking title 'royal sealer'. Clearly by receiving this exclusive ranking title they were elevated to a special status. Few of these first high priests of Amun are known, perhaps indicating that the office was not yet the most important priestly office, as it came to be in the New Kingdom. The 'royal sealer' and 'priest of Amun' Senebefni was the son of the vizier Zamont, and so son of the most important Egyptian official.[35] If we accept the possibility that the vizier Zamont was the father of the vizier Ankhu, Senebefni would have been brother of a vizier in one of the most powerful families of the early Thirteenth Dynasty. The grandfather of Senebefni, whose name is not known, also held the title 'priest of Amun', showing that the position was kept in their family for some time.

In this and the previous chapters the highest state officials have been discussed. As stated at the outset, this is a select group of about ten people at the royal court, with a slightly wider group of up to forty local governors all around the country. In the Old Kingdom the group of highest state officials also included people who held titles relating to the dress, the crowns, the hair and even the fingernails of the king. This indicates the extent to which the ruler of the Old Kingdom was treated as a god; officials in charge of the above-mentioned parts of the kings were in some way priests of kings at the highest level. It is much disputed whether the role of the king changed in the Middle Kingdom and was perceived as being less divine. However, in the Middle Kingdom there are no such highest state officials around the king with tasks related to the dress, the hair or the crowns. These tasks must still have existed, but on a different level to those in the Old Kingdom. Officials with other titles took over these duties. One example is Hetep, buried at Saqqara and well known from his block-form statues, which are amongst the earliest examples preserved. In his tomb, Hetep appears with many titles. He has the highest ranking titles and was 'overseer of sealers' beside many others. One of his titles was also 'priest of the Upper and Lower Egyptian crown'.[36] As a high official at the royal court, one of Hetep's duties was obviously also looking after the royal crowns. The title 'priest of the Upper and Lower Egyptian crown' is not very common in the Middle Kingdom. One other holder of this title was a governor at Qaw el-Kebir, providing evidence of the importance of local officials at the royal court. However, the presence of this title at a provincial court raises two questions. Did this local governor spend most of his time at the royal court or was this title more or less symbolic? The most famous example of this title-holder is the 'one in the chamber' Zemty-the-younger.[37] He is known from his stela[38] on which a biography is preserved, presenting numerous titles of which many clearly relate to the king's cult and the care of his regalia, such as 'master of the secret of the king's ornament' or 'servant of the Red Crown in the Shrine of Lower Egypt'. He is also mentioned on the stela as robing and crowning the king. On a Second Intermediate Period stela a person with the same title, 'one in the chamber', is shown directly behind king Rahotep.[39]

Another official connected with the king's regalia is the 'keeper of the diadem'.[40] People with this title are again not very well attested for the Middle Kingdom and one wonders whether the office was a regular one and it is just that the sources for establishing a line of title-holders are missing, or the title was given only sporadically to certain officials. The first one is the 'overseer of sealers' Emhat, datable to Senusret I. Here again, a high official bears a function title otherwise not related to the king's regalia. The title 'keeper of the diadem' is not his main function. In the late Middle Kingdom the picture changed and there are people with the sole function title of 'keeper of the diadem'. There was now one person at the royal court exclusively in this office. Here again, not many title-holders are known. In this instance, it might relate to the destruction of the royal cemeteries, since this is the place we would expect to find evidence for such people. It seems less likely that this class of official was sent on expeditions or for building works at Abydos, which constitute the main sources for Middle Kingdom officials.

Another title perhaps related to the regalia of the king, and this time far more common, is 'leader of all kilts'.[41] Many of the highest officials bear this title, and it is also well known for provincial governors. It is often connected with the title of a setem-priest – a position frequently recorded as principal officiant at the most solemn rituals such as burial.[42] The impression is that these officials were connected with the garments of the king, although perhaps more in a symbolic rather than a real way. The title basically disappears after the late Twelfth Dynasty.

There are two people with that function dating to the late Twelfth Dynasty,[43] but no certain example for the Thirteenth Dynasty. One wonders again who took over these functions or whether the title was just symbolic, without any real meaning. Another option is again that the title is not attested in the Thirteenth Dynasty because the royal cemeteries, where these people would have been buried, have not been located.

5

Military Officials

The military sector must have been an important part of Middle Kingdom administration. For most kings of the Eleventh and Twelfth Dynasties military campaigns are known. The kings and their armies invaded Nubia and Palestine, and war against Libyan tribes is also mentioned several times. This needed a well organised army. However, it must be admitted that we know surprisingly little about the organisation of troops and the hierarchy of military leaders.

'Overseer of troops'

The most important military official at the royal court with ranking titles was the 'overseer of troops'[1] or 'great overseer of troops'.[2] The title is known from the Old Kingdom, but it was only in the Eleventh Dynasty that it became important at the royal court. The development of the form of the title follows the patterns already seen for the 'high steward'. In the Eleventh Dynasty there was the 'overseer of troops', who could also be called 'overseer of troops in the entire land'. In the early Middle Kingdom this became the 'great overseer of troops'. However, both 'great overseer of troops' and 'overseer of troops' were always in use and in the case of the latter only the ranking titles make it possible to assign it to the royal court. As with the 'steward', the title is attested for people of a wide social spectrum, from officials in lower position to those at the top.

The 'overseer of troops' seems to have been slightly outside the hierarchies visible under the vizier and the 'treasurer'. So far there is no career path detectable for any of the officials mentioned to an 'overseer of troops', and no 'overseer of troops' seems to have been appointed to any of the offices described above. There are some stelae of these military officials mentioning other lower officials, but never any with ranking titles. An 'overseer of troops' appears in Papyrus Boulaq 18, showing at least that they were certainly part of the royal court.

The duties of the 'overseers of troops' are known from their biograph-

44. Siege of an Asian fortress, painting in the tomb of Antef, Eleventh Dynasty.

ical phrases and biographies. From these it is clear that these people not only had military functions, but were also involved in building projects. It might be concluded that basically it was the duty of the 'overseer of troops' to mobilise a high number of people for different types of projects. These were often of military character, but could also be building projects. Thus a translation of the title as 'general', as is often proposed, would be too narrow.

Some examples of the evidence for these title-holders can be given. In the tomb of Antef, dating under Mentuhotep II, the siege of an Asian fortress is shown (Fig. 44), reflecting his military duties. The stela of the 'great overseer of troops' Nesmont (p. 103) reports conflict apparently in civil war under Amenemhat I. Several 'overseers of troops' appear in military contexts in Lower Nubia, confirming the military responsibilities of these officials. However, Senebu under Senusret I reports that he was responsible for royal craftsmen. 'Overseers of troops' appear in inscriptions on pyramid blocks, indicating their involvement in pyramid building.[3] They also appear in inscriptions in Sinai, perhaps indicating that they functioned there as overseers of groups of workmen.

In the Second Intermediate Period there is evidence that royal family members were appointed to military positions, something not known from the Middle Kingdom. The best example is the 'great overseer of troops' and 'king's son' Herunefer, so far attested only from a board of his coffin.[4] He was the son of an obscure king Mentuhotep and of a 'great king's wife', proving that his title 'king's son' was not a title of honour but reflected a family connection. A stela, most likely from Denderah, mentions another 'king's son' with the name Ameny.[5] In his filiation he is called a son of a king. He was 'commander of the ruler's crew', a common title of that period, but he did not have ranking titles and therefore could not have belonged to the inner circle of people around the king.

It comes as no surprise to find that the history of the holders of the title 'overseers of troops' reads almost like the military history of the Middle Kingdom, at least for its first half. Antef has already been mentioned. He is known from his large tomb at Thebes, located directly in front of the funerary complex of Mentuhotep II. It belongs to the type known as saff tombs which, like most Egyptian tombs of officials, consisted of two parts. The front of the tomb was decorated with nine sturdy pillars which were painted, a typical feature of this kind of tomb. Behind the pillars was a transverse passageway decorated with paintings and with stelae. Cut into the middle of the back wall was a corridor decorated with reliefs of the highest quality leading to a chapel lined with fine stone slabs, which were painted. While the reliefs and the limestone slabs of the inner cult chapel were smashed in ancient times, several paintings on the pillars survived. Here, the siege of an Asiatic fortress is depicted, perhaps located in Southern Palestine. This scene indicates a military campaign of Mentuhotep II to Palestine, which is otherwise not attested. Other scenes show three boats with soldiers, hunting in the marshes and in the desert, and several workshops, with carpenters as well as leather and metal working.[6] The second part is the underground burial chamber. In the tomb chamber under the cult rooms an undecorated sarcophagus was found made from several blocks of limestone.

The successor of Antef in the office of 'overseer of troops' is not yet known and one wonders whether a direct line of officials existed with that title or whether they were put in charge only when needed. The latter seems likely since the next 'overseer of troops', who bears the name Mentuhotep, is attested in rock inscriptions in the Wadi Hammamat under Mentuhotep IV as a member of the expedition guided by the vizier Amenemhat to collect stone for a royal sarcophagus (see p. 27).

Nesmont was in office under Amenemhat I and Senusret I. He is known from several stelae and from two statues and was obviously an important official. On a stela coming from Abydos he seems to report civil war-like situations in Egypt: 'I trained the troops in ambush, and at daybreak the landing stage surrendered. When I grasped the tip of the bow, I led the battle for the two lands. I was victorious, my arms taking [so much spoil] that I had to leave [some] on the ground. I destroyed

45. Procession of offering bearers reconstructed from fragments from the tomb of Antef.

the foes, I overthrew the enemies of my lord, there being none other who will say the like.'[7] Nesmont was obviously loyal to the king. The names of Senusret I and Amenemhat I appear on the same stela, perhaps indicating that it was made by these kings for their loyal servant at the time they had joint rule.

Two '(great) overseers of troops' are known to have been involved in the Nubian campaign of Senusret I. In his eighteenth year the king sent troops to conquer the region of Lower Nubia between Aswan in the North and the Second Cataract in the South. The 'overseers of troops' under that king are Mentuhotep, appearing on a large stela found at the lower Nubian fortress of Buhen, and Dedu-Antef, known from two inscriptions. Besides these two officials, there are several other court officials mentioned in inscriptions, making Senusret I's Nubian campaign one of the best known in terms of the people involved. Mentuhotep has long title strings on the only monument mentioning him. He was 'member of the elite, foremost of action, sole friend, mouth of all people of Buto, overseer of the recruits' and finally 'overseer of troops'. His stela is a mixture of private and royal monument. In the upper half, Senusret I is shown in front of the god Mont 'receiving' ten countries or people, just conquered. The scene follows a royal inscription and at the bottom of the stela is a longer inscription with biographical phrases relating to Mentuhotep. The text is heavily destroyed, but records a 'broad mission' and the killing of people (?).[8]

The inscriptions of Dedu-Antef were found at Wadi Halfa. They are shorter, only providing the titles and his name. Here again, there is a mixture of royal and private inscriptions. On one of the stela there appears on one side the royal titulary carved in large signs, next to which are the titles of Dedu-Antef carved much smaller.[9] He had similar titles to Mentuhotep and was 'overseer of the menfat-troops,[10] overseer of the recruits'[11] and 'great overseer of troops in the whole country'.

Senusret I also employed other officials for his military campaign. The governor of the 'Antelope nome' reports in a biographical inscription in his tomb at Beni Hasan that he followed his lord to Kush (Nubia). In this action Ameny had the titles 'son of a governor, royal sealer' and 'great overseer of the troops in the Antelope nome',[12] obviously before he was appointed to the post of local governor.[13] We know that he became governor in year 18 of Senusret I and one wonders whether his appointment is connected with the mission to Nubia. Another important official with the name Mentuhotep appears on a stela found in the region of Abu Handal (Lower Nubia). He had again the high ranking titles 'member of the elite, foremost of action, royal sealer' and 'sole friend'. His function title was 'overseer of the double granary'. The stela is again dated to year 18 of Senusret I. Mentuhotep was certainly involved in the same campaign.[14] However, his main title, 'overseer of the double granary', might come as a surprise. He did not have any military titles on that

46. Two inscriptions copied from statues in Karnak. The statues are now lost, but they belonged to the 'great overseer of troops' Amenemhat (*above*) and the 'overseer of troops' Sehetepibre-seneb (*below*). Amenemhat lived under king Sobekhotep IV who dedicated the statue; the date of Sehetepibre-seneb is uncertain.

monument and is not attested on any other monument. The title 'overseer of the double granary' is mainly found in the late Middle Kingdom as a function title, although the early Middle Kingdom 'high steward' Zanofret also bears this title in a prominent position, directly before his name, on a statue found on Elephantine. Otherwise it appears most often as part of longer title strings of 'high stewards' and other important officials. Mentuhotep was most likely an official close to the king and placed on a military mission as a man the king could trust. His original court function was less important for his new mission. However, it is interesting that he does not bear any titles relating to this military mission and it can be argued that his main position was providing food for the soldiers.

The evidence indicates that four of the highest state officials were involved in the Nubian campaign of Senusret I. There were two '(great) overseers of troops', there was one local governor also provided with the same title, and there was an 'overseer of the double granary'. The responsibilities of these people are not known. They might have commanded different groups of soldiers, but it is also possible that they had different functions within one big army. At least the involvement of Ameny, who was a 'son of a mayor', might indicate that troops for the military campaign were drawn from provincial places. The 'overseer of the double granary' again makes us aware that the activities of many of the officials who were sent on special missions had nothing to do with their main function at the royal court. A similar case is known from the Thirteenth Dynasty. Ibiau was 'deputy treasurer' and recorded on his stela that he 'opened Kush', obviously referring to his involvement in a military campaign. This is unusual, as 'deputy treasurer' is not normally a title connected with military action.

The '(great) overseers of troops' after Senusret I are little known; they appear most often on stelae found at Abydos, with nothing recorded about the events of their life. Ameny may have been in office at the end of the reign of Senusret I or at the beginning of that of Amenemhat II. He is known from three magnificent stelae found at Abydos and from his tomb at Lisht, the publication of which remains incomplete.[15]

Senusret III is the most famous 'warrior' king of the Middle Kingdom. He pursued several Nubian campaigns and there is also evidence for military actions in Palestine. In contrast to the evidence for his campaigns, there are few officials known who were involved in these actions; for example, no 'overseers of troops' are securely datable under this king. However, the reign of Senusret III is a time when many new titles appeared in the administration. One of these new titles, and one common for the late Middle Kingdom and Second Intermediate Period, is 'great commander of a town'.[16] This title seems to represent an official responsible for a number of soldiers belonging to a town or fortress. Therefore it is no surprise to find the title often in Lower Nubia, where there were many fortresses. One of the first title-holders is Khusobek, known from several inscriptions and stelae. One of them has a long biographical inscription in which he reports that a place called Sekemem fell and that Retjenenu was defeated. Retjenenu appears in other Egyptian sources and was located in Palestine. The whereabouts of Sekemem is not yet attested for sure. Khusobek bears on his stela the high ranking titles 'member of the elite' and 'foremost of action'. Interestingly, no other 'great commander of a town' is known with these high titles, indicating that Khusobek gained them as a special favour for his success in the campaigns described on the stela.

In the late Middle Kingdom some 'great overseers of troops' are known in charge of Nubian fortresses. They are known from inscriptions marking the highest level of the Nile within one year:

> Level of the Nile in year seven of the King of Upper and Lower Egypt Maakherure (= Amenemhat IV), may he live for ever, according when the 'royal sealer' and 'great overseer of troops' Resseneb was in charge of Sekhem-Khakaure-maakheru (= fortress of Semnah).[17]

It appears that these 'great overseers of troops' were placed in charge of the most southerly fortresses of the territory ruled by Egyptians. In Askut the same function is attested for a 'follower of a ruler'.[18] It seems that, once again, the king chose people close to him for that task.

The few longer texts datable to the Second Intermediate Period report unrest and the invasion of foreigners into Egypt. At that time military titles became extremely important in Egypt. However, they do not appear any more often at the highest social level, for which almost no changes are visible. For example, Herunefer was 'great overseer of troops' and the son of a king with the name Mentuhotep.

'Overseer of police'

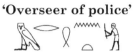

Another important official perhaps involved in military or similar tasks is the 'overseer of police'.[19] The translation may be misleading as there was in the Middle Kingdom, indeed in the whole ancient world, nothing comparable to the modern concept of police. The few sources for these people indicate a responsibility somewhere between police and judges. A list of members of a household in Lahun is compiled by an 'overseer of police'. However, the most important sources for the title, at least at the highest court level, are the monuments of Dedusobek. So far he is known from three stelae and one offering table. Their style suggests a date around the middle of the Twelfth Dynasty, perhaps the end of the reign of Amenemhat II to the first years of Senusret III. Dedusobek has the highest ranking titles. One of the inscriptions reads: 'member of the elite, foremost of action, the master of the secrets in the chamber of those who do not want to speak, who knows the man from his saying, when the stomach reveals what is in it, who causes that the heart spits out what it has swallowed, who enters in the single chamber in the front part of the palace at the day of hearing of a character'. The text is hard to understand as it uses several uncommon words, but the general impression is that Dedusobek was a man responsible for some kind of policing, perhaps even torturing people in order to discover information.

The title itself is well known from at least the First Intermediate Period. Only in the second half of the Twelfth Dynasty is it combined with ranking titles. It therefore seems that an 'overseer of police' was promoted at some point, perhaps under Senusret II, to the inner circle around the king. The evidence of several title-holders with ranking titles might point to a line of title-holders up to the end of the Twelfth Dynasty. So far there is no evidence in the Thirteenth Dynasty that these people had ranking titles. They are not well attested; basically each is known from just one source,[20] and one may wonder whether they received their ranking titles for just one specific mission.

The 'overseer of police' was placed in the administration under the vizier. There is a stela from Abydos on which the 'overseer of police' Nesmont is sitting in front of the vizier Dedumont.[21] This title also appears in the 'Duties of the Vizier'.

An 'overseer of police' Antef appears on a stela dated to year 33 of

Amenemhat III which reports the building of a wall. The stela was found in Kerma (Nubia), but perhaps originally came from Elephantine. Finally, another 'overseer of police', Senusret-seneb, appears in a rock inscription in Lower Nubia,[22] in which he is 'priest of Maat' and 'gate of Egypt, Thebes and Nubia'.[23] Again, the title priest of Maat' clearly indicates some juridical responsibility.

Provincial Officials

The administration of the provinces and towns is better known in various parts of Egypt than that of the royal court. This is largely because the decorated rock-cut tombs of some local governors are well preserved. Several of these monuments contain long biographical inscriptions, providing detailed information on the lives and duties of local governors. However, it should also be made clear that these tombs are well preserved only at some places, while at others very little remains. This leaves major gaps in our knowledge, especially for the Delta about which little is known – only at Bubastis and a few other places are some local governors attested. The oases comprise another part of Egypt, little known for this period, although some local governors are attested here too.[1]

The head of the provincial administration was the vizier. In the tomb of the New Kingdom vizier Rekhmire people are shown coming from the towns of Upper Egypt and bringing some kind of tribute or taxes. From some of the place names mentioned it seems clear that the scene or at least the list of place names goes back to the late Middle Kingdom. For example Wahsut, the town next to the tomb of Senusret III at Abydos, appears in this list. There is little evidence that the place was of importance in the Eighteenth Dynasty. However, it remains somehow obscure how, in practical terms, the vizier related to the provincial administration. The local mayors, at least in the late Middle Kingdom, came directly under the vizier, as can be seen too from the 'Duties of the Vizier', copied in this and other New Kingdom vizier tombs.[2]

Under the vizier the next officials at the royal court in charge of the provincial administration were the 'overseer of Lower Egypt'[3] and the 'overseer of Upper Egypt'.[4] The 'overseer of Lower Egypt' is well attested and it is possible to establish lines of title-holders for certain periods. The title seems to have been established in the Eleventh Dynasty, when the court was still at Thebes, far to the South. With the establishment of this office, the king seems to have aimed for closer control of the northern part of Egypt. However, the office was evidently not a powerful one, as, perhaps against modern expectations of the title, there is no indication that these people ruled as some kind of governor of the northern part of Egypt. The impression is rather that they had special, but limited, responsibilities. Many of them appear in inscriptions in Sinai, indicating that they were employed as expedition leaders.[5] The title 'overseer of Upper Egypt' appears less often, but in the early Middle Kingdom it does occur in several title strings of local and high court officials. Only in the late Middle Kingdom does it become used as sole main title. Again, there is no surviving evidence that the title implied any responsibility over local governors within the region.[6]

At a local level in the towns and regions, the people in charge held a variety of titles. At the end of the Old Kingdom at certain places there were people with the title 'overlord of a province',[7] indicating that these governors ruled a whole province. The title is still well known in the First Intermediate Period and early Middle Kingdom, but disappears in the middle of the Twelfth Dynasty. About this time, the titles 'foremost of action' (in this context better translated as 'mayor' or 'governor') and 'overseer of priests'[8] became the most important ones for local governors. At some places in the late Middle Kingdom, 'overseer of priests' was replaced by 'overseer of the temple'.[9] The local governors were obviously also the main priests of their provinces.[10] Sometimes the title 'mayor' was followed by the name of the town under his control. However, the naming of an explicit place is rather an exception and it is therefore often not possible to assign a certain governor to a specific region or place if no further information is available.

At some places special titles for local governors appear. The governors at Khemenu (Ashmunein, who were buried at Deir el-Bersheh) had the additional title 'leader of the two thrones'.[11] The governors at Abydos were often called 'god's sealer'.[12] In other regions such special titles might have existed but the sporadic preservation of inscriptions makes it hard to decide whether title combinations appearing just once are really exceptional or reflect a common title pattern that simply has not been not preserved more often. One example is Khesu the Elder, known only from his decorated tomb excavated at Kom el-Hisn in the Delta. The tomb is in many ways exceptional; no other decorated tomb of the Middle Kingdom is preserved there. Khesu bears several titles, including 'overseer of singers' and 'overseer of the temple'. He is not called 'mayor', but one wonders if he did have such a function in his province, but that it was expressed in a different way. Perhaps 'overseer of singers' was a special local title for a governor. Since there are so far no other inscribed tombs known from the town, for the moment this remains pure speculation.[13]

Especially in the first half of the Twelfth Dynasty some local rulers had impressive sequences of titles, even more striking than those of court officials, although the tombs of the latter are often too damaged to make a real comparison. Khnumhotep (II), buried at Beni Hasan, was 'member of the elite, foremost of action, royal sealer, sole friend, member of the elite at (name lost), foremost of action in the great house, member of the elite at the chapel of Geb, overlord of Elkab, setem-priest, lector priest, leader of all kilts'. His function titles were 'governor of Menat-Khufu, overseer of priests' and 'overseer of the eastern desert'.[14]

From the titles and the biographical inscriptions for these local governors four main areas of duties are visible.[15] First, they were the governors of a region, or even of just a town and its immediate surrounding region. Secondly, they were also the main or high priests of their local temples, since the religious and secular administration was not yet fully separated in the Middle Kingdom. Thirdly, they were responsible for local cults and often proudly describe their building work at local temples. This included not only temples and chapels of gods, but also of local saints, men of the past who received special, almost divine, status after they died.[16] Restoring the tombs of older governors was also not uncommon and is perhaps to be placed in the same context. Finally, they also acted as main judge in their province or town.

Some important governors were also responsible for certain administrative tasks not directly related to their own province. Khnumhotep II, buried at Beni Hasan, was also 'overseer of the eastern desert'. He was therefore an official operating at a national level. It is no surprise that the title was given not to a palace official, but to one placed in the province, as Menat-Khufu in Middle Egypt was most likely a place where it was easier to control the deserts. In his tomb one scene shows the arrival of people coming from Palestine, dressed in colourful garments. The scene clearly relates to one of Khnumhotep's tasks and most likely even to an actual event. Some governors at Rifeh and Asyut were 'overseers of Upper Egypt'. They were therefore responsible for a whole region although, as already indicated, there is little evidence that this title implied practical responsibilities. The governors on Elephantine in the South of Egypt controlled the trade between Egypt and Nubia.

It remains unclear how much these local officials were involved in the affairs in the royal court at the king's residence. However, there is good evidence from their tomb autobiographies that they were frequently present at the royal court. Nevertheless, it remains unknown whether these references report special events or regular contact with the king, or whether their stay at the palace was for long or short periods. In the palace document Papyrus Boulaq 18, no local officials from places other than in the Theban region, where the manuscript was written, are mentioned. From an earlier period we know that Wepwawetaa was governor at Abydos, at the end of the reign of Senusret I and at the beginning of the reign of Amenemhat II. He reports his visit to the royal court (p. 124), but also holds the titles 'setem-priest, leader of all kilts, mouth of Nekhen' and 'priest of Maat',[17] all of which are also often found with officials at the royal residence.

Especially in the early Middle Kingdom, the Eleventh and early Twelfth Dynasties, there are locals with function titles that are also known from the royal court. For example, there are several provincial governors at Khenemu (known from their tombs at Deir el-Bersheh) who have the titles of the vizier. At the same place there was a certain Iha[18] with the title 'overseer of the king's apartment'.[19] In Asyut the undisturbed and richly equipped tomb of the 'royal sealer' and 'treasurer' Nakht was found, also dating to the early Middle Kingdom.[20] At the moment it is difficult to place these officials in a clear context. Were they really court officials, perhaps residing at the royal court and having an office, while also serving as or under governors in name only with other people ruling the provinces for them? As already mentioned in relation to the viziers, none of these officials appear for sure on monuments at the royal court, in the mortuary temple of a king or in other documents, whereas other officials appear more than once in the mortuary temple of Mentuhotep II or in expedition inscriptions, where they are clearly on a mission for the ruling king. The only exception is perhaps the vizier Amenemhat, who was also a governor at Khenemu. He dates under Senusret I but was probably still living in the reign of Amenemhat II. There is indeed one vizier Ameny mentioned on a fragment of the annals stone of this king and it has been proposed that Amenemhat and Ameny are the same person,[21] since Ameny is a common shortened version of Amenemhat. The identification seems possible, but both names are among the most common of the Middle Kingdom, making any identification uncertain. A more secure case seems to be Kay, who was 'governor' and 'overseer of priests' in Kha-Senusret, the pyramid town of Senusret I. Kay was the father of Djehutyhotep, governor at Khenemu (Ashmunein).[22]

In the Second Intermediate Period a similar picture arises, but this time the situation is clearer. Two viziers (Iy and Iymeru from Elkab) of this period are known who certainly come from a provincial background and were, at the end of their careers, appointed to that high post. However, their situation is different to that in the early Middle Kingdom when many governors bore the titles of both vizier and governor. In the Second Intermediate Period officials first became governor and after that vizier, but never bore both titles at the same time in the same title strings, at least not on the known monuments. Both the early Middle Kingdom and the Second Intermediate Period seem to have been times when the central government was worried about its power. There are indications of civil war-like situations in the early Middle Kingdom, and in the Second Intermediate Period the state was in general on the edge of collapse. It seems that in both periods the king needed the help and support of local governors to rule the country. At the high point of the Twelfth Dynasty the opposite picture is visible. There are no locals with titles announcing important functions at the royal court. However, there is evidence that the locals sent their children to the royal residence in order to make a career there.[23]

The court of the provincial governor was almost a copy of the royal court. In the tomb of Khnumhotep (II) at Beni Hasan in front of the tomb owner are depicted a 'scribe of the king's document', several 'stewards', an 'overseer of fields', an 'overseer of sealers', a 'treasurer', an 'overseer of troops' and an 'overseer of the gateway', just to mention a few.[24] In terms of titles, it is interesting to note which officials do not appear. There was no vizier, no 'high steward', no 'leader of the broad hall' and no 'overseer of marshland dwellers', indicating that these titles were obviously restricted to the royal court. Similarly, they are not known for sure from other provincial courts.

The same range of people is known from their small burials close to the large decorated tombs of the local governors. This is again best visible at Beni Hasan where these small tombs were excavated and published in a single volume. Here there are 'treasurers', 'stewards' and 'overseers of the temple'. From the burials the wives of these men are also known, many of whom bore the simple title 'lady of the house'. These tombs do not provide much data on the family relationships of these people. A similar range of titles is known from tombs in the cemeteries at Meir, which served as the burial ground for the town of Qusae. Interestingly, here these people appear only rarely in the tombs of the governors.[25]

Local governors are attested from the Old Kingdom when it is often apparent that their office was inherited. There were strong families with local roots who ruled at several places. The same pattern is still visible in the First Intermediate Period. It has often been assumed that these families kept their influence in the Middle Kingdom and were disempowered by Senusret III, under whom the large provincial rock-cut tombs disappear. The real picture seems to be more complicated. So far, only at Asyut and Deir el-Bersheh is a line of provincial governors visible from the First Intermediate Period to the Middle Kingdom. The first governors buried at Beni Hasan were put in charge in the Eleventh Dynasty, at Meir the line starts under Amenemhat I, on Elephantine under Senusret I and at Qaw el-Kebir perhaps as late as Amenemhat II. These are the places with well attested lines of governors. At the moment it is not possible to make any statement for other places.[26]

It seems that the kings were much involved in the provincial administration, appointing people and families loyal to them. This is even visible at places were there is already an existing line of governors known from earlier Dynasties. At Asyut there are two governors attested, belonging to the Eleventh or early Twelfth Dynasty. These are Mesehti and Anu. In the Twelfth Dynasty most governors there have the name Hapidjefa. This gives the impression that the governors with the new name belong to a new line of people perhaps placed in charge under Senusret I. A similar change is visible at Beni Hasan, where there are basically two families, one dating to the Eleventh, the other to the Twelfth Dynasty. In the tombs of the first family, whose members had names like Khety and Baket, no biographical inscriptions were found. In the first tomb of the new family, belonging to a certain Khnumhotep, a long inscription records that Khnumhotep was placed in his office by Amenemhat I.

The local governors also often counted their own years and in some tombs symbols of royalty even appear. Nevertheless, in the inscriptions in their tombs and on stelae the governors quite often refer to the king. From this evidence there is little to indicate that they were actually challenging the power of the king, as has often been assumed in the past. Royal symbols appear in the whole country in the middle of the Twelfth Dynasty and are a sign of the increasing belief that the deceased would become Osiris in the next world. Osiris was the king of the Underworld and as such he was equipped with royal insignia. Becoming Osiris in the next life meant that the deceased was likewise equipped as king. Even at the royal cemeteries burials were found of officials adorned with the royal uraeus. From this interpretation of the evidence it seems that neither the governors nor anyone else challenged the power of the king. Nevertheless, for some reason the large provincial tombs certainly disappeared under Senusret III.

One of the best preserved and recorded examples for the last generation of Middle Kingdom rock-cut tombs belongs to the 'mayor' Ukhhotep (IV), son of Ukhhotep at Meir.[27] As the tomb of a governor, it is worth describing in detail. Ukhhotep was the son of another person of the same name whose position is unknown but was the brother of another Ukhhotep, who was also mayor. The word 'brother' does not mean that he was a real brother; as translated literally the word means 'the second'. It simply implies that they were of about the same generation. Ukhhotep did not have many titles. He was 'member of the elite, foremost of action, royal sealer' and 'sole friend'. These are the main ranking titles common for a high provincial local governor. His function titles were 'mayor' and 'overseer of priests'. The other few titles all have religious meanings: 'pure priest of the lady of heaven', 'setem-priest of the lady of the two lands' and 'master of the secret'. The 'lady' mentioned in these titles refers to Hathor, the main deity at Qis (the town with which the cemeteries of Meir were associated). These titles show again the important religious position of the local governors in the Middle Kingdom.

The tomb chapel of Ukhhotep consisted of two parts. There was a main chapel fully decorated with paintings and a smaller chapel serving as the centre of the cult of the deceased mayor. The paintings in his tomb are highly exceptional. The entrance was from the east. On the south wall the paintings are organised in two registers. In the lower register Ukhhotep is shown standing. He wears a long garment and holds in one hand a long staff and in the other a sceptre and an ankh sign. The ankh sign was previously almost only known from depictions of gods and royals and appears here suddenly in the hand of an official. In

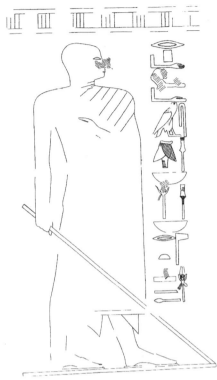

47. Ukhhotep (III) as shown in his tomb. Here the governor appears with religious titles: 'member of the elite, foremost of action, setem-priest, leader of all kilts' and 'leader of all religious titles'. The governor was certainly also the local high priest.

front of him is a marsh scene with women in it. This is again highly exceptional as we expect to see men working in the marshes. The scene in the upper register is heavily destroyed, but here Ukhhotep is sitting and in front of him are singing woman. On the west wall Ukhhotep is shown twice in a boat, once hunting birds and once fishing. Over the doorway in this wall appear royal symbols. Most remarkable is the depiction of the sign zemat-tawy, 'uniting the two countries'. This is another symbol previously known only from royal contexts or temples. The decoration on the east wall opposite is heavily destroyed, but there are remains of a scene depicting Ukhhotep hunting in the desert. On the north wall Ukhhotep is again standing with an ankh sign in his hand and before him are shown female offering bearers. In the upper register he is sitting in front of female musicians and in two registers the ten wives of Ukhhotep are depicted. On this wall there is also the entrance to the small main chapel of the tomb. Here Ukhhotep is shown together with one of his wives in front of an offering table. The scene is painted above a palace façade (Fig. 48). On the opposite wall a similar scene is shown, although this time he is with a different wife. At the back of the chapel two of his wives, Khnumhotep and Nubkau, are shown sitting on the ground.

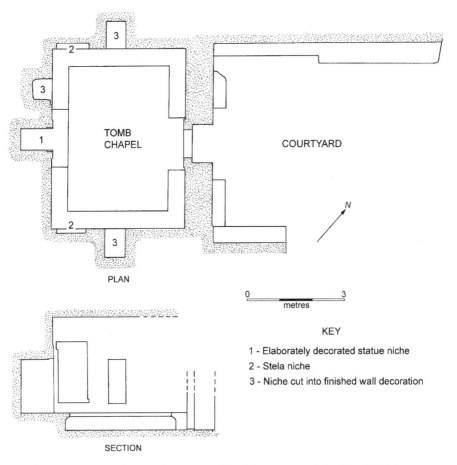

PLAN

KEY

1 - Elaborately decorated statue niche
2 - Stela niche
3 - Niche cut into finished wall decoration

SECTION

48. *Opposite*: decoration on the west wall of the statue niche (1) of Ukhhotep (IV). The scene is filled with royal symbols. At the bottom there is a palace façade, above which is a register of fertility figures, so far only known from temples. The inscription in the top register states: 'An offering for the mayor and overseer of priests Ukhhotep, may he appear as king of Upper, may he appear as king of Lower Egypt'. *Above*: plan of the tomb.

As already indicated, the scenes in the tomb are highly exceptional. First of all, with the exception of Ukhhotep himself, only women are shown in the main chapel. Only in the inner cult chapel are men shown. Several rituals could evidently be performed only by men. The high number of royal symbols is remarkable. They are known from other tombs of about this time, but not to the same extent as in this one. In this context too the high number of women and wives of Ukhhotep might be considered. Their exact status is debatable. Some are 'lady of the house', but others do not have this title. However, this high number of women around an official seems to reflect exactly the situation known from funerary monuments of kings. Mentuhotep II, Senusret I and Senusret III, just to quote the better attested examples, were buried surrounded by their wives and daughters. A still clearer example comes from the New Kingdom, where king Akhenaton is always depicted with his wife and his daughters, but never with his sons or other male members of his family.

The tomb of Ukhhotep is the last decorated example at Meir. One of the succeeding mayors with the name Khakheperre-seneb Iy, who is basically known only from his coffins, did not have a decorated tomb, thus giving the impression that local governors lost power after the time of Ukhhotep.[28] The same situation is visible at many other places. Under Senusret III large decorated provincial tombs disappear. There were obviously changes going on in the provinces, although these might not necessarily have been very dramatic. The development of new tomb architecture could be one explanation, whereby instead of large rock-cut tombs, mud brick chapels could have been built. If these chapels were built closer to the fertile land they would almost certainly have disappeared from the archaeological record. Such chapels were indeed found at Thebes.[29]

More importantly, however, governors are still well attested in the periods after Senusret III. On Elephantine, at Qaw el-Kebir and Deir el-Bersheh (Khemenu), there is a visible line of title-holders from the early Middle Kingdom to the early Thirteenth Dynasty. The difference is that the governors of the late Middle Kingdom are known not from their tombs but from other sources. On Elephantine they still adorned the local chapel of Heqaib with statues. The late Middle Kingdom governors of Qaw el-Kebir and Deir el-Bersheh are mainly known from their seals. At all three places their tombs are missing.

In terms of function titles no differences are visible. The titles of the local governors were now frequently 'mayor' and 'overseer of priests' or 'overseer of the temple'. Some of them bore ranking titles such as 'royal sealer'. The title strings seem to have been limited in comparison to the early Middle Kingdom, but it has to be remembered that high officials at the royal court also had fewer titles. It is not always clear whether under Senusret III there were new families put in charge or whether the old ones remained in power. At Qaw el-Kebir at least one governor still had the name Wahka, which was the name of two other governors belonging to the mid Twelfth Dynasty, indicating that they came from the same family. On Elephantine there appears a new family of officials, of which the first member, Heqaib (II), still had a large tomb while his successors did not.[30] The change in the late Middle Kingdom is therefore perhaps better explained as a new way expressing titles, along with other aspects of identity, on monuments, and as new funerary beliefs and practices rather than as a removal of old powerful families.

6. Provincial Officials

There is another possible explanation for the situation, for which it might be worth looking at the development of titles in the whole country, including the court. In the late Twelfth Dynasty at the royal court and in the provinces officials had fewer titles. This means that they had fewer responsibilities and therefore, arguably, fewer sources of income. With these reduced resources the local governors could no longer afford the grand style of tombs known from the early Middle Kingdom. In this context, the title 'overseer of Upper Egypt' should be mentioned as a good example. In the early Middle Kingdom it was always given to one high official with another function title, most often a local governor. In the late Middle Kingdom officials suddenly appear with this as their only title.[31] Obviously incomes and responsibilities connected with this office were no longer in the hands of local governors, but under the control of a single person with the sole title 'overseer of Upper Egypt'. This indicates that the resources for two titles were given to two people and not to one.

For the late Middle Kingdom other places become more important in terms of evidence for local administration, although this may simply indicate a shift in our sources. For the end of the Twelfth Dynasty it is possible to establish a line of title-holders at Hotep-Senusret (Lahun). The town was founded under Senusret II near to his pyramid and continued to flourish into the Thirteenth Dynasty. Its local governors are basically known from papyri found at that site. They are 'mayors' and 'overseers of the temple'. The latter title might relate to the mortuary temple of Senusret II, which was an important part of the town. At Wahsut, the town next to the tomb of Senusret III at Abydos, another sequence of local governors is visible. They are also known not from their tombs, but from seal impressions and other objects found in the governor's house at Wahsut. Although there is little evidence for their responsibilities, everything seems to indicate that each official was governor of just his town and perhaps the countryside and estates belonging to it. Especially in the case of Wahsut it can be assumed that there was also a 'mayor' at the nearby town of Abydos. The sources are sparse, but there is no evidence that the 'mayor' of one of these towns was placed over the other. For other towns local governors are sporadically attested. At Tell el-Dab'a (Hutwaret, Avaris) a seal impression was found of the 'mayor of Hutwaret'. Other governors known from seals include one from Memphis[32] and one from Kha-Senusret (a pyramid town),[33] to give just two examples.

For the mid Thirteenth Dynasty and the following Second Intermediate Period, new places with lines of local governors are again visible. This does not mean that certain places suddenly became more important while others declined, but rather seems to indicate another shift in our sources. The local governors of Djeba (Edfu) in the late Thirteenth Dynasty are well known mostly from evidence deriving from the Second Intermediate Period cemeteries of the town. The tombs of this period are simply better known than those of the Twelfth Dynasty. Many stelae were found, some of which were set up by local governors or their family members. Here no significant changes are detectable. The governors have the titles 'mayor' and 'overseer of priests'; several also have high ranking titles such as 'member of the elite' and 'foremost of action'.[34] Some of the Second Intermediate Period mayors of Edfu had links to the royal family, something that is not attested for mayors of the Middle Kingdom.

Other sources indicate a reorganisation of the provincial administration in the Thirteenth Dynasty or the Second Intermediate Period. In this respect, the already mentioned tax list in the tomb of Rekhmire is an important source. However, the list is a later copy, partly destroyed, and some titles are no longer legible. Therefore any conclusions must be arrived at with great caution. In the regions south of Thebes only three officials appear with the title 'mayor' (Kom Ombo, Edfu and Hieraconpolis). At other places different title-holders seem to be the main officials in charge. Most remarkable is that on Elephantine it was a 'commander'.[35] This fits with the evidence that no 'mayors' are attested for the Second Intermediate Period at that place, while they are well known for the Middle Kingdom. At other places just 'reporters' are listed. For the eighth Upper Egyptian nome, one 'mayor' is listed: the 'mayor of Thinis'. For the important town of Wahsut only a 'reporter' is listed. However, 'mayors' are attested for the latter town in Thirteenth Dynasty sources. The impression here is that some kind of hierarchical system existed. There were major towns with a 'mayor' and other places of lower status where officials with lower titles were in charge. However, it remains uncertain whether these major towns were administrative centres placed above other towns or their local administration was simply organised in a different way. An explanation is still wanting as to why there are no 'mayors' named for certain towns, when they are known from late Middle Kingdom sources for these places. One option is that towns were again reorganised in the Thirteenth Dynasty and 'mayors' were replaced by other officials. Therefore it is perhaps not surprising to find that no 'mayor' is known for Elephantine in the Second Intermediate Period even though 'mayors' are well attested beforehand, as the list in the tomb of Rekhmire was compiled after the reformation. However, this might be just a gap in our sources; another option is that in Rekhmire's list only 'mayors' of important towns appear, while for other places less important officials are mentioned when there was still a 'mayor' in charge.

Going back to the contemporary sources, it is important to note that the local governors of the Second Intermediate Period are in the main known only from stelae. There is one major exception, the official Sobeknakht who was buried in a fully decorated tomb at Elkab.[36]

Sobeknakht was obviously an important person. He is difficult to date within the Second Intermediate Period, but in his tomb the artist Sedjemnetjeru is named. The same artist is also known from the tomb of Horemkhauef in Hieraconpolis, on the opposite side of the river. The latter reports, on a stela found next to his tomb, a trip to Itj-tawy, the Middle Kingdom capital, indicating that Horemkhauef as well as the artist and therefore Sobeknakht did not live long after the city was abandoned (or even lived while it was still functioning). Sobeknakht reports in his tomb how he defeated the Nubians and saved Elkab. In tomb scenes Sobeknakht is shown hunting in the desert and sitting with his wife in front of an offering table before his family and officials. Sobeknakht was a member of a powerful family which ruled Elkab over several generations. Mayors of Elkab are still known from the early New Kingdom and the place seems especially important in showing that little had changed in the provinces from the late Second Intermediate Period to the New Kingdom, at least here and in terms of the titles of the officials who lived here.

Procedures, Relations, Social Mobility
and Careers

At the palace

Very little is known about rituals and proceedings at the royal court, in the throne room or in other parts of the palace or royal residence. There are no direct sources providing a description. It can be assumed that there was a certain protocol which required each official to perform specific tasks and functions, but little can be said about it.[1]

Biographical phrases provide a framework for the way officials saw themselves: the early Eleventh Dynasty 'treasurer' Tjetji said: 'I was indeed one who is truly in his lord's confidence, an exceeding wise magistrate, of quiet disposition in his lord's house, bending his arm amid the great ones.'[2]

For the highest state officials the king was obviously the centre of attention, but there are other important issues which need to be considered, such as what it meant to be simply 'treasurer'. The 'treasurer' Mentuhotep, in an inscription on a stela where he was empowered to act as a vizier, describes himself as 'one who enforces the law, who promotes offices, who establishes the boundary markers, who separates a territory from that of its neighbour', 'one who protects the unfortunate and rescues the indigent', 'one who sets the land on its proper course'.[3]

In royal and religious texts the officials next to the king are often called 'semeheru', 'friends'. This is a term most likely referring to the court officials with ranking titles. In certain royal inscriptions known as 'king's novels' they sometimes appear as people without imagination. In difficult situations the king asks for their opinion, but they always know nothing, so the king has to act alone and come up with the only good solution.[4] The intention of these texts is clearly to emphasise the intelligence and importance of the ruler at the expense of his officials. However, it seems clear from the reliefs at the mortuary temple of Mentuhotep II at Deir el-Bahari and already from the pyramid temples of the Old Kingdom that officials were regarded as an essential part of kingship.[5] In these monuments the whole court seems to have been depicted. Similar representations from other Middle Kingdom funerary temples are as yet unknown, but since they are all heavily destroyed or are still awaiting publication, this might be just a gap in our sources.

An arrival at the royal court is described on the stela of the local governor from Abydos, Wepwawetaa. 'When I had gone north to offer salutations at the great residence of his majesty, the seal-bearers who are in the palace and the persons at the portal saw me being ushered into the palace, I being made to enter unannounced. An ox was slaughtered for my meal.'[6] A shorter description is given on the stela of the 'first inspector of priests of Horus of Nekhen' and 'overseer of fields' Horemkhauef who went to the king's residence to collect a new image of Horus. 'Then I fared downstream with good dispatch and I drew forth Horus of Nekhen in my hands together with his mother, this goddess, from the Good Office of Itj-tawy in the presence of the king himself.'[7]

Day-to-day procedure is described in the 'Duties of the Vizier': 'Now, he shall enter to greet the Lord each day when the affairs of the Two Lands have been reported to him in his residence. He shall enter the Great House when the treasurer has drawn up his position at the northern flagstaff. Then the vizier shall move in from the East in the doorway of the great double-gate.'[8]

However, the most detailed description comes from a literary work, the 'Story of Sinuhe', which also reports the arrival of an official at the royal palace: 'Very early at daybreak there came the summons for me. Ten men coming, ten men going to lead me to the palace. I touched the ground between the dawn rays, as the king's children stood on the walls at my approach, the "friends" guided me to the wakhi-hall and I was placed on the way to the inner chamber. I found his majesty on the great throne on a podium of electrum, then I stretched out myself on my belly and I lost myself in his presence. This god addressed me in a friendly way.'[9]

In Papyrus Boulaq 18, the administrative document of the Theban palace dating to the Thirteenth Dynasty, some sort of banquet appears twice, confirming the impression given by the report of Wepwawetaa that a meal was an important event at the royal court. This was held in the wakhi-hall of the palace, a large hall with columns. About 65 officials are recorded in one list as participants in one such banquet. The officials are arranged in three groups, perhaps indicating some kind of social ranking. In the first group appear the vizier Ankhu, the 'overseer of troops' Ibiau, the 'high steward' (not named), the 'overseer of fields' Haankhef, the 'mouth of Nekhen' Titi and the 'personal scribe of the king's document' Iuy. Except for the vizier, they all have the ranking title 'royal sealer'. Following this group are people with titles such as 'great one of the tens of Upper Egypt', 'elder of the hall', 'commanders of the ruler's crew'. They received ten loaves of bread and some other food. At the end of the list appear military people of lower rank, three singers and a 'singer with the harp'. The former was perhaps responsible for security in the hall and the latter for providing some kind of musical

entertainment.[10] These were the staff who worked in the hall. The king
and the king's family, mentioned elsewhere in the papyrus, do not
appear in the list, the purpose of which was basically to record the food
supplies for the banquet. So far, few Middle Kingdom palace buildings
have been identified. The remains of grand buildings have been found at
Bubastis and Uronarti, which were perhaps used as temporary palaces.
Both have several columned halls, but it remains pure speculation as to
which of these was the wakhi-hall.

Some kind of competition seems to have been important among the
highest state officials. It is stated more than once that an official was
given the 'gold of praise' in front of other officials.[11] This demonstrates
an official's pride at being singled out as someone special among his fel-
low courtiers. The same is expressed in the biography of Khnumhotep
(II) in his tomb in Beni Hasan. Here it is stated that he was appointed
by the king before the dignitaries and that Khnumhotep was placed in
front of other officials, who were of higher rank.[12] These references also
reveal that appointments and the awarding of 'medals' were made in
public perhaps in some kind of throne hall or even in the wakhi-hall.

Social networks

Around the officials there is a network evident with colleagues on a similar level or other people on a slightly lower level. These associations are
work-based, but it is also likely that they are friendships formed via
families or other relationships, thus making them more stable and powerful. Several types of connections between officials are visible on monuments and in texts. In the Thirteenth Dynasty especially, numerous
members of one family in high positions or in positions of different rank
are attested several times. There are also relations between officials who
are not obviously related by family ties but were perhaps friends or at
least worked in the same branch of the administration on more or less
the same level. The most common or at least most often visible relationship is the association between a high official and a lower one. They
seem to have formed some kind of patron-client relation.

The main sources for showing relationships of people are tombs and
stelae, as these are the most common documents where several people
are depicted. Tombs of the early Middle Kingdom are often well decorated, but the decoration concentrates on the family and the people
working for the tomb owner. Few decorated tomb chapels of the late
Middle Kingdom and Second Intermediate Period are known, but they
show a different pattern of people compared to the early Middle
Kingdom. These networks are also known from contemporary stelae,[13]
but they are not apparent on stelae of the early Middle Kingdom.

One example is a stela in Cairo[14] (Fig. 49) belonging to the famous
Senebsumai (p. 63) and therefore dating to the early Thirteenth

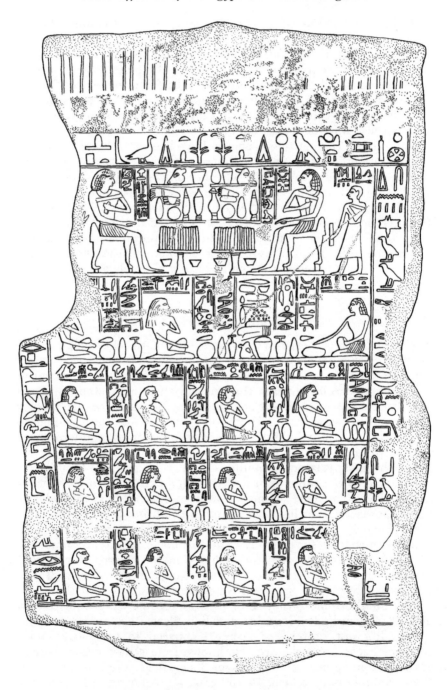

49. Stela of the 'high steward' Senebsumai.

Dynasty. On this stela Senebsumai had not yet become 'treasurer', but had reached the position of 'high steward'. The stela was most likely set up by Senebsumai, as he is the main person mentioned in the offering formula framing the central field in which various people are depicted in five registers. In the top register, Senebsumai is shown on the right, sitting on a chair in front of an offering table. On the opposite side of the main field appears the 'head of largesse'[15] Senusret, born to Zathathor. The 'high steward' Senebsumai and Senusret are not connected by family ties, or at least they are not visible in our records. However, there is some evidence that they worked closely together. The title 'head of largesse' is not common in the Middle Kingdom, although it does appear on several seals of the Thirteenth Dynasty. Of some interest is the scarab of the 'head of largesse' Nehy-senebi,[16] since a 'high steward' with the same name appears on several seals. It seems possible that they are the same person at a different stage of a successful career.[17] Here is what seems to be a close association between the two offices already indicated by the stela. Finally the famous 'treasurer' Mentuhotep should be mentioned. He was also 'head of largesse'. Senebsumai, mentioned above, later became 'treasurer', an office closely related to the 'high steward' (p. 70).

This is a new feature common on stelae and other monuments of the late Middle Kingdom. Officials and colleagues at the same level appear on the same monument. Senebsumai and Senusret were obviously working together and decided to appear on one stela. Other people in the lower register of the stela seem to work for them. One is the 'great scribe of the hearer' Zasatet. At first glance a 'great scribe of the hearer' does not seem to be connected with the 'high steward', but there are several other stelae from about the same period where a person with exactly this title appears with a 'high steward'. The 'great scribe of the hearer' was, at least in the Thirteenth Dynasty, part of the staff of the 'high steward'.[18]

Looking at the stelae set up for Senebsumai when he was promoted to 'treasurer', an even wider network of people is visible, from lower parts of the administration to the 'treasurer' Senebsumai himself (Fig. 50a-c). Most of his stelae are arranged along the same lines. At the top, most often on the right side, is the main person, in this case Senebsumai, shown standing or sitting on a chair. In front of him stands a slightly lower official making offerings, often in the role of a setem-priest.[19] In the registers below, other officials or family members of the second official are shown, but there are few relatives of Senebsumai. The stelae were evidently not set up by the main person depicted but by the second official. In the case of Senebsumai, people with the title 'overseer of the storerooms', 'overseer of the storerooms of the treasurer', 'overseer of the storerooms of the inner palace', 'chamber keeper and cupbearer' and a 'god's father of Atum' are shown in front of him. Obviously the 'overseer of the storerooms' was an important official connected to the 'treasurer'.

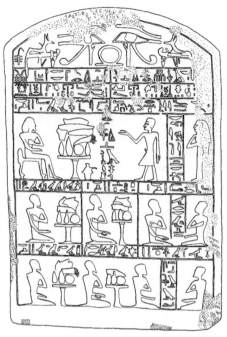

50. Officials under Senebsumai:

(a) *left* Stela (Pittsburgh) of the 'treasurer' Senebsumai with the 'overseer of storerooms' Renpyf, standing in front of him.

(b) *bottom left* Stela (Dublin) of the 'overseer of storerooms' Renpyf with the 'cupbearer' Iauemnut, standing in front of him.

(c) *below* Stela (Chicago) of the 'cupbearer' Iauemnut.

This link between 'treasurer' and 'overseer of storerooms' is attested by archaeological evidence from the beginning of the Middle Kingdom for the Theban official Meketre (Fig. 51). In front of Meketre's tomb is the smaller sepulchre of Wah, who was obviously a lower official working for the 'treasurer' Meketre and was buried close to his master. Wah was an 'overseer of the storerooms' which is the same title borne by several people on the stelae of Senebsumai, who are always depicted in front of the latter. Here is a clear example of how archaeology and depictions on monuments tell the same story.

The same 'overseers of storerooms' shown in front of Senebsumai are also known from their own stelae. On these they are shown as the main person with a lower official in front of them in exactly the same manner as the 'treasurer'. One example is the 'overseer of storerooms' Renpyf. He appears facing Senebsumai on a stela now in the British Museum

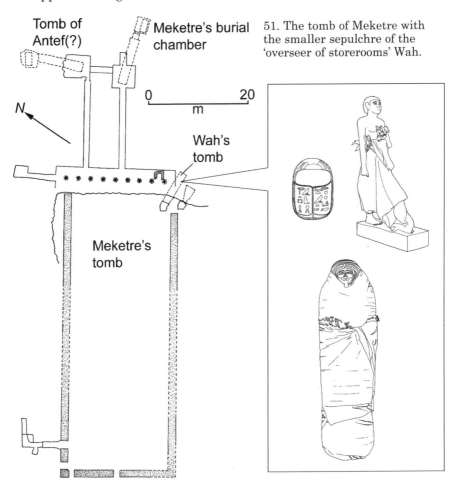

51. The tomb of Meketre with the smaller sepulchre of the 'overseer of storerooms' Wah.

and on another now in Pittsburgh, on the latter he appears with the fuller title 'overseer of the storerooms of the treasurer'. On a stela now in Dublin, Renpyf is shown as the main person. Here, the 'cupbearer' Iaumnut is depicted as the second official. The 'cupbearer' was obviously directly under the 'overseer of the storerooms' in the palace hierarchy. Finally, the 'cupbearer' Iaumnut had his own stela. From these stelae the following hierarchy is visible: the 'treasurer' was at the top, under him the 'overseer of storerooms', and beneath him the 'cupbearer'. Different hierarchies are visible on stelae of other 'treasurers' and officials. (See Fig. 50.)

Another official for whom a full social network is visible is the 'treasurer' Senebi (p. 64, compare Fig. 52), dating under Neferhotep I and Sobekhotep IV. On a stela dating to when Senebi was just 'king's acquaintance', there appears the 'steward' Ptahwer. The same person is mentioned on another stela as 'steward of the treasurer'. Obviously he kept his position as 'steward' and therefore as the administrator of Senebi's estates over a longer period. We might conclude that he worked in the private household of Senebi. The same holds true for the 'cupbearer of the chambers' Netjeremmer, who is called 'his child', most likely being a foster-child of Senebi.

People working in the administration of 'treasurer' Senebi include several 'king's acquaintances', such as Nebankh, Senen and Rehuankh. They seem to have undertaken missions for the 'treasurer' in the Aswan region and Abydos. Finally, some other high state officials bearing the ranking title 'royal sealer' appear with Senebi on stelae. They were perhaps colleagues of the treasurer rather than subordinates, although they were most likely ranked under him. Clearly the relationships recorded on stelae are important for reconstructing careers, hierarchies and social structures.

From the stelae of Senebsumai and Senebi it is clear that the 'over-

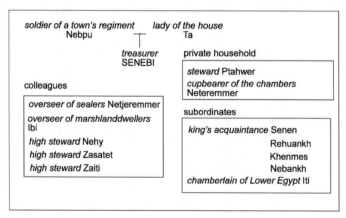

52. The social network of Senebi.

seer of the storerooms' and the 'king's acquaintance' are important officials under the 'treasurer'. They belong to the same part of the administration. Most often under these were officials working in the economic
part of the palace with titles such as 'responsible for a chamber' or 'cupbearer'. From this evidence it is known that the 'treasurer' was in charge
of the economic sector of the palace.

The relationship between officials is also visible in the arrangement
of tombs, as already seen with the tomb of Meketre and Wah. In Thebes
and Dahshur huge tombs of important officials have been found. Around
these tombs or only a short distance away were smaller ones which obviously belonged to their subordinates. Here is evidence that the working
relationship in life was visibly mirrored in the way people were buried
together. Such relationships are already clear in the Old Kingdom.
There are many tombs of 'stewards' or other officials working in the
households of high officials who were buried directly next to their master or mistress.[20] Not only do their names and titles appear in their own
tombs, but also they are shown at their duties in the tombs of their mas-
ters. A similar situation in terms of burials is well known from the
Middle Kingdom. There are many rock-cut tombs of high ranking people
with smaller tombs of their servants in front of them (e.g. Fig. 51). The
better attested examples belong to provincial officials. The 'steward'
Heny was buried in front of the tomb of the governor Hapidjefa at
Asyut.[21] Heny was most likely on the governor's staff. Another example
is the six shaft tombs in front of the rock-cut chapel of the governor
Djehutyhotep at Deir el-Bersheh. These burials obviously form the core
of Djehutyhotep's court. There was the 'steward' Zepi, the 'overseer of
troops' also called Zepi, the 'steward' Neferi, who also had the unusual
title for a provincial official of 'high steward', and there were two 'chief
physicians', one called Gua, the other Sen.[22] These men are possibly also
shown in the tomb of their master perhaps because they did not have
their own cult chapels (Fig. 53). Djehutyhotep's tomb chapel therefore
probably served their own mortuary cults as well.

Very little of the tombs belonging to Middle Kingdom court officials

53. Officials shown in the tomb of Djehutyhotep. These include 'a treasurer, an
overseer of the compound', two 'stewards of the province, an overseer of cattle'
and an 'overseer of the small cattle'.

has survived, leaving a gap in our sources for the circle of people depicted there. In the Twelfth Dynasty, the officials built their mastabas close to the royal pyramids, but today hardly anything of them remains. This is especially regrettable as there are fragments of long biographical inscriptions, which, if complete, would have provided valuable information about the tomb owners. As already indicated, much more is known about the tombs of the local officials. The paintings and reliefs at Beni Hasan, Meir and Deir el-Bersheh are well known and relatively well preserved. The circle of people shown is clear. There is the tomb owner, his family and the people working for him. In the tomb of Khnumhotep II, long rows of lower officials appear in front of the tomb owner, providing a perfect view of the local court under the governor. These include 'stewards', an 'overseer of the small cattle' and a 'treasurer'. These are basically the same kinds of people as are known from stelae of the early Middle Kingdom. They constitute the private staff of an official and are the lower officials working in the administration for him. However, it is particularly hard to decide which of these lower officials belonged to the private staff of a governor or to the administration of the province or town in general. It might further be asked whether the division of private and official administration was allocated by the state.

There are few tomb decorations known for the late Middle Kingdom and Second Intermediate Period. Here the picture and the circle of people changed and seem comparable to the people shown on contemporary stelae. In the tomb of Sobeknakht in Elkab, a similar picture is visible to that found on stelae of the late Middle Kingdom. This is the best preserved and largest tomb chapel of the Second Intermediate Period and is therefore of special importance. It remains problematic whether the tomb is typical of the period or an exception. Sobeknakht is shown with his family and servants and the people working for him. The titles of his officials are remarkably different from those of the Twelfth Dynasty, when most of the lower officials depicted are people with administrative titles. The officials under Sobeknakht were, for the greatest part, military officials, demonstrating a shift of society to military interests. In the case of Sobeknakht, this comes as no surprise as his tomb contains descriptions of a military campaign led by Nubians and the people of Punt against Egypt.[23] However, militarisation of Egyptian society is also visible on other monuments, demonstrating that the case of Sobeknakht is not unique. Besides this group of people, other high officials are recorded in the tomb of Sobeknakht, including the 'royal sealer' and 'high steward' Neferhotep, an official who certainly belonged to the royal court.[24] This is indeed similar to late Middle Kingdom stelae, on which officials of the same rank can appear together. This situation is so far unknown for the Old and early Middle Kingdom: in these periods the tomb owner, his family and servants were depicted in tombs, but not his colleagues.

Social mobility

There is no evidence that Egyptian society had anything like hereditary 'nobility', an uppermost social stratum within which honours, tasks and status were automatically transferred from one generation to the next through blood ties or marriage. Such a group of people, known as patricians, is attested in the Roman Empire, and in the Middle Ages the formation of a nobility was perhaps important for the ruling classes. Education was not widely available and not seen as essential. Even people in the highest positions were often not able to read and write. In order to maintain class distinctions, a hierarchical system using various titles was developed for the nobility. Social boundaries were, in a simple way, marked by the introduction of this class of people. The nobility had certain rights and privileges and it was not necessary to fight for them against newcomers from lower social levels. Privileges were transferred from one generation to the next without any question (though in the Middle Ages in general, there seems to be a constant struggle within the ruling class for certain titles and privileges).

In Ancient Egypt the ability to read and write was an essential part of the identity of the ruling class. It remains uncertain how the school and education system worked (see p. 147), but there was certainly no compulsory education. Access to education was therefore restricted to a small circle of people, and was an extremely useful tool for maintaining class boundaries. A 'formal' nobility was not needed.

However, there seem to have been situations and times when this class system was under threat, notably at the end of the First Intermediate Period and in the early Middle Kingdom. In the latter period it is known that the king placed new officials in the provinces.[25] Perhaps old families were replaced by new ones that the king regarded as more loyal. The few references to civil war-like situations around that time provide background information as to why the king regarded this as necessary and also reveal that there was some resistance to the changes. However, it should be pointed out first of all that there is no sign of higher social mobility. The new people chosen by the king also came mostly from well educated social backgrounds, albeit not from the top of society, such as the local governors and their families, but from a social level just under that. It seems highly improbable that anyone below this level would have been chosen, as the king needed officials who were able to read and write.

However, some of the old families seem to have felt threatened by these changes, while the new ruling families possibly felt the same, as they may have faced some resistance in their new roles. This new situation and the response from parts of the ruling class is indeed reflected in a specific way on some monuments. At least some of these people seem to have felt the need to refer to illustrious ancestors in order to demonstrate their important origins. In this period there are several examples of an official who seems to show pride in his ancestors. The most famous example is Ukhhotep (III) at Meir, who was a local governor at Qusae. The decoration in his tomb chapel includes depictions, arranged in several rows, of governors and their wives. This list goes back to the Old Kingdom and although it is partly destroyed it seems that it is essentially correct, with perhaps only some misspelling of older names. It is especially notable that for the Old Kingdom entries even the names of the wives are the same as those known from the tombs of that period. The apparent accuracy of this long list might imply that records of the local governors were kept in Qusae. However, it is also possible that Ukhhotep or the people decorating his tomb were just recording names they found in other tomb chapels at Meir. This is, after all, the only source available to a modern researcher attempting to corroborate the information on the list. Ukhhotep also restored tombs of other governors at Meir, showing some kind of piety towards his predecessors. The Middle Kingdom line of governors starts at Qusae under Amenemhat I, giving the impression that the king installed these people in order to have a trustworthy family in control of this region. One member of the new family appears to have used genealogy to confirm his position by stating that he was part of an old family, even though in reality he did not belong to it. The restoration of older tombs at Meir is also known from other places. At Deir el-Bersheh many older tombs bear inscriptions of a later date. In addition, biographical inscriptions often include phrases which mention the rebuilding of chapels of ancestors.[26]

The honouring of ancestors to confirm status and class distinctions is not only known for local governors. There are stelae of the early Twelfth Dynasty where an official proudly refers to his ancestors in the same office. This was especially popular in the late First Intermediate Period and early Middle Kingdom.[27] The 'scribe of the tema' and 'overseer of fields' Ameny reports on his stela that 'his father of his father of his father' was already in charge in the time of king Wahankh. He was obviously proud of coming from an old family. His ancestors are not named in the inscription, but on the stela several couples spanning about five generations are depicted and one wonders whether these are his ancestors. The reconstruction of the family is somehow problematic as identical names appear more than once.[28] Another example are the 'stewards' Senusret and Ameny, in office under Amenemhat III. They are depicted on their stela together with the 'high steward' Zanofret who may have lived under Senusret I or Amenemhat II, and was most likely an ancestor, thus providing further evidence of the esteem these family members displayed towards their ancestors.[29]

However, the question of whether there was any social mobility is of special interest in the context of this book. From what social background was it possible to advance to the highest positions in the state adminis-tration? As already indicated, the ability to write seems to have been important in gaining any position in the administration. Texts such as the 'Satire of Trades' point to the importance of this skill. If literacy was the basic requirement it seems unlikely that anyone from a lower back-ground would be able to climb high up the social ladder. There are almost no schools attested (p. 147) and certainly no compulsory educa-tion which would enable poor people to gain a formal education, includ-ing the knowledge of writing. The social background of all officials and especially of the highest state officials can be found only within the small literate ruling class.

Nevertheless, in comparison with other better documented ancient and pre-modern societies, there are perhaps other possibilities for peo-ple crossing class borders. First, it might be argued that not all high offi-cials were able to write, and in such cases their rise up the social and administrative ladder was perhaps the result of some special ability. However, so far no secure example of this is attested. This comes as no surprise, given that biographical inscriptions are rare. Officials whose careers can be reconstructed via different monuments are only visible at the point in their careers when they could afford their own monuments and therefore already belonged to a higher social level.

In practical terms, we could expect to find, at least in theory, higher social mobility in the military and in private households. Another option could be marriage as a way of moving from a poorer background to a richer one.

The military sector was already fully developed in the Middle Kingdom, although many unanswered questions remain about specific details. For example, it is still under discussion whether there was a standing army. Nevertheless, it is reasonable to assume that common soldiers were promoted within their troops for their special ability, whether they were used in military actions or in expeditions. However, so far there is no specific case known where this is apparent, making the point a matter of pure speculation. Another option seems to be the pri-vate household of high state officials. A person from the lowest back-ground working as a servant for a higher official might have been promoted by that official. On Middle Kingdom stelae the staff who worked under an official are sometimes depicted. Some of these lower officials are called 'his child' in relation to the main person on the stela, even when it is certain that they were not his offspring. It has been assumed that this expression refers to servants growing up in the house-hold of a high official.[30] 'His child' would be a foster-child of the higher official, perhaps from a lower background. Again, there is no certain proof of this, but it is possible that the large number foreign officials in the late Middle Kingdom may have gained their positions in this way. At the beginning, the many foreigners who came to Egypt must have lived at the bottom of society, as they often appear in lists of servants. At the very end of the Middle Kingdom, they finally appear in the highest state positions.[31] However, not all foreigners living in Egypt must necessarily have come from a poor background. The richer of them might have seen the importance of education early on and therefore given their children some kind of scribal training, thus making it possible for them to enter the Egyptian ruling class.

There is no evidence so far for any social mobility from the bottom to the top of society. In theory there seem to be ways of crossing class boundaries, but the actual data for this are missing.

For many periods of Egyptian history, there is good evidence that sons followed their fathers in office. From the Eighteenth Dynasty in particular several families are known working in the administration over many generations. The clearest evidence is for local governors. In almost every region where the sources are rich, there are strong families visible governing over many generations. Perhaps the best examples are the governors buried at Beni Hasan who left three long biographical inscriptions in their tombs. The family history of these governors in the Twelfth Dynasty is therefore well known. Under Amenemhat I, a certain Khnumhotep (I), whose origin is not known, was appointed by the king to the post of 'mayor of Menat-Khufu'. Khnumhotep I handed the office over to his son Nakht. The connection of Nakht to the next mayor Netjernakht is not known, but there must be a family relationship as Khnumhotep I was the father of Baket, mother of Khnumhotep (II), who was in office under Amenemhat II and Senusret II. Netjernakht was connected by family ties to Khnumhotep II. The latter built the tomb of Netjernakht and refers to him as 'his father', better translated in this context as 'his ancestor'. Khnumhotep II was the son of Neheri who was a local official in another place. Khnumhotep II was married to a woman called Khety. She appears several times in his tomb and bears an impressive titulary. She was 'daughter of a governor', 'foremost of action', 'priestess of Hathor' and 'priestess of Pakhet' (the local goddess in the region of Beni Hasan). Khety was the daughter of the governor of the 'Jackal nome'. Khnumhotep II had a second wife, Tjat, with less important titles, being a 'sealer', 'one who knows her lord' and 'lady of the house'. The title 'sealer' for a woman who was close to a governor is unique. Is it possible that he fell in love with a servant and appointed her to a position close to him? We do not know; and so it remains speculation.

Khnumhotep II had several children (Fig. 54). The oldest son was Nakht, who became governor of the 'Jackal nome'. However, another Khnumhotep (IV) who became successor to his father in Menat-Khufu, is known only from his unfinished tomb (Fig. 55). He does not appear in the tomb of his father. We can conclude that the eldest son died before his father or that his tomb is not yet known. The remaining sons were placed in different positions. One of them, Khnumhotep (III) was sent to

54. The family of Khnumhotep II shown in his tomb. There is evidence for some of the children outside the tomb of their father. His eldest son, Nakht, is known only from the tomb. He became governor of the 'Jackal nome'. Another son named Khnumhotep became successor and built an unfinished tomb at Beni Hasan. Yet another son named Khnumhotep made his career at the royal court and finally became vizier. Neheri, who perhaps also died as a child, is known from his funerary stela where he is shown as young boy.

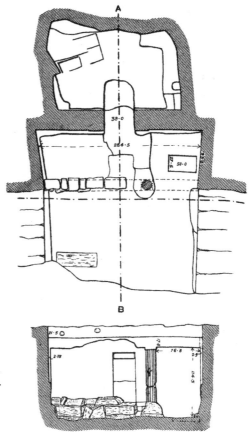

55. The tomb of Khnumhotep, son of Khnumhotep II, at Beni Hasan.

137

56. Relief block of the vizier Khnumhotep, found at Dahshur.

the royal court where he made a successful career, finally becoming vizier (p. 33, Fig. 56). A third son became a mayor in a neighbouring nome and a further one, Neheri, is known from his modest burial at Beni Hasan, where a stela with his name was found (Fig. 57). With the last generation mentioned the chain of tombs at Beni Hasan ceased and we know nothing of their successors. However, the evidence for the whole family is clear. They managed to remain in power over several generations. The oldest son most often succeeded his father, while the other sons occupied different positions or were sent to the royal court. If the eldest son died, another member of the family became governor.

There are also connections to families of mayors at other provinces, showing how they married within their own class. In the case of Khety, the wife of Khnumhotep II, one has the impression that the marriage was arranged for political reasons, while the true love of Khnumhotep II was Tjat. A similar picture is known from other provinces in Egypt. At Elephantine, Meir and Deir el-Bersheh, there are families who remained in power over several generations. These examples are well known to us only because the tombs of these people were decorated.[32]

A similar picture is found with other groups of officials. At the end of the Twelfth or the beginning of the Thirteenth Dynasty there was a family of high priests of Ptah in office over three generations. The family is mainly known from a group statue made of hard stone showing the grandfather, Sehetepibre-ankh-nedjem, his son Nebpu and his grandson Sehetepibre-khered. They all bear the title 'great one of the leader of the craftsmen', which is the main designation of the high priest of Ptah.[33] The statue was set up by Nebpu, who refers to the other priests as 'his father' and 'his son'. This seems strange as we might expect that he was still alive when he ordered the statue. It is unlikely that the son succeeded Nebpu's father into the position before Nebpu died. Nebpu and his son were obviously both high priests of Ptah, and it seems that they were both in office at the same time, or at least overlapped in office. Perhaps the father was too old to fulfil all the duties of the office and placed his son at his side.

57. Stela of Neheri.

A similar situation is known from Elephantine where two 'mayors' and 'overseers of priests' are attested, most likely father and son, who ruled together. Ameny-seneb and Khakaure-seneb lived in the early Thirteenth Dynasty at about the same time as the three high priests of Ptah.[34] They are known from several objects found on Elephantine. Their possible coregency is known because their seal impressions were found together on the same clay objects. However, it is also possible that the oldest official was already dead and, for reasons unknown, his seals continued to be used for a time after his death. The whole situation is reminiscent of Middle Kingdom kings placing their sons as co-regents at the end of their reign. It seems possible that officials copied the practice of their rulers.

However, outside the priestly families, local governors and viziers (p. 38), there is no clear evidence for father-son succession for the men around the king. This might be the result of missing sources, but the evidence, especially for the Thirteenth Dynasty, is quite strong. Often the mothers and fathers of officials are known, and come from a slightly

139

lower background. As one example, the 'treasurers' might be mentioned. The father of the 'treasurer' Senebi was a 'soldier of the town regiment', the father of the 'treasurer' Seneb was 'overseer of oils' and the father of the 'treasurer' Ameny, a simple 'steward'.[35] For other 'treasurers' where only the name of the father is attested, it might be possible that the father's high position is simply not mentioned on a preserved monument. However, most of the fathers' names do not relate to any known high official and especially not to any 'treasurer'. The famous Senebsumai had a father called Wepwawethotep. There is again no 'treasurer' attested with that name, only one official with high titles including 'royal sealer' and 'overseer of the royal production place'. However, he is well known from several monuments,[36] none of which mentions Senebsumai or Senebsumai's mother, while the wife of Wepwawethotep, Senebhenas, is well known. The mother of Senebsumai was called Serukhib. There is no relation visible between the two people with the name Wepwawethotep. The evidence seems clear: the 'treasurers' came from the families of middle and higher officials, but were most often not the sons of other highest officials with ranking titles. This is easily explained. Especially in the Thirteenth Dynasty many kings must have chosen new people when they came to power, thus always forming a new court. They chose their close officials from the wider range of officials at the palace – perhaps the same pool of people that at least some of the kings also came from.

Reconstructing careers

Especially in the Middle Kingdom, officials are often depicted with a few titles on one monument, while on another the same person appears with other titles. It is not always clear what this means. Was each stela a single element of an ensemble, on each of which some of the official's titles were placed, or were these objects made at several stages of an official's career and, therefore, the range of titles represent different stages in that career? It is also important to ask for what purpose a monument was erected. In an expedition inscription we can expect titles relating to the expedition. In the tomb of an official a wider range of titles might appear, reflecting several stages of the official's career and also perhaps the longer period in which the tomb was built during which time the official changed his titles.

Examples for all these possibilities are known and will be discussed briefly here. Evidence for changes in an official's career, as reflected in the titles found in tombs, do not appear often, but they do exist. The Eleventh Dynasty vizier Dagi (p. 26) is known from a range of objects, principally in the mortuary temple of Mentuhotep II in Deir el-Bahari and his own tomb not far from the temple. Basically, Dagi appears with two function titles. In some inscriptions he was 'overseer of the gateway', in others he was vizier and had titles relating to this office. However, titles and title strings never appear on the same monument, making it likely that they represent different stages of his career. In his tomb the title 'overseer of the gateway' is only inscribed on the beautifully decorated sarcophagus and nowhere else in the decoration of his chapel. His tomb was once greatly enlarged and it is possible to argue that the sarcophagus was made while he was 'overseer of the gateway' but before he was promoted to the post of vizier. It was only with this promotion that the tomb was heavily enlarged and the higher title included in the new decorations.

Sobekemhat (p. 31) is known from his mastaba at Dahshur, close to the pyramid of Senusret III. The tomb was excavated and published by de Morgan. In the publication only fragments of the decorated tomb are reproduced. Several titles are preserved, but only two function titles. The vizier's titles mainly appear on fragments of reliefs that may once have belonged to the decoration of a chapel on the outside of the tomb. However, on the fragments of an offering table Sobekemhat bears the title 'treasurer', suggesting that Sobekemhat prepared the offering table when he was 'treasurer', and only while he was vizier was a large part of his tomb decoration executed or at least finished.[37]

Senebni is basically only known with certainty from his tomb equipment found at Thebes. He dates perhaps to the Sixteenth Dynasty, when the royal court was at Thebes and when the capital, at least of one part of the country, was there. Senebni appears with three titles on objects of his tomb equipment. On his coffin and canopic box he is only 'king's acquaintance', a common title of the palace administration in the late Middle Kingdom and Second Intermediate Period. On a staff found in the tomb he appears as 'royal sealer' and 'overseer of the marshland dwellers'. The staff bears the name of king Sewaenre and is dedicated to Senebni. 'Royal sealer' and 'overseer of the marshland dwellers' is a common title combination, the first of which announces that Senebni was a high court official. There are so far no known officials of the late Middle Kingdom for whom all three titles appear together. It seems that Senebni made his coffin when he was 'king's acquaintance' and was later appointed to the post of the 'overseer of the marshland dwellers'.[38]

A third example concerns a person called Amenemhat who may also date to the Second Intermediate Period (p. 41). His disturbed burial was found at Deir el-Medineh, a place better known for New Kingdom activities. Several inscribed objects were found in his tomb. On two boards of his box coffin Amenemhat bears the title 'elder of the hall'. On a fragment of a cartonnage, perhaps from an anthropoid inner coffin or mummy mask, he is 'great one of the tens of Upper Egypt'; finally on a stone fragment he appears with the title of vizier. All the titles on these different items of tomb equipment are well known from other sources, but they never appear at other places together in a single title string.

Once again, the impression is that these objects were made during different stages of Amenemhat's career. The box coffin was made at the start of his career, perhaps because it was seen as the most important part of his tomb equipment. The anthropoid coffin was made after his promotion to a 'great one of the tens of Upper Egypt'. Finally he became vizier. Sadly, he is not well datable and suggestions range widely from the late Twelfth Dynasty[39] to the Second Intermediate Period; an early New Kingdom date even seems possible.

These examples also provide evidence that coffins were made quite early in the life of an official, and were not only produced just after he died. However, it is possible to argue that all these objects were made at more or less the same time and that they are not proof of changes in the careers of these officials, rather that they had all these titles at about the same time. It therefore seems sensible to look for officials with different titles, where the monuments relating to these different titles are known to have been made at different times.

Perhaps the best example is the official Nebankh (p. 78). He is known from about a dozen monuments; most often stelae and rock inscriptions, but also seals and a statue with his name. On these objects Nebankh bears basically two function titles. He is 'king's acquaintance' and on other objects he appears as 'high steward', most often in connection with the ranking title 'royal sealer', but also with other titles known for such a high official. Interestingly, it is possible to relate both titles to different kings. In this case, the reconstruction of his career seems certain. In rock inscriptions at Aswan Nebankh appears as 'king's acquaintance'. Here he is named next to king Neferhotep I and his family, whom he obviously served. Under Sobekhotep IV, successor to Neferhotep I, he appears on a stela in the Wadi el-Hudi as 'royal sealer', the title connected with the 'high steward'. He appears as 'high steward' in a rock inscription in the Wadi Hammamat, where the vizier Neferkare Iymeru (p. 38) is also mentioned. This vizier can be securely dated to the reign of Sobekhotep IV. Thus it seems certain that Nebankh was 'high steward' under the latter king. Finally, Nebankh is mentioned on a stela belonging to queen Nubkhaes. The date of the queen is disputed, but she may have been married to a king who ruled after Sobekhotep IV. On this stela Nebankh appears as 'royal sealer' and 'high steward, who follows the king', demonstrating again that this was his title after becoming 'king's acquaintance'.

In many cases it is not certain whether two people with the same name but different titles were identical or two different people. Sometimes, it is even unclear that people with the same title and same name are identical. In cases where the names of the mother and father are identical, support for the identification seems quite strong. However, in instances where a person has a common name and equally common titles, there might be some doubt over identification. Conversely, in cases where a rare title is in combination with an uncommon name, there is a higher chance of identifying two individuals with identical titles and name, even when further information on the family is missing. For example, Meketre with the variation Meket is not a common name. In the early Middle Kingdom there are several monuments, most likely belonging to high state officials, bearing the name Meketre/Meket. It seems most likely that all these monuments belong to the same person.[40] On the other hand, there are several 'treasurers' and viziers known with the name Ameny. Ameny is one of the most common names of the Middle Kingdom and without further information it seems impossible to distinguish them.

The list of Amenys with the titles 'vizier' and 'treasurer' in the table

Title	Object	Family members	Date	Possible identification
1. Vizier	appears on an annal stone	not mentioned	Amenemhat II	no. 2
2. Vizier	offering table	family mentioned, identical with former?	middle of the Twelfth Dynasty	no. 1
3. Vizier	statue	son of Seneb	Thirteenth Dynasty	no. 5
4. Vizier	rock inscriptions at Aswan*	son of Zat-iniheret	Amenemhat III	
5. 'Treasurer'	sarcophagus	not mentioned	Amenemhat III (?)	no. 6 or 7, but also 3, 4
6. 'Treasurer'		Ameny (son of the 'steward' Iy)	late Middle Kingdom	no. 5, 7
7. 'Treasurer'	statue	Ameny (son of the woman Iti)	late Middle Kingdom	no. 5, 6

*de Morgan, *Catalogue des monuments*, 12, no. 48; 31, no. 10.

gives an idea of the problem. While several associations among the above-mentioned viziers and among the 'treasurers' are possible, it is also feasible that some of the 'treasurers' became viziers. It is possible to create several other such tables, demonstrating the problems Egyptologists still face when working with ancient sources.

Notwithstanding the numerous problems just described, it is still possible to reconstruct the careers of several officials and to see a variety of career paths. First of all, there are two distinct periods visible. It seems that careers in the early Middle Kingdom were slightly different to those of the Thirteenth Dynasty and Second Intermediate Period. An official's career path seems not to have been so rigid in the early Middle Kingdom. Throughout this period a close relationship between the vizier and the 'treasurer' is clear. Two 'treasurers' from this time also had the title of vizier, perhaps just for honorific purposes, which demonstrates the close relationship between these offices. Khnumhotep was 'high steward' before becoming vizier, while the 'scribe of the royal document' Antefiqer (p. 73) became 'high steward', and the 'high steward' Siese (p. 56) became 'treasurer'. Nothing similar is known for an official of the Thirteenth Dynasty, when the two parts of the administration were more clearly separated.

In the late Middle Kingdom two groups of officials are at the palace. Several careers are visible within these two groups, as already discussed (see p. 68). These are the officials under the vizier belonging to the scribal and juridical part of the palace, and the officials under the vizier who belong to the palace's economic sector. Interestingly, so far there are almost no known officials who crossed from one group to the other. This seems a sign of specialisation within the administration and also perhaps of a more rigid structure compared to the early Middle Kingdom.

The careers of the officials under the 'treasurer' are better known, simply because more stelae of these people with information on family members are preserved. The starting point of their careers, or at least the point where these people are first visible, is that of a 'king's acquaintance'. The important 'high steward' Nebankh, the 'overseer of marshland dwellers' Senebni and the 'treasurer' Senebi were first appointed to this office. However, several other less well attested 'high stewards' also started their careers in that office, such as Senebikhered and Rehuankh. The office of the 'high steward' was also closely connected to that of the 'overseer of sealers'. At least seven of the latter became 'high stewards' later in their careers. With the official Senebsumai there is at least one case of a 'high steward' who was promoted to the position of 'treasurer'.

Under the vizier in the late Middle Kingdom there were the 'overseer of fields', the 'personal scribe of the king's document', the 'leader of the broad hall' and the 'overseer of the compound'. For each of these officials with ranking titles a promotion to the position of vizier seems to be attested. Under these officials with ranking titles, there are the 'zab-official', the 'great one of the tens of Upper Egypt' and the 'elder of the hall'. Again, there are several indications that viziers and officials under viziers started their careers with these functions, but were never appointed to the position of 'treasurer'.

Finally, it should again be acknowledged that our sources are very fragmentary. Many of the relationships visible might mirror a particular situation, which may not necessarily reflect normal circumstances. One of the main sources is the corpus of Abydos stelae, which provide evidence for hierarchies and careers. Yet the officials depicted came together for a single project. In reviewing such evidence it should always be borne in mind that modern reconstructions are highly speculative.

The Lives of Court Officials

Given the number of sources, it is surprisingly hard to gain anything other than the vaguest picture of the life of an Egyptian official.[1] In general, certain stages in the life of an ancient Egyptian, such as rituals around birth or death, are well documented, while others, including training and daily life, are poorly attested. It is not known how long on average an official stayed in one office before he was appointed to another, higher position. This book deals basically with the highest level of administration. Some sources indicate that officials underwent a long career before reaching the top. Many of the individuals discussed here may therefore have been quite old when they reached the peak of their careers.

The mortality rate for mother and child was probably as high as in all pre-industrial societies. Thus the very moment of childbirth needed special protection for both mother and child. It is known from texts that during childbirth the mother squatted with her feet on special bricks. The ancient Egyptians called these bricks 'meskhenet' and considered them to be the personification of a goddess who served as a protector of mother and child during the delivery. For a long time the birth bricks were known only from Egyptian texts, but in 2001 one was found in the house of the local governor at Wahsut, in South Abydos. Another object often used for child protection was a magical wand. This is made from a long section of a hippopotamus tooth decorated with fantastic animals and certain deities. These creatures are also known as protectors of the sun god while he passed through the underworld during the night. Evidently the belief was that these deities, who could protect the sun god, could also protect mother and child.

In their early years, children of the highest officials were placed under the protection and care of a wet nurse (menat).[2] These women seem sometimes to have attained relatively high status and in some respects were regarded as part of the family. They are often shown on stelae together with the whole family and in those instances are clearly not regarded as a mere servants. Men could also bear the same title, indicating that the meaning was not just 'wet nurse', but also some kind of educator.[3] Another title was 'atju' for men or 'atjyt' for women, also meaning 'nurse', perhaps a person in charge for the slighter older children.[4]

There is evidence that at a certain age young men were circumcised. In the tomb of the Old Kingdom vizier Ankhmahor there is a depiction

58 The nurse Nebiderenkha, shown on the stela of the 'bowman' Nefernay. She is depicted in front of the stela owner and one wonders whether his mother died early and the nurse occupied the position of mother.

of two men undergoing this procedure. An inscription from the First Intermediate Period[5] mentions that a man was circumcised together with 120 other men, indicating that the practice was took place in some kind of ritual or celebration involving all young men of a certain age or position. From the Middle Kingdom three texts are known which mention circumcision, showing that it was still practised. It is not really known at what age the procedure was done, and therefore it is unclear whether it was a ritual of childhood, a rite of passage into puberty, or even specific to a particular age.[6]

Another ritual is attested several times in the Old, and twice in the Middle Kingdom. The stela of the 'scribe of the king's document' Zamont says: 'I was a child when I knotted the head band in front of his majesty.' A similar phrase is found in a much destroyed biographical text discovered at Lisht.[7] The translation of this passage is rather vague and, as it includes several unusual words, is more a guess than a certainty. However, it seems clear that it relates to a ritual for a growing boy on his way to manhood.[8]

Amazingly little is known about the Middle Kingdom school system or indeed any kind of scribal education. There are only a few references to schools in Middle Kingdom texts, the most famous one being the beginning of the 'Teaching of Duau-Khety', where it is stated:

> the man of Tjaru (?) called Duau-Khety
> for his son called Pepy,
> while he was sailing south to the Residence
> to place him in the writing school
> among the children of officials, of the foremost of the Residence.[9]

This indicates that there was some kind of school system in Middle Kingdom Egypt, but it remains unknown how common schools were. It seems remarkable that there are no further references to schools in the Middle Kingdom. The only other reference before the New Kingdom dates to the First Intermediate Period and comes from a biographical inscription at Asyut.[10] It therefore seems unlikely that the school was an institution as we know it today. There is no evidence that there was a building maintained by the state, temple or any other institution reserved solely for teaching children. From New Kingdom texts it can be assumed that there was a school or place of teaching close to the Mut complex in the Karnak temple as well as others at various locations in western Thebes,[11] while the quote from Duau-Khety above speaks in general terms of the 'residence', perhaps referring to a school located at the royal palace, which would almost certainly have been available to only a select number of people.

Nevertheless, there is also some evidence that there was another system functioning beside schools. For the Old Kingdom it has been assumed that a famulus system was in operation. This means a father or a single person teaching a son or student, not in a proper school but as a tutor.[12] However, the Old Kingdom evidence for this system comes only from works of literature, the 'Teachings'. More recent research has shown that all these works date from the Middle Kingdom and therefore this evidence tells us more about the situation in the Middle than the Old Kingdom. Furthermore, there are many stelae known which list family members with professions and titles from the same sector of administration, such as those working under the vizier or working under the 'treasurer'. In general one gets the impression that people in the same family worked in the same part of the administration. Conversely, however, other family stelae record various scribal titles which come from different parts of the administration.[13] For example, there is a 'great scribe of a treasurer' next to a 'scribe of the great compound',[14] while on another stela there is a 'scribe of the great compound' next to a 'scribe of the cattle stall'.[15] These are all people whom we would not expect to find working together in the same branch of the administration. There is an impression from this latter group that the members of the family who were scribes were perhaps specially trained and therefore able to work in different parts of the administration. It has always been assumed that all 'officials' were able to read and write. But this is not really proven and there may have been different levels of literacy. High court officials were almost certainly able to write, but quite often they also had a 'secretary' doing the day-to-day scribal work and acting as their deputy. For example, many 'scribes of the vizier' are known. Perhaps these people were especially well trained in the writing of formal documents.

Taking the evidence of the scribal families and the 'Teachings' together, it would seem that there was another way of becoming a scribe besides attending a special school. Is it possible that a father trained his son in writing and reading and that in certain families this ability was especially well inculcated, enabling the young boys to become specialised scribes? Were private teachers more the rule than the exception? This may not seem that unlikely when we consider that even the Egyptologist Flinders Petrie was trained not at school but by his father at home.[16] In many cultures this practice was more common than we might expect today.

It can therefore be argued with caution that in the Middle Kingdom there were two ways of training young boys. One was a school at the royal residence or perhaps just an official in charge of educating the children of the king and those of a few high officials. Such schools might have also existed in the provinces, but are not yet firmly attested. Other children were simply taught by their parents or were 'thrown' into a lower position at an early age and learned their profession by copying the work of older colleagues. In this way, their education was perhaps not very different to learning a craft which was also most likely learned in a father's workshop.

There is evidence that some of the highest officials grew up at the royal palace and were placed under a special teacher or an official who acted as their educator, which suggests that a school system was not seen as essential. The 'overseer of the king's apartments' Iha, buried at Deir el-Bersheh, reports: 'I have become one truly favoured, a teacher of the king's children'.[17] The vizier Antefiqer bears the title 'foster-child of the king'.[18] The 'treasurer' Iykhernofret reports on his famous Abydos stela that he was educated as the only pupil at the palace, while the 'follower of the King' Nebipusenusret 'grew up as child at the feet of the king, a pupil of Horus, lord of the palace'.[19] Some of these men were perhaps brought up at the palace together with the 'king's sons'. In this context it should be mentioned that several Middle Kingdom high officials had the title 'god's father'. This title could have had several meanings. It was given to priests, but the title also indicated a non-royal father of a king. In the New Kingdom it was the title for a teacher of a 'king's son'.[20] The same might be assumed for the Middle Kingdom, although it must be admitted that concrete evidence for this period is still missing.

Little is known of exactly when young men took up their first positions in the administration. From biographical inscriptions of the New Kingdom it can be assumed that this was already some time before puberty. They started in a low position in the administration and had to work their way up. Several careers are mentioned (p. 140), although the age of each official is unknown. However, most officials become visible to us only after rising to a high position in which they were able to set up their own monuments. Therefore it can be assumed, as already mentioned, that officials at the very top already had long careers behind them. Interestingly, the human remains of the vizier Khnumhotep, buried at Dahshur and found by de Morgan, are described as those of an old man of around 60-65 years of age at the time of his death. His career is to a certain extent possible to reconstruct and was certainly very long, from his beginnings as a lower official (though coming from an important family) to his rise to the top of society (p. 33).

At some point, perhaps before reaching the age of twenty, most officials married. This essential part of life is described in the 'Teaching of Hordedef': 'When you are excellent, found your house, take yourself a wife as a lady of the house(hold), so that a son might be born to you. May you build your house for your son, after you have made a place where you can live, adorn your house in the cemetery.'[21] Nothing is known about any form of wedding ceremony and it seems that a woman simply moved into the house of her husband without any ritual or contract. At about the same time the young man may also have founded his own house. The houses of the highest officials, so far as they can be identified, look rather stereotypical. The known examples were excavated in planned settlements and one wonders whether they were intentionally built from the beginning for the highest state officials and assigned to them when they reached their positions. From this very vague evidence it might be argued that houses of a certain size were given to officials with their appointment to a higher position. However, the reference to founding a house in Hordedef's teaching is ambiguous as the word 'per' is used, which could also mean 'household' or even 'estate'. Nevertheless, the reference shows clearly the essentials for the start of an adult life: a wife, a house and a son.

How did these highest state officials live? A number of houses have been excavated that certainly belonged to men in the highest positions. Several large houses were found at Tell el-Dab'a and at Lahun. A large house belongs to the local governor at Wahsut, a town built next to the mortuary temple of Senusret III at Abydos. The whole house complex under discussion is more than 60 x 90 m in area. It is one of the rare cases where it is possible to connect an Egyptian house with the name and title of an official. All these houses, dating to the late Middle Kingdom, are built along the same lines. As an example, it is worth describing the recently excavated house of the governor of Wahsut (see Fig. 62). The actual living quarters of the house owner were located at the back of the building. From a court-yard fronted with columns, an entrance led to a hall with four columns. This was the main hall of the house, the place where the governor gave audience, met with clients and received petitions from people working under him. It was some kind of public place. It is like-ly that the governor acted here as a judge for the people of his town. In the house of a vizier or a 'treasurer' this room might have been the 'office' (p. 17). Around this main hall several other rooms were arranged. On the left side there was a long room at the end of which was a niche for a bed. This was the main bedroom of the house owner. Other rooms are not so easy to identify. Next to the main hall was another room with two columns. Here, another entrance led to a small group of rooms, again of unknown function. The area in front of the house was built up with several structures. There are two rows of columns and it seems possible that the buildings next to it were at least partly later additions. Apartments on the north-west side of the residence were evidently used for the wife of the governor, indicated by the many seal impressions found there for a 'member of the elite' and 'king's daughter' Renseneb. The central feature here was a small hall with two columns. The function of each room in this part of the complex is again uncertain, partly because areas still await further investigation. The remaining part of the complex most likely included granaries, as is known from the houses at Lahun, although only fur-ther excavation will confirm this.

Almost identical houses were found at Lahun, in the town close to the pyramid of Senusret II at the entrance to the Fayum. Here nine houses of similar size and layout were excavated, one of which was built on a platform. The last building of this group, placed on a platform has often been regarded as a palace, but perhaps it was the house of the local gov-ernor. The number of nine large houses in the town corresponds to the number of high court officials and one wonders whether they were indeed originally built for people with ranking titles at the court of Senusret II. Each of these houses had huge granary installations that were certainly not intended for the sole use of the house owner and his family, but also for other people. It remains uncertain whether the grain stored here was used to feed the servants and serfs of the house owners, or whether the officials living here stored food for the general population of the town, thus serving as an example of the redistribution system of the Egyptian economy.

The highest state officials certainly had large estates administrated by their own 'stewards' and other officials. In the tomb of Meketre wood-en models of ships were found, some of which obviously represent the fleet of this official. However, others are fishing boats which, it could be argued, were simply placed in the tomb to secure the eternal food sup-ply of Meketre and do not represent ships of his own fleet. Ships belonging to officials are also shown in provincial tombs, again demonstrating the resources these people controlled.

It is unclear whether high officials controlled their own farmlands or whether these belonged in practical terms to the king and therefore to the state. Money was not yet known. It is unlikely that officials received a monthly or annual payment. It seems more likely that certain estates were attached to each office and title, providing an income for the officials. An inscription in the tomb of the local governor Hapidjefa states that he took resources from the estate of his father and not from the estate of his office as 'mayor'.[22] This reveals a separation of the estates of an official, whereby some belonged to the family and some to the state. The ka-priest Heqanakht, known from his letters found in a tomb at Thebes, always talks about 'my land', which gives the impression that he was its legal owner. However, such a conclusion is not entirely logical. It should be remembered from modern parallels that in economies in which people rent flats or houses, they invariably refer to 'my house' or 'my flat', although they are in no way legal owners of them.

As already indicated, many servants or serfs worked on the estates and households of officials. A list of such people is preserved on a papyrus now in the Brooklyn Museum. The servants listed include many Asiatics, people entitled as 'king's servants' and 'female servants'. Professions listed for some of them include that of 'field worker', 'organiser of the household', 'hairdresser', 'gardener' and 'weaver'.[23] Several inscriptions describe how local governors as well as military officials such as Khusobek received large numbers of people. Most of them were perhaps farm workers on the estates of the officials, but they provide further evidence that the people owned by an official as his slaves or serfs could amount to several hundred.

Tomb depictions and literary compositions provide some evidence for an official's leisure time. Hunting in the desert and the marshes and fishing are popular scenes in tomb chapels of the Middle Kingdom and all other periods. These scenes on chapel walls may be interpreted on several levels. It has been argued that hunting scenes in which the wife of the tomb owner is depicted have a strong sexual meaning. Hunting in the desert might also indicate the power of bringing order into the world. However, these scenes are certainly also a reflection of a leisured lifestyle of these people. Texts inform us that dinner banquets must have played an important part in their leisure activities, although scenes showing such events mostly date from the New Kingdom.

Virtually nothing is really known about the duties and functions of high officials in their old age. For the New Kingdom there is some evidence that elderly officials occupied some high, but perhaps not very demanding, positions, such as high priests of certain gods. For example, it is known that at the end of their careers some viziers became high priests of a particular god. For the Middle Kingdom little of this is visible in the sources. However, few people in Ancient Egypt reached very old age in the first place. The average age at death was just over twenty, although such statistics include the high rate infant mortality, and someone living into their twenties was quite likely to survive into their thirties or beyond. This means that officials who survived into their twenties were likely to rise very high in their careers. The high officials under discussion here were all people at the very top of the administration. It has been mentioned that there is evidence that some officials were in office together with their sons (p. 138). Is it possible in these cases that they chose their successor while still alive, but were too old to fulfil all their duties?

It is not known when high officials started to prepare a tomb, but there are quite a few indications that it was early in their careers. There are several examples of coffin or sarcophagus inscriptions which include titles lower in rank than those known from other monuments belonging to the same person, demonstrating that these objects were made before their appointment to the higher position (see p. 142). There are also cases in which the enlargement of a tomb may have gone with a promotion, as in the tomb of Dagi, who was first 'overseer of the gateway' and later became vizier. His tomb shows two building phases.[24] A similar impression is provided by other items made for the tombs of officials. On fragments of an offering table found at the mastaba of the vizier Sobekemhat, he appears as 'treasurer', obviously carved before he was appointed vizier. High officials seem to have been flexible in changing the location of their tombs in order to be close to a new king after an old king died. For example, Meketre is mentioned in the funerary temple of Mentuhotep II. The tombs of the officials of this king are placed around the temple. However, Meketre was finally buried next to another unfinished royal funerary temple quite far away from the king under whom he started his career. It seems unlikely that the 'treasurer', being the second man in the administration after the vizier, did not arrange a tomb under Mentuhotep II. It is possible therefore that he had prepared one overlooking Mentuhotep II's funerary temple, but abandoned it to erect a new one under a new king. A similar circumstance may be seen with the vizier Antefiqer. Senet, the mother of Antefiqer, had a large tomb unique for a woman at Thebes. It seems likely that this was originally prepared for the vizier and given to his mother and decorated for her when the royal court moved to the North. Accordingly, Antefiqer received a new tomb at Lisht.

In general, the highest officials belonged to a small group of people who could afford the full set of burial rituals known from different sources, especially the 'Coffin Texts' and depictions in tomb chapels. One of the first concerns after the death of a high official must have been the preparation of the body for mummification. The body of the deceased was therefore brought by boat to the house of mummifica-

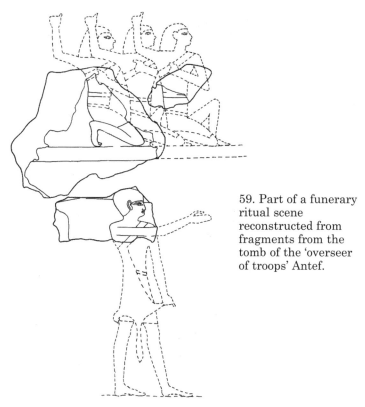

59. Part of a funerary ritual scene reconstructed from fragments from the tomb of the 'overseer of troops' Antef.

tion. During the mummification process many liturgies were spoken and performed. Several of these are preserved as 'Coffin Texts' on the inner faces of coffins. As few bodies of Middle Kingdom officials have survived, it is hard to say whether mummification was a regular feature of burial at that time, although for lower officials it was certainly not yet common. The mummy of the local governor Djehutynakht, who was buried at Deir el-Bersheh and dates to the Eleventh Dynasty, is a rare example of a mummified body of an individual of high status.[25] Following mummification offerings were made, after which the coffin containing the deceased travelled by boat to Abydos, Sais and from there to the ancient town of Buto. Here, the Muu dancers appeared whose depictions in several Middle Kingdom tombs indicate their special importance. However, it is hard to say whether the mummy was really brought to Abydos, Sais and Buto or whether the journey was simply a symbolic performance. After that, one of the most important rituals took place. The Opening of the Mouth ceremony ensured that the mummy was brought back to life. It followed the mysterious Tekenu procession in which an object called 'Tekenu' was drawn on a sledge. Then followed the canopic

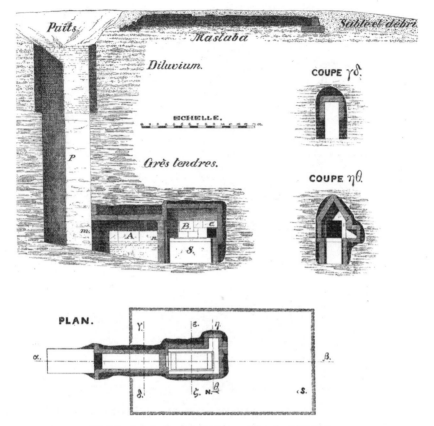

60. Mastaba of an unknown official at Dahshur.

procession in which the canopic jars were brought to the tomb. Finally, the remaining burial equipment was deposited in the tomb which was then sealed.

Chronological and regional variations in rituals and liturgies certainly occurred. Officials at the royal court were treated differently to those in local centres, where perhaps there were local traditions. Rituals of the early Middle Kingdom were different to those of the late Middle Kingdom or Second Intermediate Period. It is also likely that officials or their family members chose a selection of these rituals and therefore not all of them were used for each burial.

In general, officials with ranking titles always received the grandest tombs in the cemeteries. This is perhaps best seen at the mastaba cemetery next to the pyramid of Senusret III at Dahshur. Sixteen mastabas were excavated at the end of the nineteenth century. In general, there are three sizes of building. The biggest mastabas occupy an area of around 150 square metres. Of the three mastabas of this size found, two belong to viziers, and although the title of the tomb owner of the third remains unknown, he must have been an official at the same high level. The second size type is around 30 to 40 square metres. The largest of these belongs to the 'high steward' and vizier Khnumhotep. He bears ranking titles. It might be argued that he built the tomb while still in the lower rank of a 'high steward' or even lower, and became vizier at the very end of his career without enough time to prepare a bigger tomb. Another tomb of similar size belongs to the 'controller of the phyle' Khnumhotep, who lacked any ranking titles and was obviously of lower status than the vizier Khnumhotep. The smallest mastabas are around 5 square metres and seem to belong to the lowest ranked people still able to afford a mastaba. The only example where the name of the owner has survived is the mastaba of the 'embalming priest' Khentyemsaef. His title and the place of his tomb in a pyramid cemetery certainly suggest that his office was located at the royal funerary complex.

Next in importance to the size of the mastaba was the equipment of the burial apartments. Mastaba no. 1 (Figs 60 and 61), belonging to the second size type, had a paved burial chamber and a sarcophagus. It

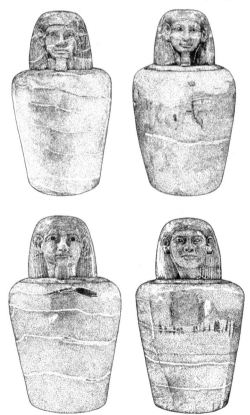

61. Canopic jars from the mastaba of an unknown official at Dahshur.

seems possible that this was the burial place of a ranking title official. Sadly, no inscriptions from the tomb are preserved, or if they are remain to be published. Mastaba no. 7 is about the same size, but its burial apartments were poorly equipped, suggesting that it belonged to a person of lower status.[26]

The burial equipment of the highest state officials was always of the finest quality. In the early Middle Kingdom, wooden models were typical for burials. Indeed, the highest quality examples of the Middle Kingdom were those found in the Theban tomb of the 'high steward' and 'treasurer' Meketre and in the tomb of the local governor Mesehti, buried at Asyut. Most of the preserved sarcophagi (coffins made of stone) belong to this range of people, such as that of Dagi, and Mentuhotep's fine example from his tomb at Lisht, or the sarcophagus of the 'treasurer' Ameny found re-used at Tanis. In the Second Intermediate Period, black coffins were common at Thebes. One of the few examples with gilding again belongs to a high court official, in this case to the 'overseer of marshland dwellers' Senebni, who was 'king's acquaintance' when the coffin was made. High officials were equipped with a set of canopic jars, while for lower officials this custom was in no way common.

The Heqanakht letters show that after the death of an official there was for a certain time a cult. Texts in the tomb of Hapidjefa at Asyut regulate this cult.[27] However, it is doubtful that the cult lasted very long. The next generation were already more interested in their own burials and did not spend resources on their ancestors.

9

Women Related to Court Officials

What is known about the women related to these court officials? Do we have enough information to gain a picture of their position and life? Although it is sometimes stated that women in Ancient Egypt had almost the same rights as men, there are clear differences visible in the position and status of men and women. Most monuments, such as stelae or decorated tombs, are set up by and decorated for men. Women appear there as secondary figures, usually as the wife or mother of the main person depicted. There are some decorated tombs and stelae just for women, but these are rather the exception. The most famous example is the tomb of Senet in Thebes. The tomb clearly belongs to her: she is the main person depicted in the inner chapel, where she appears on the false door. However, in the corridor she is shown with the vizier Antefiqer, her son or husband, and there she is always depicted behind him.

Several titles for women are known, but these occur infrequently. It is therefore often hard to follow the life of one woman as recorded on several monuments. Common names and common titles make identifications difficult. In the Old Kingdom women sometimes bore long title strings reflecting their social role and function. At that time, one woman even bore the title 'vizier', although it is disputed whether this was an honorific title or one given to an actual female vizier in charge.[1] Other common titles for women in the Old Kingdom include 'priestess of Hathor' and the ranking title 'king's acquaintance'. Women obviously enjoyed a certain status, but it seems that in practical terms they were excluded from exercising any real power in the state administration.

There was very little change in the situation during the Middle Kingdom. In the Eleventh and early Twelfth Dynasties some ongoing traditions of the Old Kingdom are still visible. In the Theban tomb of Senet, Zatzasobek, wife of Antefiqer, is referred to as a 'priestess of Hathor'. The same title is attested for many other women of the early Middle Kingdom, such as the wife of the 'great overseer of troops' Nesmont, datable to the beginning of the Twelfth Dynasty,[2] and the wife of the 'great overseer of troops' Ameny who most likely dates under Amenemhat II.[3] However, in the middle of the Twelfth Dynasty this title disappears from the women at the royal court, but is still common for the wives of local governors for at least one or two further generations. Even so, most often the wives of high officials are not mentioned with any title at all and are called simply 'his beloved wife at the place of his heart'.[4] In the middle of the Twelfth Dynasty the title 'lady of the house' appears. At first it is mostly attested for women at the provincial courts and only sporadically for women at the royal court. However, by the late Twelfth and into the Thirteenth Dynasty it becomes the most common title for woman of a higher social level.

In the Thirteenth Dynasty three other female titles appear. Many women are called 'one adorning the king', or have a title combined with the word 'young woman',[5] such as 'first young woman of the king',[6] while others, most often married to lower officials, are called 'servant of a ruler'.[7] The exact meaning and function of these titles are mostly a matter of guesswork. However, 'lady of the house' seems to have a strong economic meaning, indicating that the woman was really in charge of the house as an economic unit. Other titles might indicate a woman's high social status in relation to the king, which clearly relates to male titles of the late Middle Kingdom and Second Intermediate Period. This is when a higher number of titles denoting social status also appear, which contrasts with those indicating a purely economic or administrative function, more commonly found in the Twelfth Dynasty.

'One adorning the king' was a common title for women in the First Intermediate Period and often belonged to those not directly associated with the king's house.[8] In the early Middle Kingdom it became rare and was perhaps restricted to women directly connected to the king. The women buried in the mortuary temple of Mentuhotep II at Deir el-Bahari had this title, next to the title 'king's wife'.[9] The title disappears almost completely in the Twelfth Dynasty only to reappear late in the same dynasty, yet again for women of the highest social status who were likely to have been connected to the king and palace. In the late Thirteenth Dynasty and Second Intermediate Period the title becomes one of the most common for women. It appears among the wives of palace officials and also women in the provinces.[10] In both cases it seems to have functioned as a status marker rather than a title announcing a specific function, and perhaps refers to women who had some kind of contact with the king. In this respect 'the one adorning the king' Sobeknakht is of some interest. She lived in the late Thirteenth Dynasty at Hierakonpolis, far removed from the royal court. At first glance it seems unlikely that she would have had any contact with the king. However, her husband was the 'first inspector of the priests of Horus of Nekhen' and 'overseer of fields' Horemkhauef, who reports on his stela that he travelled to the royal court at Lisht. One wonders whether his wife Sobeknakht followed him on that trip and came in close contact with the king, receiving an honour expressed with that title.[11]

The economic power of women, at least at the highest social level, is demonstrated by a papyrus found in Thebes dating to the Thirteenth Dynasty. On its verso there is a list of 95 servants who were transferred

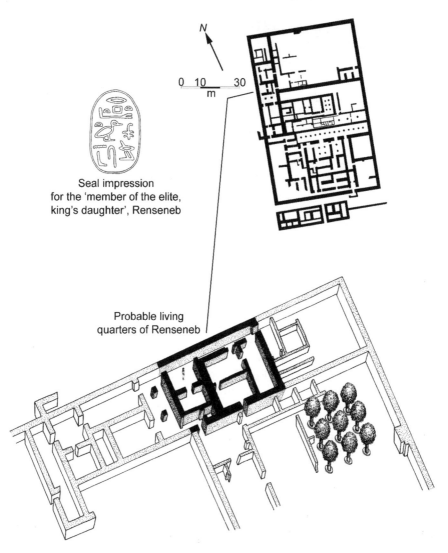

Seal impression
for the 'member of the elite,
king's daughter', Renseneb

Probable living
quarters of Renseneb

62. The governor's house at Wahsut with the women's quarters.

to a woman called Senebtisi.[12] Women had their own seals, obviously for marking their own property, although often this might be only jewellery. However, in the case of Senebtisi, her seal is explicitly mentioned in connection with the signing of a contract for the transfer of the servants.[13] In the elite houses at Lahun and Wahsut women had their own living quarters (Fig. 62). Renseneb lived in the governor's grand house at Wahsut in the Thirteenth Dynasty. She is mainly known from seal impressions found there. Her seal impressions were 'peg' sealings,

159

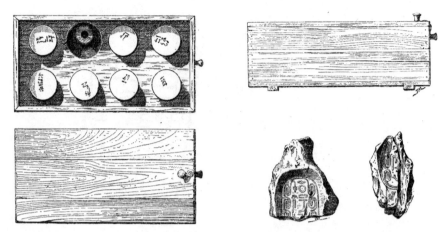

63. Sealed box from the tomb of the 'king's daughter' Nubhetepti-khered; the seal belongs to the 'true (?) king's acquaintance' Senebtifi.

meaning that they were once attached to wooden boxes or doors. In the former case they might indicate that she sealed her jewellery box. The large number of seal impressions found in this part of the house, most likely her living quarters, might not indicate her economic power, but rather the care she exercised over her jewellery. A sealed box was found in the tomb of the 'king's daughter' Nubhetepti-khered, showing how such a box was once locked (Fig. 63).

It is unknown whether women, and in particular those at the highest social level, were able to write. However, there are indications that at least some of them could. In this respect, an inscription on a stela now in Paris[14] raises an interesting point. The stela shows an official and his wife and lists several family members including a woman, of whom it is said that she was taught by her father. This reference is unusual and open to several interpretations, but the word used for 'taught', 'seba', is the same word used to describe schools – 'at-seba', meaning 'chamber of teaching'. One wonders whether this is a reference to a woman taught to write by her father.

The women of the local governors are better known than those of the court officials, simply because they appear in the tombs of their husbands with their long title strings and with fuller filiations. Khety, a woman whose name was more typical for men, appears in the tomb of Khnumhotep (II) at Beni Hasan, dating under Amenemhat II and Senusret II. She was his wife and had the titles 'daughter of a governor', 'foremost of action', 'king's acquaintance', 'priestess of Hathor', 'priestess of Pakhet' and 'lady of the house'. As one of her titles announces, Khety was the daughter of a governor, while a text in the tomb also informs us that she was the daughter of the ruler of the 'Jackal nome' (the name of the seventeenth Upper Egyptian nome). Her father is not mentioned by name. However, one of her sons was installed as governor at that place, providing evidence for a close connection between the 'Jackal nome' and the sixteenth Upper Egyptian nome.[15]

The case of Khety is perhaps also important for understanding how a marriage was arranged. It is clear from her titles that she came from another nome. For that reason alone one might conclude that the marriage between Khety and Khnumhotep was a political arrangement, with the intention of cementing the relationship between two influential families of governors in two neighbouring nomes. However, there are many other options. First of all, it seems very likely that the sons of governors were married to women of the same social status and these could have been most readily found at other provincial courts. We know that Egyptian officials were quite mobile, making it possible that the two met accidentally while their parents were on an expedition or while Khnumhotep, as a young man, was visiting the other nome. Indeed, some teachings give the impression that sons of high officials chose their wives out of love and not for political reasons. In the 'Teaching of Ptahhotep' it is written that: 'If you are excellent, found your house, love your wife within reckoning.'[16] However, there are indeed indications that some marriages were arranged. The clearest examples come from the New Kingdom royal family. There are several cases where daughters of Near Eastern kings were married to the Egyptian king as a diplomatic arrangement between their fathers and their future husband. Such clear cases are not known from Middle Kingdom Egypt. However, going back to the case of Khety and Khnumhotep, there is a second woman next to Khnumhotep. This is the '(female) sealer' Tjat. She is always shown next to Khnumhotep, but does not have any important titles, only that of 'sealer', which is more commonly known for men from several social levels. Since Khety had important titles and was the 'lady of the house', she was evidently the main wife of Khnumhotep. The title announced that she was the main person in charge of Khnumhotep's house as an economic unit (while his 'stewards' might be in charge of his whole estate). Tjat appears to have been just a part of his household. The impression here is that Tjat was the lover of Khnumhotep, but did not come from the highest social background. She also became mother of some important children of Khnumhotep. Later she may have become the main wife of Khnumhotep, perhaps after the death of the first wife.[17]

Women could also have female versions of the high ranking titles 'member of the elite' and 'foremost of action'. However, very few examples are known of women with these titles. They certainly indicate an extremely high position. 'Member of the elite' appears in the Middle Kingdom for the first time as a title of the 'king's wife' Neferu, the wife and sister of Mentuhotep II.[18] Another woman with this title belonging to the early Middle Kingdom is Zatipi, wife of Khnumhotep I from Beni Hasan, although nothing is known about her origins.[19] In the Second

Intermediate Period the title is attested for several women, but their exact status and origin is not always clear.[20] Hatshepsut, the wife of the 'royal sealer' and 'overseer of fields' Dedetu, bears the title.[21] Nothing is known about her family background, but one wonders whether she had royal connections. Indeed, most importantly, the title is sometimes held by women related to the royal family. It is certainly possible that the title always relates to woman connected to royalty, though perhaps not necessarily a queen or 'king's daughter', but other less direct relationships, such as that of Sobekhotep, who was the mother of a queen and the wife of a vizier.[22] Merestekh was the sister of a king (see p. 87). The title is also attested for Neferu, wife of the governor of Elkab Sobeknahkt (I) and mother of the governor with the same name.[23] There are indeed several connections within this family to the royal family and Neferu seems to be an offspring of a queen, confirming the royal connection with her title. Reditnes, perhaps the daughter of Sobeknakht (I) and wife of Sobeknakht (II), also bears the same title. A further well documented example is the 'member of the elite' and 'king's daughter' Renseneb,[24] known from her seal impressions found in the house of the governor of Wahsut. Not all 'king's daughters' had the title 'member of the elite' and it remains uncertain why some had it and others not.

The slightly lower, but still important, ranking title 'foremost of action' is mainly attested for several wives of local governors. As the title can also be translated as '(female) governor', this is perhaps not surprising as it indicates a woman of high position next to a local governor. However, it should be clearly stated that the title is not very common and once again it remains completely unknown why some women were given this title and others not.

At the present time there are no known occurrences of women with the two other ranking titles, 'royal sealer' and 'sole friend'. In the late Middle Kingdom 'royal sealer' was the most important title for announcing an administrative connection at the highest level to the royal court. Women did not have any administrative function there, at least not at the top level. It is therefore hardly surprising that the title was not given to them.

As an example of women within a distinct social group, the wives of the viziers deserve to be discussed and presented in more detail. The first known wife of a Middle Kingdom vizier is Maatnemty, wife of the vizier Dagi. Only her name is known and no titles for her are preserved in Dagi's tomb, where she is shown standing behind him (Fig. 64). The partly destroyed inscription calls her simply 'his beloved [wife]' (the word 'wife' is not preserved).[25]

Information about the women around the vizier Antefiqer is rather confusing. Of the two depicted in the tomb of Senet at Thebes, one is the 'priestess of Hathor' Zatzasobek (Fig. 65); the other is Senet, begotten of Dui, the tomb owner. Both are called 'his beloved wife', while Antefiqer

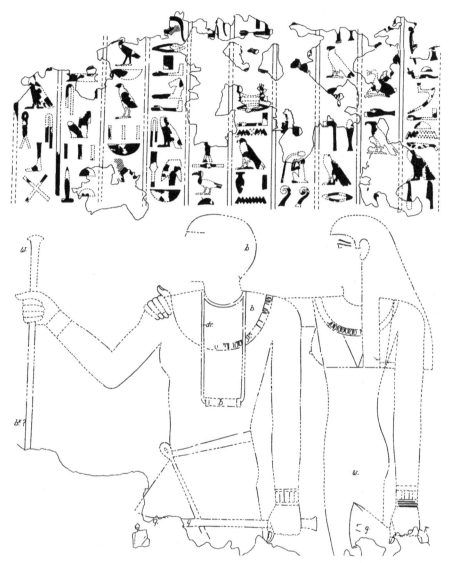

64. Dagi and his wife Maatnemti.

is also called 'born to Senet'. This has fuelled much speculation, especially because one large figure depicted in the tomb has been erased several times. However, nothing can be said about their parents or social origin (compare the discussion on p. 28).

So far there are no women connected to viziers attested for most of the Twelfth Dynasty, generally reflecting our limited sources for these officials. It is only at the very end of that Dynasty that the sources become

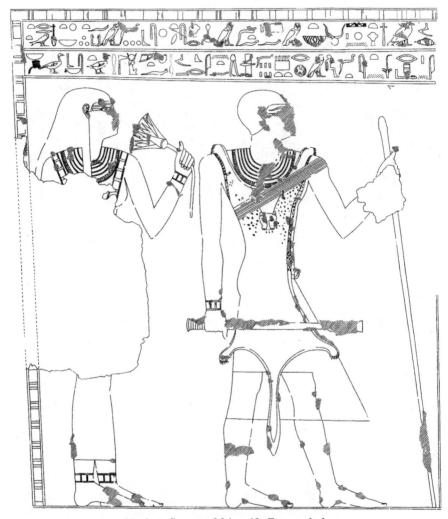

65. Antefiqer and his wife Zatzasobek.

richer. There is more information about a woman with the double name Sehetepibre Nehy, born of a lady called Senebtisi. She was the daughter of the 'great overseer of troops' Ameny and married to the vizier Ameny who was in charge under Amenemhat III. Sehetepibre Nehy appears on a stela of the 'great overseer of troops' Ameny as 'his beloved daughter'. On rock inscriptions of the vizier Ameny she appears as 'his wife.[26] The connection between the two attestations is only possible to make because the woman has a double name, a common feature in the late Middle Kingdom.[27] However, in this instance the combination of these two names is unique; therefore there seems little doubt about these relationships. Here, then, is one of the few Twelfth Dynasty examples of how the daughter of one important person was married to another high official. Another interesting point should be mentioned. Both names of the lady are basically male names. This might come as a surprise, but it was a common practice in the late Middle Kingdom and especially in the Second Intermediate Period to give women names that in other periods were given to men. The reason for this practice is so far unknown. It has been assumed that these women were named after a male member of the family, most likely a grandfather.[28] This seems possible, but positive evidence is rare and in most cases simply missing. For the moment we can only state that it was common in the late Middle Kingdom and Second Intermediate Period to give male names to women. With Sehetepibre Nehy we are also moving into the late Middle Kingdom when, in general, family members and the wider family are mentioned more often on monuments and in inscriptions.

The well known family of Senusret-ankh also belongs to around the late Twelfth Dynasty. His wife is a woman called Henutsen, daughter of a woman called Peret with the second name Zatzemay. The social background of Henutsen remains unknown. She names her mother, but not her father.

Another important wife of a vizier is Henutpu, who was also the mother of the vizier Ankhu. On a statue belonging to her husband she is called 'vizier's wife' and daughter of the 'royal sealer' and 'priest of Amun'. Her husband is not identified for sure, but he was perhaps Zamont (see p. 36) who again had a son with the same high priestly titles.[29] Henutpu was obviously regarded as an important woman. She is the only woman of the Middle Kingdom known who had a statue in the temple of Amun-Re at Thebes.[30] This was perhaps commissioned by her son, who placed three statues in the temple; one for himself, one for his mother and one for his father.

The wife of the famous vizier Ankhu was Mereryt,[31] whose social background remains again obscure. However, their daughter Senebhenas was married to the 'royal sealer' and 'overseer of the royal production place' called Wepwawethotep, who was closely related to the 'king's wife' Iy, a consort of king Sobekhotep II.

More is known about Reditnes, wife of the vizier Iy, who also bore the title 'king's daughter'. She was the daughter of an unknown king. Iy became vizier in year 1 of king Merhetepre and it is possible that this explains the royal origins of his wife. When her father, who was perhaps an official, became king, he appointed several family members or friends to higher positions. One wonders whether this was a general practice in the Second Intermediate Period, with its many short-reigned kings. It would explain the large number of officials for this period, much higher than for the longer Twelfth Dynasty.

Finally, the wife of the vizier Senebhenaf should be discussed. She is

66. Stela and canopic jar heads of Neni, found at Dahshur.
(a) Stela

known only from the coffin of his daughter, queen Mentuhotep, and was
the 'member of the elite' Sobekhotep.[32] Her high ranking title might at
first indicate that she comes from a high social background or even perhaps from the royal family (see p. 162). However, it is possible to argue
that she could have received this title as the mother of queen

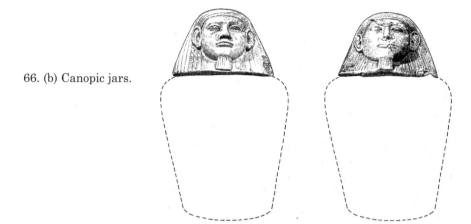

66. (b) Canopic jars.

Mentuhotep, and likewise her husband might have been appointed vizier upon his daughter's accession. In the Second Intermediate in particular, there is a close connection between the wives of the viziers and the royal family, as can be seen from the examples presented.

Finally, the burial places of women of high status should be discussed. The wives of high officials were sometimes buried in the same tombs as their husbands, although evidence for this is not abundant. In the burial chamber of the local governor Djehutynakht, buried at Deir el-Bersheh, his coffin and that of his wife were found side by side.[33] The burial, which dates to the late Eleventh Dynasty, had been robbed but still contained a large number of objects, including a set of wooden models characteristic of the period. From the Second Intermediate Period, parts of the burial equipment belonging to the 'overseer of marshland dwellers' Senebni and a woman with the title 'one adorning the king', named Khons, have survived. Although little is known about the circumstances in which their objects were found, it seems likely that they come from one burial chamber as the objects are in a similar state of preservation and they entered the collections of the Cairo and Moscow museums at roughly the same time.[34]

In many other cases it seems likely that a woman had her own shaft within a mastaba or rock-cut tomb of her husband. One well preserved, but yet not fully published, mastaba excavated at Dahshur provides some evidence. The main title of its owner Horkherty has not survived, but looking at the size of his tomb he was most likely a vizier or 'treasurer'. His burial chamber was found looted, although it still contained an uninscribed sarcophagus. The shaft also contained the undisturbed burial chamber with the remains of 'the one adorning the king' Zatwerut.[35] Although it is nowhere stated, it seems likely that she was his wife.

Archaeological evidence indicates that the wives of officials were not always buried close to their partners, but often interred somewhere else. The excavation of several large mastabas at Dahshur has revealed that the underground parts of the tombs show no sign of a space for a second burial. The wives of these officials must be sought elsewhere, perhaps not too far away. They were most likely buried in shafts, yet to be located, near these mastabas, although small burial complexes for women are also well known in the Middle Kingdom. The most famous example is the rock-cut tomb of Senet, the mother of the vizier Antefiqer. In the tomb the vizier appears most often next to his wife; in the scenes of daily life he is always shown first with the tomb owner Senet behind him. Only in the innermost chapel does Senet appear as the main person. The tomb's size and the quality of its decoration are exceptional for that of a woman. There are no other Middle Kingdom tombs of women of the same scale and quality, perhaps with the exception of royal ones. Nevertheless, at Dahshur and Lisht there are quite a number of burials of women only and one wonders whether at least some of them were family members of high state officials. The most famous example is the almost untouched burial of the 'lady of the house' Senebtisi, also called Zathapy. Her burial still contained a wonderful set of high quality jewellery making it likely that her husband came from the highest social level. Frustratingly, as Senebtisi is one of the most common names of the late Middle Kingdom, it remains for the moment impossible to identify any family relationships. So far the highest women known with that name is the wife of the early Thirteenth Dynasty vizier Khenmes (p. 38), although another option is that she was the wife of the 'great overseer of troops' Ameny, dating to the reign of Amenemhat III (p. 35).

At Dahshur, two stelae were found inscribed with the names of women, perhaps placed at a mastaba which had completely disappeared at the time of excavation. No further family affiliations are provided. The context of these women remains uncertain. They might be concubines of the king, high status female servants, or the wives of some officials also buried at Dahshur or elsewhere. At least one of them was Nubian and seems to be an interesting case of a foreigner in Egypt at a higher social level than expected (Fig. 66).[36]

To conclude, it can be said that the wives of the highest state officials came from the same background as the officials themselves. They had a certain amount of economic power and sometimes bore high ranking titles. However, there is little evidence that they ever carried out any of the highest administrative duties. Their power may have been more hidden, as informal advisers and participants in the work of their husbands.

Appendix: List of Officials

I. Viziers[1]

Eleventh and Twelfth Dynasties

Bebi (relief fragment from Deir el-Bahri; Mentuhotep II)[2]

Ahanakht (governor of Khemenu buried at Deir el-Bersheh; the title of vizier is mentioned only once in his tomb; Mentuhotep II?)[3]

Dagi ('overseer of the gateway' → vizier; relief fragments from Deir el-Bahri, tomb; Mentuhotep II and later)[4]

Amenemhat (rock inscriptions at the Wadi Hammamat; Mentuhotep IV)[5]

Ipi (tomb at Thebes; end of Eleventh or early Twelfth Dynasty)[6]

Neheri I (governor of Khemenu known from rock inscriptions at Hatnub, once appearing with the title vizier; Amenemhat I)[7]

Kay (known from rock inscriptions at Hatnub, once appearing with the title vizier; son of Neheri I; Amenemhat I)[8]

Antefiqer (tomb at Lisht, tomb of his mother/wife Senet at Thebes, several rock inscriptions, Reisner papyri; end of Amenemhat I – Senusret I)[9]

Amenemhat (governor of Khemenu buried at Deir el-Bersheh, also bearing the title vizier; Senusret I)[10]

Senusret (mentioned in a tomb at Beni Hasan, stela, tomb at Lisht; Senusret I – Amenemhat II)[11]

Ameny (mentioned on the annal fragment of Amenemhat II; Amenemhat II)[12]

Ameny (offering table; Senusret II? identical with previous entry?)[13]

Amenemhat-ankh (fragments of false door; Twelfth Dynasty)[14]

Sobekemhat ('treasurer' → vizier; tomb at Dahshur; Senusret III)[15]

Nebit (tomb at Dahshur; Senusret III)[16]

Khnumhotep ('chamberlain' → 'high steward' → vizier; tomb at Dahshur; Senusret III – Amenemhat III)[17]

Ameny (rock inscriptions at Aswan; Amenemhat III)[18]

Khety (Lahun papyrus; Amenemhat III, 29th year)[19]

Zamont/Resuseneb ('mouth of Nekhen' → vizier; two stelae, rock inscriptions; end of Twelfth or beginning of Thirteenth Dynasty)[20]

Qemeny (bronze ship mast-finial; end of Twelfth or beginning of Thirteenth Dynasty)[21]

Senusret-ankh ('overseer of fields' → 'personal scribe of the king's document' → vizier; rock inscriptions, statue (found at Ugarit), stela; end of Twelfth or beginning of Thirteenth Dynasty)[22]

Thirteenth Dynasty

Khenmes (rock inscription, statue with the name of the king, now in London, BM; Sekhemkare)[23]

Ankhu (son of a vizier, perhaps of Zamont) (several stelae, pBoulaq 18, papyrus

in Brooklyn, statues, cylinder seal, seal impressions from Nubia, statue of his father; Sekhemre-Khutauy Sobekhotep Amenemhat – Khendjer)²⁴
Iymeru (of Ankhu) (stela, statue; about Neferhotep I)²⁵
Resseneb (son of Ankhu) (stela)²⁶
Neferkare Iymeru (several statues, stelae, rock inscription, seal impression; Sobekhotep IV)²⁷
Djed-Ptah/Dedtuseneb (seal impressions from Uronarti; perhaps under king Horus Khabau and Horus Djed-Kheperu)²⁸
Ibiau ('overseer of a compound' → vizier; stelae,²⁹ as vizier only mentioned in the filiations of his sons; Ibiau?)

Late Twelfth or Thirteenth Dynasty
(not more precisely datable)
Ameny (statue, London, BM, see Fig. 17)³⁰
Iwy (seal)³¹
Minhotep (seal)³²
[Neb-su]menu (seal impression)³³
Hori (seal)³⁴
Sebekaa Bebi (overseer of the compound → vizier; seals)³⁵
Dedu-Mentu Senebtyfy (stela, statue)³⁶

Second Intermediate Period
Senebhenaf (coffin of his daughter, queen Mentuhotep, wife of king Djehuty)³⁷
Amenemhat (elder of the hall → great one of the tens of Upper Egypt → vizier; tomb in Thebes, papyrus)³⁸
Iy ('overseer of the royal domain' → 'governor of Elkab' → vizier; stela from Karnak, mentioned in the tomb of Sobeknakht at Elkab; king Merhetepre)³⁹
Sobeknakht (stela from Karnak)⁴⁰
Iymeru (governor of Elkab → vizier; stela from Karnak)⁴¹

II. 'Treasurers'⁴²

Eleventh and Twelfth Dynasties
Khety (tomb at Thebes, rock inscriptions, mentioned in the mortuary temple of king Mentuhotep II; Mentuhotep II)⁴³
Meketre (sealer → 'high steward'/treasurer; tomb at Thebes, mentioned in the mortuary temple of king Mentuhotep II, rock inscription; Mentuhotep II – early Twelfth Dynasty)⁴⁴
Antef (tomb at Thebes; early Twelfth Dynasty)⁴⁵
Ipi (rock inscription, coffin fragments; Amenemhat I)⁴⁶
Rehuerdjersen (tomb at Lisht, stela; Amenemhat I?)⁴⁷
Sobekhotep (rock inscription; Senusret I year 22)⁴⁸
Mentuhotep (tomb at Lisht, statues from Karnak, stela at Abydos; he also bears the title vizier, but this may just be honorific; Senusret I)⁴⁹
Merykau (stela from the Eastern desert; Amenemhat II)⁵⁰
Siese (chamberlain → 'high steward' → treasurer, perhaps vizier; stelae, offering table, tomb at Dahshur; Amenemhat II)⁵¹
Sen-ankh (rock inscription; Senusret III year 8)⁵²
Sobekemhat (tomb at Dahshur; identical with the vizier of the same name; Senusret III)
Iykhernofret (several stelae; Senusret III – Amenemhat III)⁵³

Ameny (statue; son of the steward Iy)[54]
Ameny (statue; son of Iti)[55]
Senusret (papyrus fragment from Lahun dated to a year 10)[56]
Hor (seal; late Twelfth Dynasty)[57]

Thirteenth Dynasty

Senebef (seal, stela)[58]
Ameny-seneb (relief from Abydos, seal impression from Mirgissa)[59]
Herfu (seals, weight, statue in Brooklyn)[60]
Khentykhetyemsaf Seneb (statue, stela found at Harageh)[61]
Seneb (stela)[62]
Senebsumai ('high steward' → treasurer; seals, stelae, statue, bronze statue, papyrus fragments from Lahun; Sobekhotep II – Neferhotep I)[63]
Senebi (king's acquaintance → treasurer; seals, stelae, rock inscription; Nefehotep I – Sobekhotep IV)[64]
Amenhotep (seals, tomb at Dahshur, faience vase; after Sobekhotep IV)[65]

Fourteenth and Seventeenth Dynasty

Nubmerut (offering table)[66]
Teti (tomb at Thebes; Nubkheperre Antef)[67]
Neshi (Kamose stela)[68]
Renseneb (Merdjefare)[69]

Late Twelfth or Thirteenth Dynasty
(known only from seals)
Ibt,[70] Isi,[71] Adj-zehui,[72] Wepemhab,[73] Win, Nebsumnu,[74] Redienptah[75]

Hyksos or at least northern Egypt

Ihuir[76]
Aperbaal[77]
Perimhezut[78]
Rediha[79]
Har[80]
Sadi[81]
Nebrazehui (?)

IIb. 'Deputy treasurers'

Sehetepibre (stela; Senusret III/Amenemhat III)[82]
Ameny-seneb (lintel, Cambridge, see Fig. 19)
Sehetepibre (Senusret III/Amenemhat III, see Plate 5)[83]
Ibjau (Thirteenth Dynasty)[84]
It (Thirteenth Dynasty)[85]
Khakheperre-seneb (late Middle Kingdom)[86]

III. 'High stewards'[87]

Eleventh Dynasty
Henenu (tomb, expedition inscription in the Wadi Hammamat; Mentuhotep II Mentuhotep III)[88]
Buau /Mentuhotep (decorated coffin; end of Eleventh Dynasty?)[89]

Twelfth Dynasty
Meketre (same as the treasurer)
Ipi (same as treasurer)
Sobeknakht (tomb at Lisht, statue)[90]
Hor (stelae, one found at the Wadi el-Hudi; Senusret year 9)[91]
Nakht (statue, control note on pyramid block)[92]
Antef, son of Zatamun (stelae, tomb at Lisht; Senusret I year 24, 25)[93]
Antef, son of Zatuser (statue; Senusret?)[94]
Kheperkare (stelae; Amenemhat II)[95]
Zanofret (statue, stela; Amenemhat II?)[96]
Sobekemhat (statue; Amenemhat II?)[97]
Siese (same as 'treasurer'; Amenemhat II)
Khenty-khety-wer (statues, stelae; Senusret II?)[98]
Antefiqer (statues, relief fragments; 'scribe of the royal document' → 'high steward'; Senusret II – Senusret III?)[99]
Khnumhotep (same as vizier; Senusret III)
Nesmont (statue; Senusret III?)[100]
Senmeri (Semnah despatches; Amenemhat III)
Meketankhu (stela, rock inscription; Amenemhat III, year 4)[101]
Senebef (stela; Amenemhat III)[102]
Ameny-seneb (also 'deputy treasurer', stela)[103]
Senusret (bronze statue, relief fragment, seal, stela)[104]
Hor (stela in eastern desert; Twelfth Dynasty)[105]
Renseneb (rock inscription, stela)[106]

Thirteenth Dynasty
Aabni (stela, weight, pBoulaq 18; Sobekhotep II)[107]
Gebu (statue)[108]
Nebsekhut (statue)[109]
Anekef ('overseer of sealers' → 'high steward'; stela, seals; about Neferhotep)[110]
Nehy ('overseer of sealers' → 'high steward', stelae; about Neferhotep I – Sobekhotep IV)[111]
Zaitiit (stela; about Neferhotep I – Sobekhotep IV)[112]
Res ('king's acquaintance' → 'high steward'; stela, seals)[113]
Ameny (stelae, seals; about Neferhotep I and earlier)[114]
Senebikhered ('king's acquaintance' → 'high steward'; statue base, stela, offering table; about Neferhotep I and earlier)[115]
Titi ('cupbearer' → 'chamberlain of the inner palace' → 'overseer of sealer' → 'high steward'; statue, stelae, seals; about Sobekhotep III – Neferhotep I)[116]
Nebankh (stelae, rock inscriptions, seals; king's acquaintance under Neferhotep I; 'high steward' under Sobekhotep IV)[117]
Rehuankh ('king's acquaintance' → 'overseer of sealers' → 'high steward'; statue, seals, rock inscription; Sobekhotep IV or shortly after)[118]
Amenemhat Zasatet (stelae; Neferhotep I – Sobekhotep IV)[119]

Not securely datable
Akef (seal)[120]
Aki (also 'overseer of sealers'; seals, stela; Thirteenth Dynasty)[121]
Amenemhat-seneb Nemtyemweskhet (model coffin, stelae, seals)[122]
Amenemhat Nehy-senebi (rock inscription, statue, seals)[123]

Antef (seal)[124]
Hepetrehu (stela)[125]
Ibt (seal)[126]
Imbu[127]
Irgemetef (statue base, statue, stela)[128]
Iufseneb[129]
Iy ('overseer of sealers' → 'high steward'; seals)[130]
Khnumhotep[131]
Mentuser[132]
Neberzehwy (seal)[133]
Nehy (stela)[134]
Nehy-senebi (seals)[135]
Nemtyhotep[136]
Ptahwer (statue)[137]
Redi(n)ptah[138]
Renefemib[139]
Senaa-ib (stelae, statue)[140]
Senankh[141]
Senusret, son of Zahathor[142]
Sobekhotep[143]
Sobekhotep-merytef[144]
Sobekhotep-wer[145]
Wenen[146]
... i (stela)[147]

Second Intermediate Period

Khonsmes (canopic box)[148]
Neferhotep (shown in the tomb of Sobeknakht in Elkab)[149]

IV. 'Overseer of sealers'[150]

Khety (rock inscription; Mentuhotep II, year 41)[151]
Meru (tomb, stela, rock inscription; Mentuhotep II, year 46)[152]
Rahershefnakht (tomb at Saqqara South; Amenemhat I?)[153]
Sokarhotep (tomb at Helwan; Amenemhat I?)[154]
Emhat (stela; Senusret I, year 9)[155]
Ptahwer (stela; Twelfth Dynasty)[156]
Netjeriemmer ('cupbearer of the chambers' → 'overseer of sealers'; stelae; Neferhotep I)[157]
Herunefer (statue, stela, rock inscription; Neferhotep I and shortly before)[158]
Nenkhemsen (stela; Neferhotep I)[159]
Jahnefer (stela, shown together with the king; Nubkheperre Antef)[160]
Ptahmose[161]

Thirteenth Dynasty, later 'high stewards'

Aki
Anekef
Iy
Nehy
Rehu-ankh

173

Res
Titi
Aki

Known from seals
Ameny[162]
Ashau[163]
Iuseneb[164]
Keki[165]
Nebsumenu[166]
Resu[167]
Senebi-hetep[168]
Sobekweser[169]
Seshenunefer[170]
Rehu-ankh (same as 'high steward'?)

V. 'Personal scribe of the king's document'[171]

Iai (rock inscriptions; Mentuhotep II)[172]
Zamont (stela)[173]
Dedusobek (statue)[174]
Antefiqer (the later 'high steward')

Thirteenth Dynasty

Iuy (pBoulaq 18)
Iymeru (stela)[175]
Zaamun (stela)[176]
Senebefni (statue)[177]
Seneb (rock inscription)[178]
Nebsun (stela; about Sobekotep IV)[179]
Itib (?) (seal)[180]
Senebtifi Ptahemsaf (stela, statue)[181]
Tershenuah (seal)[182]

VI. 'Overseer of the marshland dwellers'

Ameny (Senusret I – Amenemhat II)[183]
Khakheperraseneb (stelae)[184]
Ibi (Neferhotep I)[185]
Senebni ('king's acquaintance' → 'overseer of sealers'; burial at Thebes; king Sewahenra, Sixteenth Dynasty?)[186]
Aamu (Sekhemre-wadjkau Sobekemsaf)[187]

Known only from seals

Ini[188]
Dedu[189]
Senen[190]
Semerti[191] (late Thirteenth Dynasty or Hyksos period)
Neferhotep[192]
Nen[193]

Resunefer[194]
Rediniptah[195]

VII. 'Overseer of troops' or 'Great overseer of troops'[196]

Antef (stela, tomb; Mentuhotep II)[197]
Mentuhotep (Wadi Hammamat; Mentuhotep IV)[198]
Nesmont (statue, stelae; Amenemhat I/Senusret I)[199]
Mentuhotep (stela Florence 2540; Senusret I; year 18)[200]
Dedu-Antef (inscriptions, Wadi Halfa; Senusret I)[201]
Senebebu (statue; about Senusret I)[202]
Ameny (stelae, tomb at Lisht; about Amenemhat II)[203]
Montemhat (stela)[204]
Ameny (stelae, offering table; Senusret III/Amenemhat III)[205]
Seni (Wadi Hammamat inscription)[206]
Resseneb (rock inscription; Amenemhat IV, year 4)[207]
Sehetepibreseneb (statue found in Karnak temple)[208]
Renseneb (rock inscription; Sekhemre-khutawy)[209]
Ibiau (pBoulaq 18)
Sobekherhab (stela)[210]
Amenemhat (statue found in Karnak temple; Sobekhotep IV)[211]
Herunefer (coffin board, son of a king Mentuhotep)[212]

Seals

Hori[213]
In[214]
Mentuhotep ('great overseer of troops')[215]
Nemu[216]
Saiu[217]
Saneb[218]
Sapath ('great overseer of troops')[219]
Sethi ('great overseer of troops')[220]
Sobeknakht[221]
Wegaf ('great overseer of troops')[222]

VIII. 'Overseer of fields'[223]

Imhotep (tomb at Lisht; about Senusret I to Amenemhat II)[224]
Mentuhotep (statue)[225]
Ankhu (seal, tomb inscription, statues), end of Twelfth/beginning of Thirteenth
    Dynasty[226]
Senusretankh (identical with the later vizier)
Senusretseneb (Nerkare, rock inscription)[227]
Nehy (rock inscription)[228]
Amenemhat, son of Hapyu (stela, Liverpool)[229]
Haankhef (pBoulaq18, and perhaps in another papyrus; Sobekhotep II)[230]
Amenemhat, son of Zathathor (stela in Munich)[231]
Panetyni (double name, first part hard to read, rock inscription)[232]
Kheperka (statue in Turin)[233]
Ameny (stela)[234]
Antef (stela)[235]

Dedetu (stela)[236]
Zahathor (stela)[237]
Mentuhotep (seal)[238]
Senebni (seal)[239]
Senebhenaf (later 'controller of the broad hall', q.v.)
Nebiryrau (stela)[240]
Ibiau (coffin fragments)[241]
Redinptah (seal)[242]
Redinamun (gilded canopic chest, Thebes; Sixteenth-Seventeenth Dynasty)[243]

XI. 'Overseer of the compound'[244]

Ibiau (stela, statue; king Ibiau)[245]
Seneb (statue, seal)[246]
Bebi (see vizier Bebi Sobekaa)
Mentuhotep (rock inscription)[247]
Senebi (statue of father, vizier Ameny, fig. 17)[248]

Known from seals[249]
Ptahhotep
Zaamun
Seneb
Senebtifi
Sobekhotepkhuf [250]

X. 'Controller of the broad hall'[251]

Seneb (two stelae)[252]
Renseneb ('commander of the ruler's crew' → 'great one of the tens of Upper Egypt' → 'controller of the broad hall'; stelae)[253]
Senebhenaf (stela, statue; son of the vizier Ibiau)[254]
Neferhotep (stela)[255]
Iymeru (father of the vizier Neferkare Iymeru; before Sobekhotep IV)[256]
Ibiau (scribal board)[257]
Menuhotep (seal)[258]
Redienheqyt (stela)[259]
Khons (stela) (Fig. 42)

XI. 'Overseer of the gateway'[260]

Dagi (Mentuhotep II, the later vizier)
Hor (see 'high steward' Hor; under Senusret I)
Inherethetep (block from tomb found at Lisht)[261]
Ipi (tomb at Lisht, stela, statue; late Senusret I to first half of Amenemhat II)[262]
Khentykhetywer (block from tomb at Dahshur, stela; Amenemhat II year 28)[263]
Inpy (stela, tomb at Lahun; Senusret II – Senusret III)[264]
Ankhpuptah (seal)[265]
Senusret-ankh (seal impressions)[266]

XII. 'Overseer of the police'

Dedusobek (about Senusret II)[267]
Amenhotep[268]
Antef[269] (Amenemhat III year 33)
Dedy (seal)[270]
Senusret (seal)[271]
Senusretseneb (rock inscription)[272]

XIII. High priests of Ptah

Senusret-ankh (tomb at Lisht)[273]
Sehetepibre-ankh (statue base, offering table, stela)[274]

Late Twelfth Dynasty
Sehetepibre-ankh-nedjem (offering table, statue)[275]
Nebpu (son of Sehetepibre-ankh-nedjem) (statue)[276]
Sehetepibre-khered (son of Nebpu) (statue)[277]

Late Middle Kingdom
Sobekhotep Haku (statue, seal)[278]
Senebui (stela)[279]
Seneber[...] (papyrus fragment)[280]
Impy (statuette)[281]

XIV. High priests of Amun

Senebefni[282]
Redini[283]

XV. High priests of Heliopolis

Nubkaure-ankh (offering table, rock inscription)[284]
Khakaureemhat (mentioned on papyrus fragment from Lahun)[285]
Maakherure-emhutaat (seal)[286]
Ra (seal)[287]
Khentykhetyhetep Iymiatib (seal)[288]
Iufseneb (seal)[289]

Notes

For full publication details of short references see
the Bibliography and Abbreviations.

Preface

1. Recent exceptions aimed at a wider audience are M. Rice, *Who's Who in Ancient Egypt*, London 1999; C. Booth, *People of Ancient Egypt*, Stroud 2006; T. Wilkinson, *Lives of the Ancient Egyptians: Pharaohs, Queens, Courtiers and Commoners*, London 2007.
2. P. Stanworth, 'Elites', in Geoff Payne (ed.), *Social Divisions*, Houndsmills and New York 2000, 173-93.

1. Historical Background

1. T. Wilkinson, *Early Dynastic Egypt*, London & New York 1999, 137.
2. Strudwick, *Administration*.
3. J. Padró, *Études Historico-Archéologiques sur Héracléopolis Magna*, Barcelona 1999.
4. Ward, *Index*, no. 845.
5. Ward, *Index*, 18a.
6. For the reading *semeher*, see Quack, 'Zum Lautwert von Gardiner Sign-List U 23', *Lingua Aegyptia* 11, 2003, 113-16.
7. Doxey, *Egyptian Non-Royal Epithets in the Middle Kingdom*, 125.
8. Grajetzki, 'Der Gebrauch von Rangtiteln in der Provinzialverwaltung der 1. Zwischenzeit und des frühen Mittleren Reiches', in C.-B. Arnst, I. Hafemann & A. Lohwasser (eds), *Begegnungen, Antike Kulturen im Niltal*, Leipzig 2001, 161-70.
9. Ward, *Index*, no. 400 (*imi-ra kat nebet*).
10. Janssen, *Autobiografie*, 66-8.
11. Janssen, *Autobiografie*, 134-5.
12. Janssen, *Autobiografie*, 126-8.
13. C. Raedler: 'Zur Struktur der Hofgesellschaft Ramses II', in R. Gundlach & A. Klug (eds), *Der ägyptische Hof des Neuen Reiches, seine Gesellschaft und Kultur im Spannungsfeld zwischen Innen- und Außenpolitik,* Wiesbaden 2006, S. 40-64 (Raedler applies the works of Norbert Elias to Ancient Egypt).
14. Fr. 82; Fay, *The Louvre Sphinx*, 50-2.
15. D. Franke, 'Middle Kingdom Hymns and other sundry religious texts – an inventory', in S. Meyer (ed.), *Egypt – Temple of the Whole World: Studies in Honour of Jan Assmann*, Leiden 2003, 95-135.
16. Freed, 'Stela workshops', 297-336.
17. Martin, *Seals*, no. 234; the early Twelfth Dynasty scarab seal of Wah (Martin, *Seals*, no. 390) is atypical. The inscriptions are not for sealing.

18. Cairo CG 20181.
19. Ben-Tor, *Scarabs, Chronology, and Interconnections*, 36-8.
20. Martin, *Seals*, 6 (back type 6).
21. Martin, *Seals*, no. 1111.
22. Martin, *Seals*, no. 1247.
23. Grajetzki, 'Der Schatzmeister Amenhotep und eine weitere Datierungshilfe für Denkmäler des Mittleren Reiches', *BSEG* 19 (1995), 5-11; Martin, *Seals,* no. 1722 ('high steward' Titi), no. 1514 ('treasurer' Senebsumai), nos 213-14 ('high steward' Ameny).
24. Berlev, *JEA* 60 (1974), pl. XXVIII.
25. H. Goedicke, 'An ancient naval finial of the Middle Kingdom', *Ägypten und Levante* 10 (2000), 77-81.

2. The Vizier, 'Prime Minister' of Egypt

1. P. Lacau & J.Ph. Lauer, *La pyramide à degrés V*, Cairo 1965, 1-3, pl. 1; Strudwick, *Administration*, 300
2. For the Old Kingdom viziers, see Strudwick, *Administration*, 300-35.
3. Martin-Pardey, 'Die Datierung der "Dienstanweisung für den Wesir" und die Problematik von Tp rsj im Neuen Reich', in N. Kloth (ed.), *Es werde niedergelegt als Schriftstück, Festschrift für Hartwig Altenmüller zum 65. Geburtstag, Studien zur altägyptischen Kultur*, SAK-Beihefte 9, Hamburg 2003, 323-34; Quirke, *Titles and Bureaux*, 18.
4. den Boorn, *Duties of the Vizier*, 309-31.
5. Martin, *Seals*, no. 1848.
6. Martin, *Seals*, no. 1849.
7. Martin, *Seals*, nos 1846, 1847, 1847a.
8. Newberry, *PSBA* 22 (1900), 99-105.
9. Quirke, *Administration*, 117.
10. Lorton, 'What was the *per-nsw* and who managed it?: aspects of royal administration in "The Duties of the Vizier"', *SAK* 18 (1991), 291-3.
11. Ward, *Index*, no. 192.
12. Ward, *Index*, no. 224.
13. Ward, *Index*, no. 1263.
14. Ward, *Index*, no. 1563.
15. Ward, *Index*, no. 248.
16. Ward, *Index*, no. 1176.
17. Ward, *Index*, no. 1465.
18. Ward, *Index*, no. 523 (Ward reads 'Keeper of Nekhen').
19. Ward, *Index*, no. 1449; Quirke, *Titles and Bureaux*, 88.
20. Ward, *Index*, no. 87.
21. Quirke, *Titles and Bureaux*, 86-87.
22. Willems, *Dayr al-Barshâ*, 109.
23. Borchardt, 'Der zweite Papyrusfund von Kahun und die zeitliche Festlegung des mittleren Reiches der ägyptischen Geschichte', *ZÄS* 37 (1899), 96-7.
24. von Beckerath, *Untersuchungen*, 95-7.
25. B. Fay, 'Custodian of the Seal, Mentuhotep', *GM* 133 (1993), 19 n. 3.
26. Jaroš-Deckert, *Das Grab des Jnj-jtj.f*, pl. 33, fr. 227.
27. The only exception is perhaps the tomb of Senet, where the husband/son of the tomb owner is a high official. However, this tomb is in many ways unique, belonging to a woman (see discussion on p. 28).

28. Davies, *Antefoker*, pls VII, XIV.

29. B. Fay, 'Tell me, Richard – did the ancient Egyptians really wear suspenders? (Thoughts on the vizier's insignia and one of the men who wore it during Amenhotep III's reign)', in *Servant of Mut, Studies in Honor of Richard A. Fazzini*, Leiden & Boston 2008, p. 98 figs 9, 10, 12 (fig. 12 might date to the Thirteenth Dynasty; the kilt is much higher than in the other two examples).

30. Allen, 'High officials of the early Middle Kingdom', 22.

31. Arnold, *Das Grab des Jnj-jtj.f*, 40.

32. Simpson, 'Lepsius Pyramid LV at Dahschur: the mastaba of Si-Ese, vizier of Amenemhet II', in *Pyramid Studies,* 60.

33. Bröckelmann, 'Zwei Wesire namens Antefoqer? Nochmals zur Inhaberfrage des thebanischen Grabes Nr. 60', in D. Bröckelmann (ed.), *Pharaos Staat, Festschrift für Rolf Gundlach zum 75. Geburtstag*, Wiesbaden 2006, 3-18.

34. Arnold, 'Two new mastabas of the Twelfth Dynasty at Dahshur', *Egyptian Archaeology* 9 (1996), 23-5.

35. Franke, 'The career of Khnumhotep III', 56-67.

36. Grajetzki, *Beamten*, 21.

37. Habachi, 'The family of the vizier Ibi and his place among the viziers of the Thirteenth Dynasty', *SAK* 11 (1984), 122-3.

38. Cairo CG 42034.

39. Ryholt, *Second Intermediate Period*, 319.

40. Cairo CG 20690.

41. G. Jéquier, *Le monument funéraire de Pepi II, III*, Cairo 1940, fig. 29.

42. Habachi, 'The family of the vizier Ibi and his place among the viziers of the Thirteenth Dynasty', *SAK* 11 (1984), 114-22; compare Ryholt, *Second Intermediate Period*, 259-60.

43. Geisen, *Mentuhotep*, pl. 1-4.

44. Geisen, 'Zur zeitlichen Einordnung des Königs Djehuti an das Ende der 13. Dynastie', *SAK* 32 (2004), 154.

45. Discussed by Spalinger, *RdE* 32 (1980); Ryholt, *Second Intermediate Period*, 233-5.

3. The 'Treasurer' or 'Chancellor'

1. Note that in the Old Kingdom the title was *sehed khetemet*. At the very end of the Old Kingdom it changes to *imy-ra khetemet*; Grajetzki, *Beamten*, 66.

2. Franke, 'Review of Grajetzki, *Beamten*', *JEA* 87 (2001), 197.

3. Blackman, *JEA* 17 (1931), 55-61.

4. Winlock, 'The Egyptian Expedition 1922-1923', *BMMA* 1923, 12, fig. 2.

5. Willems, *Dayr al-Barshâ*, 93.

6. Grajetzki, *Beamten*, 67-8.

7. Ward, *Index*, no. 576; Quirke, *Titles and Bureaux*, 49-50.

8. Quirke, *Titles and Bureaux*, 115 ('overseer of the half-domain').

9. Winlock, 'The Egyptian Expedition 1922-1923', *BMMA* 1923, 12, fig. 2.

10. Willems, *Chests of Life,* 109-10 (the dating rests on the king's titulary which seems to have changed with the unification of the country. However, it is possible that he changed it shortly after, thus dating the queen's burial after unification and the beginning of Khety's career after that, while Bebi was in power before and promoted to the position of vizier upon unification).

11. Jaroš-Deckert, *Das Grab des Jnj-jtj.f*, 130-1; PM I (I), 386-7.

12. For the Nubian campaigns of Mentuhotep II see Postel, 'Une nouvelle

mention des campagnes nubiennes de Montouhotep II à Karnak', in L. Gabolde (ed.), *Hommages à Jean-Claude Goyon*, Cairo 2008, 329-39.

13. Arnold, *Das Grab des Jnj-jtj.f*, 40-1.

14. Arnold, 'Amenemhet I and the early Twelfth Dynasty at Thebes', *MMJ* 26 (1991), 1-32; Willems, *Heqata*, 23 n. 58; Grajetzki, *Beamten*, 241-3.

15. Allen, 'High officials of the early Middle Kingdom' (not included in the list of officials).

16. Allen, 'High officials of the early Middle Kingdom', 20.

17. A more recent translation of the text: Parkinson, *Voices from Ancient Egypt*, 40-3.

18. See the discussion in Willems, *Dayr al-Barshâ*, 100-5.

19. Willems, *Dayr al-Barshâ*, 107.

20. Vernus, *Le surnom au moyen Empire*.

21. H. Schäfer, *Die Mysterien des Osiris in Abydos unter König Sesostris III*, Leipzig 1904; Lichtheim, *Egyptian Autobiographies*, 98-100.

22. D. Polz & A. Seiler, *Die Pyramidenanlage des Königs Nub-Cheper-Re Intef in Dra' Abu el-Naga*, Mainz am Rhein 2003, 11-12, pl. 1c.

4. Other Important Officials

1. Borchardt, *ZÄS* 37 (1899), 96-7.

2. Leiden V,5 (ANOC 23.2); Louvre C 2 (ANOC 29.1).

3. Ward, *Index*, no. 1523.

4. Ward, *Index*, no. 775.

5. Ward, *Index*, no. 23.

6. Jørgensen, *Catalogue, Egypt I*, 124-51.

7. ANOC 29.1, Louvre 2.

8. Cairo CG 20473.

9. Cairo CG 20474.

10. ANOC 23.

11. See for example the young looking face of Amenemhatankh, dated under Amenemhat III, Louvre E 11053 (Delange, *Catalogue,* 69-71).

12. Ward, *Index*, no. 93.

13. Grajetzki, *Two Treasurers*, 21.

14. On stela Leyden 34 three 'high stewards' are depicted side by side.

15. For the dating compare ANOC 19, and especially the stela 19.3 which seems close in style to stela 46.1 belonging to the 'high steward' Nebankh who dates under Sobekhotep IV.

16. Quirke, *Titles and Bureaux*, 50-1.

17. Petrie, *Season*, VIII, 213.

18. Quirke, *Titles and Bureaux*, 70-1.

19. Stela London BM 828, *HTBM* 2, pl. 21.

20. Smither, 'A tax-assesor's journal of the Middle Kingdom', *JEA* 27 (1941), 74-6.

21. Hayes, *JEA* 33 (1947), 3-11.

22. Sams, *Ancient Egypt*, pl. 25.

23. Habachi, *Heqaib*, 106-7, no. 92; Franke, *Heqaib*, 67.

24. Quirke, *Titles and Bureaux*, 64-5.

25. Strudwick, *Administration*, 178-80.

26. Quirke, *Titles and Bureaux*, 30-1.

27. These are the tombs of Senebsumai (p. 63), Amenhotep (p. 64) and a 'king's acquaintance' with highest ranking titles. For the latter see Schiestl, *Sokar* 16 (2008), 66-7.
28. R. Buongarzone, '*La rw(y).t e il mr rw(y).t*', *EVO* 18 (1995), 45-63.
29. Ward, *Index*, no. 1156 (*kherep rekhu nisut*).
30. R. Buongarzone, '*La rw(y).t e il mr rw(y).t*', *EVO* 18 (1995), 45-63.
31. Ward, *Index*, no. 72 (*imy-ra akhenuty*).
32. Ward, *Index*, no. 741 (*wehemu*).
33. Ward, *Index*, no. 721 (*wer medju shemau*).
34. Ward, *Index*, no. 729 (*wer kherep hemuty*).
35. Cairo CG 20102.
36. Ward, *Index*, no. 934.
37. Ward, *Index*, no. 425; Quirke, *Titles and Bureaux*, 34.
38. BM EA 564, *HTBM* II, 8.
39. BM EA 855, *HTBM* IV, 24.
40. Ward, *Index*, no. 521 (*iri nefer hat*), compare no. 522.
41. Ward, *Index*, no. 1176.
42. Ward, *Index*, no. 1465.
43. Simpson, *Inscribed Material*, 36-9, fig. 61 (datable under Amenemhat III); Martin, *Seals*, no. 1247.

5. Military Officials

1. Quirke, *Titles and Bureaux*, 98.
2. Quirke, *Titles and Bureaux*, 97-8.
3. Arnold, *Control Notes*, 68, 70-1, 93, 103.
4. Parkinson & Quirke, 'The coffin of Prince Herunefer'.
5. H.M. Stewart, *Egyptian Stelae, Reliefs and Paintings II*, Warminster 1979, 79, pl. 15.2.
6. Jaroš-Deckert, *Das Grab des Jnj-jtj.f*.
7. Following Arnold, 'Amenemhet I and the Early Twelfth Dynasty at Thebes', *MMJ* 26 (1991), 18.
8. Obsomer, 'Les lignes 8 à 24 de la stèle de Mentouhotep (Florence 2540) érigée à Bouhen en l'an 18 de Sésostris Ier', *GM* 130 (1992), 57-74.
9. MacAdam, 'Gleanings from the Bankes MSS', *JEA* 32 (1946), 60-1, pl. IX.
10. Ward, *Index*, no. 194; Stefanović, *The Holders of the Regular Military Titles*, 207-8.
11. Ward, *Index*, no. 231.
12. Newberry, *Beni Hasan I*, pl. 8.
13. Ward, *Index*, no. 208.
14. Žába, *The Rock Inscriptions of Lower Nubia*, 109-15.
15. ANOC 2.1-3; D. Farout, 'Le monument abydénien du général en chef Amény engendré pour Qebou', *Egypte, Afrique & Orient* 37 (2005), 25-32.
16. Ward, *Index*, no. 695; Stefanović, *The Holders of the Regular Military Titles*, 49-57 (*atju aa en nut*).
17. Hintze/Reineke, *Felsinschriften*, 150, no. 504.
18. S.T. Smith, *Askut in Nubia*, London 1995, 27.
19. Ward, *Index*, no. 695; Quirke, *Titles and Bureaux*, 106-7; for the title in the Middle Kingdom: Philip-Stéphan, *Dire le droit*, 81-4.
20. The stelae and offering table of Dedusobek come from one chapel.
21. Cairo CG 20570.

22. Hintze & Reineke, *Felsinschriften*, 126, no. 451.
23. Ward, *Index*, no. 844a.

6. Provincial Officials

1. M. Baud, F. Colin & P. Tallet, 'Les gouverneurs de l'oasis de Dakhla au Moyen Empire', *BIFAO* 99 (1999), 1-19.
2. den Boorn, *Duties of the Vizier*, 108-9.
3. Ward, *Index*, no. 415.
4. Ward, *Index*, no. 374.
5. D. Stefanović, *The Title* mr t3-mHw *in the Middle Kingdom Documents*, Belgrade 2003.
6. See Grajetzki, *British Museum Studies in Ancient Egypt and Sudan*, forthcoming.
7. Ward, *Index*, no. 1061.
8. Ward, *Index*, no. 259.
9. Ward, *Index*, no. 250.
10. V. Selve, 'Les fonctions religieuses des nomarques au Moyen Empire', *CRIPEL* 15 (1993), 73-81.
11. Ward, *Index*, no. 1151 (*kherep nesty*).
12. Ward, *Index*, no. 1480; compare Sauneron, 'Le "Chancelier du Dieu" [...] dans son double rôle d'embaumeur et de prêtre d'Abydos', *BIFAO* 51 (1952), 156-71.
13. D.P. Silverman, *The Tomb Chamber of Hsw the Elder*, Winona Lake 1988.
14. Newberry, *Beni Hasan I*, pl. XXXV.
15. Favry, *Le normaque*, 341-77.
16. Franke, *Heqaib*, 131-46.
17. Stela Leiden V 4; Lichtheim, *Egyptian Autobiographies*, 75.
18. Newberry, *El Bersheh I*, 38-41, pl. XXI.
19. Ward, *Index*, no. 36.
20. J.P. Allen dates Nakht under Amenemhat I and places him in the sequence of court treasurers. See J.P. Allen in N. Strudwick & J.H. Taylor (eds), *The Theban Necropolis*, London 2003, 20.
21. Brovarski, 'Ahanakht of Bersheh and the Hare Nome in the First Intermediate Period and Middle Kingdom', in W.K. Simpson & W.M. Davies (eds), *Studies in Ancient Egypt, the Aegean, and the Sudan: Essays in Honor of Dows Dunham on the Occasion of his 90th birthday, June 1, 1980*, Boston 1981, 24 n. 60.
22. Newberry, *El Bersheh I*, 39, pl. XXXIII.
23. Franke, 'The career of Khnumhotep III'.
24. Newberry, *Beni Hasan I*, pl. XXX.
25. Garstang, *Burial Customs*, pls VII-VIII.
26. Franke, 'The career of Khnumhotep III', 51-67; Franke, *Heqaib*, 13.
27. A.M. Blackman, *The Rock Tombs of Meir VI*, London 1953; Willems, *Chests of Life*, 86.
28. A.B. Kamal, 'Rapport sur les fouilles exécutées dans la zone comprise entre Deîrout, au nord, et Déîr-el-Ganadlah, au sud', *ASAE* 12 (1912), 75-7.
29. M. Nelson; M. Kalos, 'Concessions funéraires du Moyen Empire découvertes au nord-ouest du Ramesseum', *Memnonia* XI (2000), 131-51.
30. Franke, *Heqaib*, 41-2.
31. Simpson, 'The stela of Amun-wosre', *JEA* 51 (1965), 63-8; Simpson,

'Provenance and date of the stela of Amun-wosre', *JEA* 51 (1966), 174; A. el-Sawi, 'Die Stele des Nbw-K3w-r-śnb, genannt Iw-śnb, und der Śnb-rn.ś', *GM* 92 (1986), 87-90; Cairo CG 23033.
32. Martin, *Seals*, no. 182.
33. Martin, *Seals*, no. 1544.
34. Cairo CG 20530.
35. Ward, *Index*, no. 1595 (tjesu).
36. Tylor, *Tomb of Sebeknekht*; V. Davies, 'Sobeknakht of Elkab and the coming of Kush', in *Egyptian Archaeology* 23 (2003), 3-6.

7. Procedures, Relations, Social Mobility and Careers

1. Helck, *Verwaltung*, 279-89.
2. Blackman, *JEA* 17 (1931), 56.
3. Simpson, *MDAIK* 47 (1991), 333.
4. J. Brophy, 'Die Königsnovelle: an Egyptian literary form', *Bulletin of the Australian Centre for Egyptology* 2 (1991), 16; B. Hofmann, *Die Königsnovelle*, Wiesbaden 2004, 7.
5. G. Jéquier, *Le Monument Funéraire de Pepi II, Tome III*, Cairo 1940, pl. 35.
6. Lichtheim, *Egyptian Autobiographies*, 79.
7. Hayes, *JEA* 33 (1947), 4.
8. Translation after den Boorn, *The Duties of the Vizier*, 55.
9. Translation after Quirke, *Egyptian Literature*, 67.
10. pBoulaq 18, XXXVII-XXXIX; XLV-XLVI.
11. P. Montet, 'Note sur les inscriptions de Sanousrit-ankh', *Syria* 15 (1934), 132; de Morgan, *Fouilles à Dahchour1894*, 19, fig. 23.
12. Lloyd, 'Khnumhotep II', 23.
13. Leprohon, 'The personnel of the Middle Kingdom funerary stelae', *JARCE* 15 (1978), 33-8.
14. Cairo CG 20075.
15. Ward, *Index*, no. 974.
16. Martin, *Seals*, no. 780.
17. Martin, *Seals*, nos 774-9.
18. Grajetzki, *Two Treasurers*, 12-13.
19. Franke, 'Sem-priest on duty', in S. Quirke (ed.), *Discovering Egypt from the Neva: The Legacy of Oleg D. Berlev*, Berlin 2003, 65-78.
20. e.g. H. Junker, *Gîza VI*, Wien & Leipzig 1943, 74.
21. B. Gunn, 'The coffins of Heny', *ASAE* 26 (1926), 166-8.
22. Willems, *Chests of Life,* 75-7.
23. Tylor, *The Tomb of Sebeknekht.*
24. Tylor, *The Tomb of Sebeknekht,* pl. IX.
25. Franke, *Heqaib,* 12-13.
26. Favry, *Le nomarque,* 338-9.
27. Franke, 'The good shepherd Antef (stela BM EA 1628)', *JEA* 93 (2007), 164-5.
28. Leiden, n. 3.
29. Leiden, n. 30; compare the discussion in Franke, *Heqaib,* 58.
30. Franke, *Verwandtschaftsbezeichnungen,* 304-8.
31. Schneider, *Ausländer.*
32. Newberry, *Beni Hasan II,* 7-16.
33. Delange, *Catalogue,* 81-3.

34. von Pilgrim, *Elephantine XVIII*, 235, fig. 93e, 251-2.
35. Grajetzki, *Beamten*, 78.
36. Fr. 207; Cairo CG 20690.
37. de Morgan, *Fouilles à Dahchour1894*, 33.
38. Berlev, *JEA* 60 (1974), 106-13.
39. Lüscher, *Kanopenkästen*, 53.
40. P. Tallet, 'Meket/Meketrê', *Revue d'égyptologie* 54 (2003), 288-94.

8. The Lives of Court Officials

1. Compare R. Janssen & J. Janssen, *Growing Up and Getting Old in Ancient Egypt* (London 2007).
2. Stefanović, 'The Non-Royal Women of the Middle Kingdom I – *mnat*', *GM* 216 (2008), 79-90.
3. Ward, *Essays on Feminine Titles*, 8.
4. Ward, *Essays on Feminine Titles*, 3.
5. D. Dunham, *Naga-ed-Dêr Stelae of the First Intermediate Period*, Boston 1937, 102, no. 84.
6. Feucht, *Kind*, 248-4.
7. Allen in Arnold, *Middle Kingdom Tomb Architecture at Lisht*, 89.
8. Feucht, *Kind*, 238-45.
9. Translation follows Quirke, *Egyptian Literature*, 121. The text was composed in the Middle Kingdom. The known copies of the text date to the New Kingdom and it might be argued that the reference to the school was added later, when the text was updated.
10. H. Brunner, *Die Texte aus den Gräbern der Herakleopolitenzeit aus Siut*, Glückstadt 1937, 29.
11. Feucht, *Kind*, 227-8.
12. Brunner, *Erziehung*, 10-13.
13. A few examples: Cairo CG 20056; Cairo CG 20084; Fischer, *Egyptian Titles*, frontispiece; Petrie, *Season*, no. 86; G. Andreu, 'La stèle Louvre C.249: un complément à la reconstitution d'une chapelle abydénienne', *BIFAO* 80 (1980), 139-47, pl. XXXVIII; for a fuller list see Grajetzki, 'Zwei Fallbeispiele für Genealogien im Mittleren Reich', in M. Fitzenreiter (ed.), *Genealogie, Realität und Fiktion von Identität,* London 2005, 66-57.
14. On a stela in Chiddingstone Castle; Grajetzki, 'Zwei Fallbeispiele für Genealogien im Mittleren Reich', in M. Fitzenreiter (ed.), *Genealogie, Realität und Fiktion von Identität,* 60-7.
15. Stela Vienna ÄS 136, Hein & Satzinger, *Stelen I*, 4, 48-54.
16. M.S. Drower, *Flinders Petrie: A Life in Archaeology*, Madison 1985, 14-15.
17. Willems, *Dayr al-Barshâ*, 65.
18. Ward, *Index*, 174, no. 1506; Davies, *Five Theban Tombs*, pl. XIV.
19. London BM EA 101; Blackman, 'The stela of Nebipusenwosret: British Museum No. 101', *JEA* 21 (1935), 1-9, pl. 1; Parkinson, *Voices from Ancient Egypt*, 140, 160; sources in general are listed in Brunner, *Erziehung*, 163.
20. H. Brunner, 'Der "Gottesvater" als Erzieher des Kronprinzen', *ZÄS* 86 (1961), 90-100.
21. Quirke, *Egyptian Literature*, 171.
22. F.Ll. Griffith, *Siut*, London 1889, lines 279, 284, 288, 303, 313, 321; Franke, *Verwandtschaftsbezeichnungen*, 273.
23. Hayes, *A Papyrus of the Late Middle Kingdom*, 87-109, pls VIII-XIII.

24. Arnold, *Das Grab des Jnj-jtj.f*, 40.

25. S. D'Auria, P. Lacovara & C.H. Roehrig, *Mummies & Magic*, Boston 1988, 111-12.

26. de Morgan, *Fouilles à Dahchour1894*, 15-42. Note that the publication is very selective. The new excavations at the cemetery might change the picture provided there.

27. A. J. Spalinger, 'A redistributive pattern at Assiut', *Journal of the American Oriental Society* 105.1 (1985), 7-19.

9. Women Related to Court Officials

1. Strudwick, *Administration*, 303.

2. Louvre C1 (ANOC 6.2).

3. Stela Cairo CG 20546; BM 162 (ANOC 2.2-3).

4. Cairo CG 20542, 20561, Louvre C 167 (ANOC 4.1, 3-4); BM 566 (ANOC 3.1).

5. Ward, *Index*, no. 613.

6. Ward, *Index*, no. 616.

7. Ward, *Essays on Feminine Titles*, 7.

8. Willems, *Dayr al-Barshâ*, 73.

9. Ward, *Essays on Feminine Titles*, 110.

10. Grajetzki, *Two Treasurers*, 48-51.

11. Hayes, *JEA* 33 (1947), 4.

12. Quirke, *Administration*, 147-9.

13. Hayes, *A Papyrus of the Late Middle Kingdom*, 116.

14. P. Vernus, 'Quelques exemples du type du "parvenú" dans l'Egypte ancienne', *BSFDÉ* 1970 (59), 37.

15. Newberry, *Beni Hasan I*, pl. XXXV, reference to biographical inscription.

16. Translation follows Quirke, *Egyptian Literature*, 95 (Ptahhotep, 24).

17. Ward, 'The case of Mrs Tchat and her sons at Beni Hasan', *GM* 71 (1984), 51-9.

18. Ward, *Essays on Feminine Titles*, 45.

19. Newberry, *Beni Hasan I*, pl. XLVI.

20. Daressy, 'Monuments d'Edfou datant du Moyen Empire', *ASAE* XVII (1917), 240 (wife of governor, Second Intermediate Period); Engelbach, *ASAE* XXII (1922), 'Steles and tables of offerings of the late Middle Kingdom from Tell Edfû', 116 (a 'king's daughter' and another one, but related and therefore part of the royal family).

21. Stela, Louvre C 58.

22. Geisen, *Mentuhotep*, 2-3.

23. Tylor, *The Tomb of Sebeknekht*, pl. VII; Davies, *ASAE* 80 (2006), 142, fig. 7.

24. J. Wegner, 'Social and historical implications of sealings of the King's daughter Reniseneb and other women at the town of Wah-Sut', in M. Bietak & E. Czerny (eds), *Scarabs of the Second Millennium BC from Egypt, Nubia, Crete and the Levant: Chronological and Historical Implications*, Vienna 2004, 227-30.

25. Davies, *Five Theban Tombs*, pl. XXXIV.

26. de Meulenaere, *BIFAO* 81s (1981), 77-9.

27. Vernus, *Le surnom au moyen Empire*, 66, no. 310.

28. Ryholt, *Second Intermediate Period*, 269.

29. CG 42034 (statue); CG 20102 (stela).

30. Cairo CG 42035.
31. Cairo CG 20690.
32. Geisen, *Mentuhotep*, 2-3.
33. Dunham, 'The tomb of Dehuti-nekht and his wife', *BMFA* 19, no. 114 (August 1921), 43-6.
34. Berlev, *JEA* 60 (1974), 106-13.
35. Arnold, *Egyptian Archaeology* 9 (1996), 23-5; D. Arnold, *Antike Welt* 6 (2002), 623-4.
36. de Morgan, *Fouilles à Dahchour1894*, 38-9, fig. 80.

Appendix

1. After Grajetzki, *Beamten*, 7-31; for additional discussions of the viziers of the early Middle Kingdom, see J.P. Allen, in N. Strudwick & J.H. Taylor (eds), *The Theban Necropolis*, London 2003, 21-6.
2. Gr. 10 (I.1); Allen, in *The Theban Necropolis*, 22; *HTBM* 6, pl. 24 (see Fig. 8).
3. Allen, in *The Theban Necropolis*, 21-2.
4. Gr. 10-11 (I.2); Allen, in *The Theban Necropolis*, 22; Davies, *Five Theban Tombs*, 39, pls XXX-XXXII, XXXIV, XXXVIII (tomb and Deir el-Bahari fragments); CG 28024 (sarcophagus).
5. Gr. 11-12 (I.3); Allen, in *The Theban Necropolis*, 22-3; Couyat, Montet, *Ouâdi Hammâmât*, 77-8 (no. 110), 79-81 (no. 113), 98-100 (no. 192), 103 (no. 205).
6. Gr. 12 (I.4); Allen, in *The Theban Necropolis*, 23; Bull, *JEA* 10 (1924), 15.
7. Allen, in *The Theban Necropolis*, 23.
8. Allen, in *The Theban Necropolis*, 23.
9. Fr. 146/Gr. 12-15 (I.6); Allen, in *The Theban Necropolis*, 23-4; Simpson, in *Pyramid Studies*, 60. Žába, *The Rock Inscriptions of Lower Nubia*, 39 (no. 10a); 98-109 (no.73) (rock inscriptions in Nubia); A.M.A.H. Sayed, *RdE* 29 (1977), 170 (rock inscription at the Red Sea); Sadek, *Wadi el-Hudi I*, 22-4, no. 8; *Wadi el-Hudi II*, pl. IV (rock inscriptions in the Wadi el Hudi); W.K. Simpson, *Papyrus Reisner II*, Boston 1965, 20-3, pls 7-8, 10; G. Posener, 'Le vizier Antef-oqer', in J. Baines (ed.), *Pyramid Studies and Other Essays Presented to I.E.S. Edwards, Egypt Exploration Society*, London 1988, 73-7 (execration text); Arnold, *Middle Kingdom Tomb Architecture at Lisht*, 69-71, pls 129-33.
10. Allen, in *The Theban Necropolis*, 24-5.
11. Fr. 490/ Gr. 15 (I.7); Allen, in *The Theban Necropolis*, 25; Louvre C.4, Gayet, *Stèles*, pl. III; Arnold, *Middle Kingdom Tomb Architecture at Lisht*, 77-82, pls 146b, 147-58 (tomb).
12. Fr. 117/Gr. 16 (I.8); Petrie, *Memphis I*, pl. 5.
13. Gr. 16 (I.9); Cairo CG 23027.
14. Grajetzki, 'A new vizier of the Middle Kingdom: Amenemhat-ankh', *Cahiers Caribéen d'Egyptologie* 11, février-mars 2008, 145-7.
15. Gr. 16-17 (I.10); de Morgan, *Fouilles à Dahchour 1894*, 33; Simpson, 'Sobkemhet, a vizier of Sesostris III', *JEA* 43 (1957), 26-9.
16. Gr. 17 (I.11); D. Arnold, 'Two new mastabas of the Twelfth Dynasty at Dahshur', *Egyptian Archaeology* 9 (1996), 23-5; D. Arnold, 'Die letzte Ruhestätte ägyptischer Beamter: ein Mastaba-Feld des Mittleren Reiches in Dahschur, Ägypten', *Antike Welt* 6 (2002), 623-4.
17. Gr. 17-19 (I.12); Franke, 'The career of Khnumhotep III of Beni Hasan and

the so-called "decline of the nomarchs"', in *Middle Kingdom Studies*, 56-67; de Morgan, *Fouilles à Dahchour1894*, 19-23; D. Arnold, 'Die letzte Ruhestätte ägyptischer Beamter: ein Mastaba-Feld des Mittleren Reiches in Dahschur, Ägypten', *Antike Welt* 6 (2002), 624-8.

18. Fr. 116/Gr. 19 (I.13); de Morgan, *Catalogue des monuments*, 12, no. 41; 31, no. 10 = Petrie, *Season*, VI, 137; the same: XVII, 594.

19. Gr. 19 (I.14); Collier & Quirke, *The UCL Lahun Papyri: Religious, Literary, Legal, Mathematical and Medical*, 118-19.

20. Fr. 526/Gr. 19 (I.15); Cairo CG 20102 (vizier) Hintze & Reineke, *Felsinschriften*, 143-7, nos 495, 498-9 ('mouth of Nekhen').

21. Gr. 20 (I.16); Goedicke, 'An ancient naval finial of the Middle Kingdom', *Ägypten und Levante* 10 (2000), 77-81.

22. Fr. 501-3/Gr. 20-1 (I.17); de Morgan, *Catalogue des monuments*, 11, no. 43; 22, no. 153; 26, no. 192; Petrie, *Season*, V, 116; de Morgan, *Catalogue des monuments*, 13, nos 51, 55; 23 no. 156; Petrie, *Season*, III, 86, 87, V, 114, VI, 141 ('overseer of fields', 'personal scribe of the king's document'); Bosticco, *Stele*, no. 39; Montet, 'Note sur les inscriptions de Sanousrit-ankh', *Syria* 15 (1934), 131-3 (vizier).

23. Fr. 461/Gr. 24 (I.25); Delia, 'Nine rock inscriptions near the First Cataract', *BES* 10 (1989/90), 48-51; Newberry, *PSBA* 23 (1901), 222-3.

24. Fr. 173, 178/Gr. 24-6 (I.26) Cairo CG 20690; Bolshakov & Quirke, *The Middle Kingdom Stelae*, 94-102, pls 21-2 (Hermitage 1063-4) Cairo CG 42034; Hayes, *A Papyrus of the Late Middle Kingdom*, 71-2, pls V, VI; Martin, *Seals*, no. 337; Gratien, *Prosopographie*, 62 (seal impression found at Mirgissa).

25. Fr. 24; Cairo CG 20690.

26. Fr. 398; Cairo CG 20690.

27. Fr. 26/Gr. 26-7 (I.29); Habachi, *Heqaib*, 67-8, no. 40; Delange, *Catalogue*, 66-8 (Louvre A 125); Verbrovsek, *Als Gunsterweis*, 380-5; Martin, *Seals*, no. 49 (perhaps this vizier).

28. Martin, *Seals*, nos 1775, 1778.

29. Fr. 62c-e; Habachi, *Heqaib*, 69, no. 43; Habachi, *SAK* 11 (1984), pl. 4a (stela, MMA 22.3.307).

30. Gr. 23 (I.23); Petrie, *Abydos II*, pl. XXVI.

31. Gr. 22 (I.18); Martin, *Seals*, no. 90.

32. Gr. 22 (I.19); Martin, *Seals*, no. 555.

33. Gr. 22-23 (I.20); Martin, *Seals*, no. 683 (name and title partly destroyed).

34. Gr. 23 (I.21); Martin, *Seals*, no. 1130.

35. Gr. 23 (I.22); Martin, *Seals*, nos 1383-4 (448-9 as 'overseer of the compound' Bebi; 1385 'overseer of the compound' Sobekaa Bebi).

36. Fr. 745/Gr. 24 (I.24); ANOC 51; Verbrovsek, *Als Gunsterweis*, 192-3.

37. Gr. 29 (I.33); Geisen, *Mentuhotep*, 2.

38. Fr. 80/Gr. 30-1 (I.36); Bruyère, *Deir el Médineh* (1929), 103-15 (tomb); Smither, 'The report concerning the slave-girl Senbet', *JEA* 34 (1948), 31-4 (papyrus).

39. Fr. 11-12/Gr. 28-9; Lacau, *Stele*, 35, 40; Tylor, *The Tomb of Sebeknekht*, pl. 11.

40. Gr. 30 (I.34); Lacau, *Stele*, 19.

41. Gr. 29 (I.32); Lacau, *Stele*, 24, 35.

42. After Grajetzki, *Two Treasurers*.

43. Gr. 44-5 (II.1); Allen, 'The high officials of the early Middle Kingdom', *The Theban Necropolis*, 18-19; Verbrovsek, *Als Gunsterweis*, 420-1; Winlock, 'The

Museums Excavations at Thebes', *BMMA* 1923, 11-19 (tomb); Petrie, *Season*, XV, 443, XVI, 489 (rock inscriptions).

44. Gr. 45-6 (II.2); P. Tallet, 'Meket/Meketrê', *RdE* 54 (2003), 288-94.

45. Gr. 46 (II.3); E.P. Uphill, 'The office sd3wty-bity', *JEA* 61 (1975), 250.

46. P. Tallet, 'The treasurer Ipi, early Twelfth Dynasty', *GM* 193 (2003), 59-64.

47. Fr. 391/Gr. 49-50 (II.7); Allen, in *The Theban Necropolis*, 20; Hayes, *The Scepter of Egypt I*, 333, fig. 221 (stela); Arnold, *Middle Kingdom Tomb Architecture at Lisht*, 63-9, pls 115-28 (tomb).

48. Gr. 47 (II.5); G. Posener, 'Une stèle de Hatnoub', *JEA* 54 (1968), 67-70, pl. IX.

49. Fr. 262/Gr. 47-49 (II.6); W.K. Simpson, 'Mentuhotep, Vizier of Sesostris I, Patron of Art and Architecture', *MDAIK* 47 (1991), 331-40; Allen, in *The Theban Necropolis*, 20-1, 25; Delange, *Catalogue*, 55-65 (statues Louvre A122, 123, 124); Cairo CG 42037, 44, 45; Verbrovsek, *Als Gunsterweis*, 393-415; Arnold, *Middle Kingdom Tomb Architecture at Lisht*, 38-50, pls 62-92 (tomb); Cairo CG 20539 (Abydos stela); uncertain: stela H.G. Fischer, *Egyptian Studies I*, 59-67.

50. Gr. 50 (II.8); B. Mathieu, 'Une stèle du règne d'Amenemhat II au ouadi Um Balad (désert Oriental)', *BIFAO* 98 (1998), 235-46, fig. 1.

51. Fr. 511/Gr. 50-1 (II.9); ANOC 41.1, 41.2, Cairo CG 23006 (as overseer of the chamber); Simpson, in *Pyramid Studies*, 57-60, pls 14-15.

52. Gr. 51 (II. 10); de Morgan, *Catalogue des monuments*, 86, no. 20; Gasse/Rondot, *Séhel*, 79, 456-57.

53. Fr. 27/Gr. 52-3; ANOC 1.

54. Gr. 54 (II.15); Reisner, *Kerma*, 524-5, no. 47.

55. Gr. 54 (II.16); S. Adam, 'Report on the excavation of the Department of Antiquities at Ezbet Rushdi', *ASAE* LVI (1959), 214-15, pl. VIII; Verbrovsek, *Als Gunsterweis*, 353-4. There is a 'treasurer' Ameny attested on a sarcophagus found at Tanis (P. Montet, *Fouilles de Tanis, Les Constructions et le tombeau d'Osorkin II a Tanis*, Paris 1947, 81-2, pl. XLVII), but originally perhaps from Hawara. The sarcophagus might belong to one of the 'treasurers' with this name. A possible third 'treasurer' with the name Ameny is known from a stela found at Abydos (Petrie, *Abydos I*, pl. LX, 3). However, the title is only partly preserved. The identification as 'treasurer' at the royal court remains uncertain.

56. Gr. 51 (II.11); Collier & Quirke, *The UCL Lahun Papyri: Accounts*, Oxford 2006, 96-7.

57. Martin, *Seals*, no. 1111.

58. Gr. 53 (II.13); Bosticco, *Stele*, 33-5, no. 30.

59. Gr. 55 (II.17), Grajetzki, *Middle Kingdom*, pl. XX; B. Gratien, 'Scellements et contrescellements au Moyen Empire en Nubie: l'apport de Mirgissa', *CRIPEL* 22 (2001), 50, fig. 11.

60. Gr. 55 (II.18); Martin, *Seals*, nos 1142-3; Trope, *Excavating Egypt*, 116 (no. 86) (weight); Brooklyn 36.617, T.G. James, *Corpus*, 49, pl. XXXVI (statue); for the reconstruction of the titles see Grajetzki, *Beamten*, 55.

61. Gr. 55-6 (II.19); Cairo CG 408 (statue); Jørgensen, *Catalogue, Egypt I*, 196-7, no. 82 (stela).

62. Gr. 59 (II.23); Hein & Satzinger, *Stelen I*, 4, 81-3.

63. Fr. 667-8/Gr. 57-9 (II.22); Gratien, *Prosopographie*, 165 (found at Mirgissa); Ben-Tor, *Scarabs, Chronology, and Interconnections*, pl. 23, 8; Martin, *Seals*, nos 1513-41a ('treasurer'), 1512 ('high steward'); Wegner, *Abydos*, 344, nos 16-17 (Abydos, as 'treasurer'); ANOC 17.1-2 (as 'high steward'); ANOC 17.4,

25.1-2; Roccati, *Discovering Egypt from the Neva*, 111-12; Bolshakov & Quirke, *The Middle Kingdom Stelae*, 53-7, pl. 11 (Hermitage 1084); Franke, 'Die Hockerstatue des Sonbso-mei in Leiden und Statuen mit nach oben gerichteten Handflächen', *OMRO* 68 (1988), 59-76 (statue, as 'high steward', perhaps found at Ballas, as mentioned in a notebook of Flinders Petrie from this place, information kindly provided by S. Quirke); Collier & Quirke, *The UCL Lahun Papyri: Accounts*, Oxford 2006, 162-3, 170-1; Mariette, *Mastabas*, 583 (fragment found at Dagshur).

64. Fr. 634/Gr. 56-7 (II.21); Wegner, *JARCE* XXXV (1998), 39, fig. 19, 8; Grajetzki, *Two Treasurers*, plate 1 (Liverpool Museum M 13661), plate 2 (Liverpool Museum M 13635); Hein & Satzinger, *Stelen I*, 4, 55-61 (Vienna ÄS 140).

65. Fr. 87A/Gr. 60 (II.24); Newberry, *PSBA* 36 (1914), 35 (vase); de Morgan, *Fouilles à Dahchour en 1894-1895*, 70, fig. 113 (tomb); Martin, *Seals*, nos 189-92.

66. Gr. 61 (II.26); Petrie, *Tanis II*, 29, pl. IX, 1.

67. D. Polz, A. Seiler, *Die Pyramidenanlage des Königs Nub-Cheper-Re Intef in Dra' Abu el-Naga*, Mainz am Rhein 2003, 12.

68. L. Habachi, *The Second Stela of Kamose*, Abhandlungen des Deutschen Archäologischen Instituts Kairo 8, Glückstadt 1975.

69. Yoyotte, *BSFE* 114 (1989), 17-63.

70. Martin, *Seals*, nos 109-11.

71. Martin, *Seals*, nos 274-6.

72. Martin, *Seals*, no. 388.

73. Martin, *Seals*, no. 407.

74. Martin, *Seals*, no. 682.

75. Martin, *Seals*, nos 898-902.

76. Gr. 61 (II.27); Fay, *The Louvre Sphinx*, 66, no. 32, pl. 86e-h (London BM 1849).

77. Gr. 61 (II.28); R. Krauss, *Orientalia* 62 (1993), 28, fig. 2, n. 80; M. Abd el-Maksoud, *Tell Heboua (1981-1991)*, Paris 1998, 271-2, pl. 1.

78. Martin, *Seals*, nos 477-506.

79. Martin, *Seals*, nos 904-12 (he does not bear ranking titles).

80. Martin, *Seals*, nos 984-1088a; Mlinar, in Bietak & Czerny (eds), *Scarabs of the Second Millennium BC from Egypt, Nubia, Crete and the Levant: Chronological and Historical Implications*, Vienna 2004, 129-32.

81. Martin, *Seals*, no. 1672, Ward, *Orientalia Lovaniensia Periodica* 6-7 (1975-6), 589-94.

82. Fr. 692/Cairo CG 20538.

83. Cairo CG 20538 (stela).

84. Cairo CG 20086 (stela).

85. Brunner-Traut & Brunner, *Tübingen*, 84-5, pl. 54.

86. Jaroš-Deckert, *Wien*, 72-8.

87. Grajetzki, *Beamten*, 80-105.

88. Allen, in *The Theban Necropolis*, 16.

89. Allen, in *The Theban Necropolis*, 16.

90. Allen, in *The Theban Necropolis*, 17; Hayes, *The Scepter of Egypt I*, 178, fig. 109 (tomb); Cairo CG 390 (statue); Arnold, *Middle Kingdom Tomb Architecture at Lisht*, 85-6, pls 162-4.

91. Fr. 424/ANOC 29; Allen, in *The Theban Necropolis*, 17.

92. Allen, in *The Theban Necropolis*, 18; Arnold, *Control Notes*, 110 (N19); Arnold, *Middle Kingdom Tomb Architecture at Lisht*, 73-7, pl. 146a.

93. Fr. 133/ANOC 4; Allen, in *The Theban Necropolis*, 18, tomb mentioned in Franke, *Heqaib*, 58.

94. Eggebrecht & Seidel, *Antike Welt* (2000), 1, 1-8.

95. Fr. 457/Gr. 83-84 (III.7); ANOC 23; Allen, in *The Theban Necropolis*, 18; Leiden V,5; Guimet 11324, Cairo CG 20541.

96. Habachi, *Heqaib*, 92, no. 67; Leiden n. 30.

97. de Morgan, *Fouilles à Dahchour en 1894-1895*, 36, fig. 84.

98. Fr. 468/ANOC 40; Delange, *Catalogue*, 91-93 (A 30).

99. Fr. 145/Gr. 86-97 (III.12); Petrie, *Illahun, Kahun and Gurob*, pl. XII, 1; Page, *Archaic to Saite,* 31 (as 'high steward'); Petrie, *Kahun, Gurob and Hawara,* pl. XI, 15.

100. de Morgan, *Fouilles à Dahchour1894*, 53.

101. Simpson, *Inscribed Material*, 36-9, n. C5, pl. 7; Petrie, *Season*, pl. III, 21.

102. Fattovich & Bard, *Egypte, Afrique & Orient* 41, April 2006, 25; R. Pirelli, *RdE* 58 (2007), 88-9, pl. XVII.

103. Fr. 128/Cairo CG 20435.

104. Fr. 491/Gr. 88 (III.16); Martin, *Seals*, no. 1258.

105. Engelbach, *ASAE* XXXIII (1933), 73.

106. Petrie, *Season*, VII, 160, Cairo CG 20317 (stela).

107. Fr. 167/Gr. 89 (III.17), Cairo CG 20391 (stela); Flinders Petrie, *Ancient Weights and Measures*, London 1926, pl. XXXVI (3785A, the weight).

108. Jørgensen, *Catalogue, Egypt I*, 188-9, no. 78; Verbrovsek, *Als Gunsterweis*, 429-30.

109. Cairo CG 42039; Verbrovsek, *Als Gunsterweis*, 416-17.

110. Cairo CG 20023 ('overseer of sealers'); Martin, *Seals*, nos. 345-7.

111. Fr. 331/Gr. 91 (III.22), stela Leiden 34; Habachi, *Heqaib*, 73-7, no. 47.

112. Stela Leiden 34.

113. Fr. 395/Kitchen & Beltrão, *Rio de Janeiro*, no. 6; Martin, *Seals*, nos 859-60, 862-3; Wegner, *Abydos*, 344, no. 22; Martin, *Seals*, no. 864 ('overseer of sealers'); Cairo CG 20735.

114. Fr. 98/ANOC 10; Roccati, *Discovering Egypt from the Neva*, 111-16; Martin, *Seals*, nos 213-14.

115. Grajetzki, *Two Treasurers*, pl. 5 (St Petersburg Hermitage 5010); Hein & Satzinger, *Stelen I*, 4, 114-17 (as 'king's acquaintance'); Bolshakov & Quirke, *The Middle Kingdom Stelae*, 53-7, pl. 11 (Hermitage 1084); S. Aufrère, N. Bosson, C. Landes (eds), *Portes pour l'au delà. L'Égypte, le Nil et le 'Champ des offrandes'*, Lattes 1992, 147, 192, no. 37.

116. Fr. 732/Habachi, *Heqaib*, 77, no. 51; Martin, *Stelae*, 45-7; Louvre C.199, Gayet, *Stèles*, pl. XLIII; Hein & Satzinger, *Stelen I,* 4, 68-73 (as 'cupbearer'); Habachi, *Heqaib*, 77, no. 50; Martin, *Seals*, nos. 1721-4.

117. Fr. 294/Habachi, *Heqaib*, 70, no. 44; 71-2, no. 46; Gasse/Rondot, *Séhel*, 89-90, 459; 92-3, 462 (as 'king's acquaintance'); Spalinger, *RdE* 32 (1980), pl. 8; ANOC 46.1; Sadek, *Wadi el-Hudi I*, 52, no. 25, Sadek; *Wadi el-Hudi II*, pl. XII; Wegner, *JARCE* XXXV (1998), 39, fig. 19, 6; Ben-Tor, *Scarabs, Chronology, and Interconnections*, pl. 24, 15; Martin, *Seals*, no. 653 (seals).

118. Fr. 389; Cairo CG 20104, 20147; Berlin 7311 (ANOC 22), (Hein & Satzinger, *Stelen I*, 4, 55-61) ('king's acquaintance'); Sadek, *Wadi el-Hudi I*, 51, no. 24, pl. XII; *Wadi el-Hudi II*, pl. XII; Martin, *Seals*, nos. 857-8 ('overseer of sealers'); Grajetzki, *Two Treasurers*, 43 (from Černy's notebook, compare PM VIII, 404, 801-438-920 – as 'high steward').

119. Fr. 85/Gr. 90 (III.19); Kitchen & Beltrão, *Rio de Janeiro*, 60-3, pls 39-40; stela Leiden 34.

120. Martin, *Seals*, nos 384-84a.

121. Fr. 192/Cairo CG 20087; Martin, *Seals*, nos 371-6, 379 (as 'overseer of sealers); Ben-Tor, *Scarabs, Chronology, and Interconnections*, pl. 23, 4.

122. Fr. 326/Gr. 96 (III.32); Bourriau, *Pharaohs and Mortals*, 93-4, no. 74 (the model coffin); ANOC 19.1-2 (stelae); Martin, *Seals*, nos 353-56a (seals).

123. Gr. 97 (III.33); Petrie, *Season*, pl. IX, 267; Martin, *Seals*, nos 774-9; M. Vallogia, 'À propos du titre [*wd wpt*] "Économe"', *BIFAO* 76 (1976), 344, no. 8.

124. Martin, *Seals*, nos. 253 (Anef is written), 241-6; Ben-Tor, *Scarabs, Chronology, and Interconnections*, pl. 25, 2.

125. Cairo CG 20765.

126. Martin, *Seals*, no 109 (just 'royal sealer' and 'steward').

127. Gr. 95 (III.29); Flinders Petrie, *Tools and Weapons*, London 1917, pl. XXII, no. 80; A.E.P. Weigall, 'Upper Egyptian Notes, *ASAE* 9 (1908), 111.

128. Fr. 156/Habachi, *Heqaib*, 84-5, no. 57 (statue base), Cairo CG 20460 (stela); S. Wenig, 'Zur Inschrift auf der Statue des Berliner Ägyptischen Museums Nr. 22463', *ZÄS* 96 (1970), 139-42 (statue base).

129. Martin, *Seals*, no. 89.

130. Martin, *Seals*, nos 4-6.

131. Petrie, *Abydos II*, pl. XXXI (bottom).

132. Martin, *Seals*, nos 562-3.

133. Gratien, *Prosopographie*, 99 (found at Mirgissa).

134. Habachi, *Heqaib*, 106, no. 91.

135. Martin, *Seals*, nos 774-9.

136. Martin, *Seals*, no. 360; Ben-Tor, *Scarabs, Chronology, and Interconnections*, pl. 23, 11.

137. Fr. 240/Berlin 1913, 146.

138. Martin, *Seals*, nos 873, 890-96a.

139. Martin, *Seals*, nos 846-7; Wegner, *Abydos*, 344, no. 19.

140. Fr. 607/Grajetzki, 'Two monuments of the High Steward Senaa-ib of the Middle Kingdom', *RdE* 54 (2003), 270-4.

141. Stela Cairo CG 20284.

142. Martin, *Seals*, no. 1258.

143. Martin, *Seals*, no. 1433.

144. Martin, *Seals*, no. 1439.

145. Martin, *Seals*, no. 1437.

146. Martin, *Seals*, no. 409.

147. Bolshakov & Quirke, *The Middle Kingdom Stelae*, 39-41, pl. 7 (Hermitage 1082).

148. Cairo CG 4732 (canopic box); Lüscher, *Kanopenkästen*, 57, 103.

149. Tylor, *The Tomb of Sebeknekht*, pl. IX.

150. Grajetzki, *Beamten*, 147-54.

151. Gr. 147 (VII.1); Petrie, *Season*, VIII, 213.

152. Gr. 147 (VII.2); Lepsius, *Denkmäler* II, pl. 148c, d (tomb); Petrie, *Season*, XV, 459, 472 (rock inscription).

153. His tomb and titles are not yet fully published, N. Berger-el Naggar, A. Labrouse, 'La tombe de Rêhérychefnakht à Saqqâra-Sud, un chaînon manquant?', *BSFE* 164 (2005), 14-28, compare fig. 11 on p. 24 for his title 'overseer of sealers'.

154. Gr. 147-8 (VII.3); Z. Saad, *Royal Excavations at Saqqara and Helwan (1941-1945)*, Cairo 1947, 168-9.

155. Gr. 148 (VII.4), stela Leiden 7.

156. Gr. 149 (VII.7), stela, Cairo CG 20061.

157. Gr. 150 (VII.11), Cairo CG 20225 (as 'cupbearer'), Cairo CG 20614.

158. Fr. 408/Gr. 150 (VII.12); Cairo CG 431;Verbrovsek, *Als Gunsterweis*, 451-2 (statue); Leyden 14; Cairo CG 20616 (stelae); de Morgan, *Catalogue des monuments*, 38, no. 137 (rock inscription).

159. Gr. 150 (VII.13); Leyden 34.

160. Gr. 151 (VII.14); Petrie, *Abydos II*, 34, pl. XXXII, 3.

161. Gr. 152 (VII.19).

162. Martin, *Seals*, nos 215.

163. Martin, *Seals*, nos 367-9.

164. Martin, *Seals*, nos 80-2.

165. Martin, *Seals*, no. 1706.

166. Martin, *Seals*, no. 1118.

167. Martin, *Seals*, no. 864.

168. Wegner, *Abydos*, 344, no. 23; the reading on the seals is unclear, but fits better to the title 'overseer of sealers' with a bird written after the 'seal' (*khetem*) sign.

169. Martin, *Seals*, nos 428, 1396, 1397; Ben-Tor, *Scarabs, Chronology, and Interconnections*, 23, 9.

170. *Scarabs and Design Amulets: A Glimpse of Ancient Egypt in Miniature*, New York 1991, no. 105.

171. Grajetzki, *Beamten*, 169-73.

172. Gr. 169 (X.1); Petrie, *Season*, XV, 438, 463; Winlock, *AJSL* 57 (1939-40), 151.

173. *HTBM* II, pl. 21.

174. Cairo CG 887.

175. Grajetzki, *Two Treasurers*, pl. 6 (Berlin 7288).

176. A. Leahy, 'A stela of the Second Intermediate Period', *GM* 44 (1981), 23-30.

177. PM VIII, 268 (801-413-600).

178. de Morgan, *Catalogue des monuments*, 41, no. 1; Petrie, *Season*, XI, 287.

179. Spalinger, *RdE* 32 (1980), pl. 8.

180. Martin, *Seals*, no. 297.

181. Gr. 172-3 (X.11); Hein & Satzinger, *Stelen I*, 4, 48-54.

182. Martin, *Seals*, no. 1726a.

183. Fr. 91/Gr. 178-9 (XI.2); H. Altenmüller & A.M. Moussa, 'Die Inschrift Amenemhets II. aus dem Ptah-Tempel von Memphis: Vorbericht', *SAK* 18 (1991), 8.

184. Fr. 447/Gr. 179 (XI.4); Cairo CG 20520; Bosticco, *Stele*, 40-1, no. 35 (Florence 2559); 41, no. 36 (Florence 2561).

185. Fr. 54/Gr. 179-80 (XI.5), Cairo CG 20614; Leyden 33.

186. Fr. 655/Gr. 180 (XI.6), Cairo CG 28029 (coffin); Berlev, *JEA* 60 (1974), 103-16, pl. XXVII-XXVIII (canopic box and staff).

187. A. Gasse, 'Une expédition au Ouadi Hammamat sous le règne de Sebekemsaf Ier', *BIFAO* 87 (1987), pl. XXXIX-XLII (Aamu does not bear ranking titles).

188. Martin, *Seals*, nos 227, 303, 635.

189. Martin, *Seals*, no. 1749.

190. Martin, *Seals*, no. 1623.

191. Martin, *Seals*, no. 1450.

192. Martin, *Seals*, nos 723-4.

193. Martin, *Seals*, no. 753.

194. Martin, *Seals*, nos 870-1.

195. G. Wozencroft, 'A scarab of the mid Thirteenth dynasty attested to Redinptah', *GM* 213 (2007), 101-4.

196. Grajetzki, *Beamten*, 117-25.

197. Jørgensen, *Catalogue, Egypt I*, 122-3, no. 47; Jaroš-Deckert, *Das Grab des Jnj-jtj.f.*

198. Goyon, *Wadi Hammamat*, 77, pl. XXXII.

199. Louvre C.1, Gayet, *Stèles*, pl. I; ANOC 6.2, 4; Bourriau, *Pharaohs and Mortals*, 31-2, no. 21 (Cambridge, Fitzwilliam Museum E16.1969); D. Wildung, 'Ein Würfelhocker des Generals Nes-Month', *MDAIK* 37 (1981), 503-7 (block statue, Munich).

200. C. Obsomer, 'Les lignes 8 à 24 de la stèle de Mentouhotep (Florence 2540) érigée à Bouhen en l'an 18 de Sésostris Ier', *GM* 130 (1992), 57-74.

201. M.F.L. MacAdam, 'Gleanings from the Bankes MSS', *JEA* 32 (1946), 60-1, pl. IX.

202. Habachi, *Heqaib*, 75-8, no. 49.

203. Fr. 100/ANOC 2.1-3; Farout, 'Le monument abydénien du général en chef Amény engendré pour Qebou', *Egypte, Afrique & Orient* 37 (2005), 25-32.

204. J.D. Leprohon, *Stelae I, The Early Dynastic Period to the Late Middle Kingdom*, CAA Museum of Fine Arts 2, Boston, Mainz 1985, 153-5 (stela MFA 29.1130).

205. Fr. 101/Gr. 120 (IV.9).

206. Couyat, Montet, *Ouâdi Hammâmât*, no. 74, pl. XVIII.

207. Hintze & Reineke, *Felsinschriften*, 150-1, no. 504.

208. Mariette, *Karnak*, pl. 8q; Verbrovsek, *Als Gunsterweis*, 428.

209. Fr. 374/Hintze & Reineke, *Felsinschriften*, 152, no. 509; de Morgan, *Catalogue des monuments*, 25, no. 182.

210. ANOC 44.1.

211. Mariette, *Karnak*, pl. 8p; Verbrovsek, *Als Gunsterweis*, 388.

212. Parkinson/Quirke, The Coffin of Prince Herunefer.

213. Martin, *Seals*, nos 1134-8.

214. Martin, *Seals*, no. 224.

215. Martin, *Seals*, no. 596.

216. Martin, *Seals*, no. 743.

217. Martin, *Seals*, no. 1272.

218. Martin, *Seals*, no. 1301.

219. Gratien, *Prosopographie*, 165 (found at Mirgissa).

220. Martin, *Seals*, no. 1294.

221. Martin, *Seals*, no. 1412; Ben-Tor, *Scarabs, Chronology, and Interconnections*, pl. 25, 3.

222. Martin, *Seals*, no. 439.

223. Grajetzki, *Beamten*, 130-6.

224. Arnold, *Middle Kingdom Tomb Architecture at Lisht*, 36-9 (tomb).

225. Cairo CG 526.

226. Fr. 177/Gr. 131-2 (V.3); Martin, *Seals*, no. 339; Franke, in H. Altenmüller & R. Germer, *Miscellanea Aegyptologica, Wolfgang Helck zum 75. Geburtstag*, Hamburg 1989, 67-87 (relief from tomb).

227. Hintze & Reineke, *Felsinschriften*, 152, no. 510.

228. Fr. 333/de Morgan, *Catalogue des monuments*, 13, no. 55, 23, no. 156 = Petrie, *Season*, III, 87, V, 114.

229. Sams, *Ancient Egypt*, pl. 25.

230. Hayes, *A Papyrus of the Late Middle Kingdom*, 72, pl. VI.

231. K. Dyroff & B. Pörtner, *Aegyptische Grabsteine und Denksteine aus süddeutschen Sammlungen*, 2, *München*. Strassburg, 1904, pl. IV, 6.

232. de Morgan, *Catalogue des monuments*, 11, no. 43; 23, no. 156.

233. W. Grajetzki & G. Miniaci, 'The statue of "royal sealer" and "overseer of fields" Kheperka, Turin Museum Cat. 3064', *EVO* 30 (2007), 69-75.

234. Kitchen & Beltrão, *Rio de Janeiro*, 46-49, pls 25-6.

235. Kitchen & Beltrão, *Rio de Janeiro*, 46-49, pls 25-6.

236. Fr. 769/G. Andreu, 'Recherches sur la classe moyenne au Moyen Empire', in *Geschichte, Verwaltungs- und Wirtschaftsgeschichte, Rechtsgeschichte, Nachbarkulturen, Akten des 4. Internationalen Ägyptologen-Kongresses*, München 1985, Studien zur altägyptischen Kultur Beihefte, SAK-Beihefte 4, 15-26 (stelae Odessa GAM no. 52970 and Louvre C58).

237. Habachi, *Heqaib*, 106-7, no. 92, Franke, *Heqaib*, 67.

238. Martin, *Seals*, no. 595.

239. Martin, *MDAIK* 35 (1979), 224, no. 71.

240. Hayes, *The Scepter of Egypt I*, 346, fig. 227 (bottom left).

241. Grajetzki, *Beamten*, 136, no. V.18.

242. Martin, *Seals*, no. 897.

243. E. Graefe, *Das Grab des Padihorresnet, Obervermögensverwalter der Gottesgemahlin des Amun*, Brussels 2003, pls 117-18 (Kat. No. 541-4).

244. Grajetzki, *Beamten*, 158-61.

245. Habachi, *Heqaib*, 68, no. 41; Bourriau, *Pharaohs and Mortals,* 57-9, no. 45 (BM EA.1348).

246. Martin, *Seals*, no. 1499; Franke, *Heqaib*, 67; compare fig. 37.

247. Quirke, *RdE* 39 (1988), 103, no. 8.

248. Gr. 160 (VIII.7); Petrie, *Abydos II*, pl. XXVI.

249. Martin, *Seals*, nos 526-8 (Ptahhotep); no. 1277 (Zaamun); nos 1603-5 (Senebtifi).

250. Martin, *MDAIK* 35 (1979), 216, no. 8 (reading of name uncertain).

251. Grajetzki, *Beamten*, 164-7.

252. Fr. 623, Brunner-Traut & Brunner, *Tübingen*, 81-2, pl. 51.

253. Fr. 373/ANOC 59, Jørgensen, *Catalogue, Egypt I*, 190-1, no. 79 (Copenhagen Ny Carlsberg Glyptotek AEIN 964); H.G. Fischer, *Varia nova, Egyptian Studies* 3, New York 1996, pl. 26 on 139 (MMA 63.154).

254. Fr. 661/Habachi, *Heqaib*, 69, no. 43; Habachi, *SAK* 11 (1984), pl. 4a (MMA 22.3.307); Habachi, *Heqaib*, 68-9, no. 42 (statue).

255. Hein & Satzinger, *Stelen II*, 157 (Vienna ÄS 5897).

256. Fr. 25.

257. Nash, *PSBA* 36 (1914), 249, pl. XV (no. 76).

258. Martin, *Seals*, no. 557.

259. Franke, 'Middle Kingdom hymns and other sundry religious texts – an inventory', in S. Meyer (ed.) *Egypt – Temple of the World*, Leiden, Boston 2003, 100-2 (stela Cairo JE 39755, CG 20825).

260. Grajetzki, *Beamten*, 142-4.

261. Arnold, *Middle Kingdom Tomb Architecture at Lisht*, 86, pl. 165.

262. Gr. 142 (VI.1); Cairo CG 20288 (stela); Habachi, *Heqaib*, 88-9, no. 61, Franke, *Heqaib*, 55-6 (statue); Arnold, *Middle Kingdom Tomb Architecture at Lisht*, 55-7, pls 93, 101-6 (tomb); Freed, in *Studies*, 327-9 (dating).

263. Fr. 469/Gr. 142-3 (VI.2) de Morgan, *Fouilles à Dahchour en 1894-1895,*

38, fig. 88 (fragment from tomb); A. Nibbi, 'Remarks on two stelae from Wadi Gasus', *JEA* 62 (1976), 50, pl. IX (stela).

264. Fr. 155/Gr. 143 (VI.3); Cairo CG 20683 (stela), Petrie, *Illahun, Kahun and Gurob*, pl. XII, 11; Petrie/Brunton, *Lahun II*, 26-7, pl. XXVII-XXIX.

265. Gr. 144 (VI.4); Martin, *Seals*, no. 325.

266. Wegner, *Abydos*, 344, no. 18 (there translated as 'treasurer'; the writing of the signs with two reeds, a 't' and the 'house' sign at the end fits better with *rwyt*; the 'kh' (Gardiner Aa1) and 't' (Gardiner X1) there are a misreading of the 'rw' (Gardiner E23).

267. Fr. 764/ANOC 3; Cairo CG 23035; Philip-Stéphan, *Dire le droit*, 242.

268. Delia, 'First Cataract rock inscriptions: some comments, maps, and a new group', *JARCE* XXX (1993), 90.

269. Reisner, *Kerma*, 511-12, no. 30 (stela).

270. Martin, *Seals*, no. 1746.

271. Martin, *Seals*, no. 1247.

272. Hintze & Reineke, *Felsinschriften*, 126, no. 451.

273. Arnold, *Middle Kingdom Tomb Architecture at Lisht*, 14, pl. 25.

274. Fr. 696; H.G. Fischer, *Egyptian Studies I*, 60, fig. 1, XVII; James, *Corpus*, 39-40, pl. XXXIV (statue base and offering table); Berlin 1913, 208.

275. Fr. 697; Berlin 1913, 208; Delange, *Catalogue*, 81-3.

276. Delange, *Catalogue*, 81-3.

277. Delange, *Catalogue*, 81-3.

278. Verbrovsek, *Als Gunsterweis*, 472-5; Martin, *Seals*, no. 1149.

279. Martin, *Stelae*, 48-9.

280. Collier & Quirke, *The UCL Lahun Papyri: Religious, Literary, Legal, Mathematical and Medical*, 136-7.

281. Delange, *Catalogue*, 180-1.

282. Cairo CG 20102.

283. Martin, *Seals*, no. 874 (the reading as 'priest of Amun' is not certain).

284. R. Engelbach & T.C. Townsend, 'A XIIth Dynasty Inscription near the Cairo-Suez Road', *ASAE* 33 (1933), 1-5; G. Gabra & N. Ramsy, 'Zu einem Opferständer eines Hohenpriesters von Heliopolis des Mittleren Reiches', *Varia Aegyptiaca*, 10 (2-3) (1995), 101-4.

285. Borchardt, *ZÄS* 37 (1899), 90.

286. Martin, *Seals*, no. 537.

287. Martin, *Seals*, no. 811.

288. Martin, *Seals*, no. 1234.

289. Martin, *Seals*, no. 87.

Further Reading

General

J. P. Allen, 'The high officials of the early Middle Kingdom', in N. Strudwick & J. Taylor, *The Theban Necropolis*, London 2003, 14-29.

D.M. Doxey, *Egyptian Non-Royal Epithets in the Middle Kingdom*, Leiden, Boston, Köln 1998.

D. Franke, *Personendaten aus dem Mittleren Reich (20.-16. Jahrhundert v. Chr.), Dossiers 1-796*, Wiesbaden 1984.

W. Grajetzki, *Die höchsten Beamten der ägyptischen Zentralverwaltung zur Zeit des Mittleren Reiches*, Berlin 2000.

W. Helck, *Zur Verwaltung des Mittleren und Neuen Reiches*, Leiden, Köln 1958.

S. Quirke, *The Administration of Egypt in the Late Middle Kingdom*, Whitstable 1990.

A. Philip-Stéphan, *Dire le droit en Égypte pharaonique*, Brussels 2008.

N. Strudwick, *The Administration of Egypt in the Old Kingdom*, London 1985.

D. Valbelle & G. Husson, *L'état et les institutions en Égypte, des premiers Pharaons aux empereurs romains*, Paris 1992.

Dictionaries of titles

H.G. Fischer, *Egyptian Titles of the Middle Kingdom, A Supplement to Wm. Ward's Index*, 2nd edn, New York 1997 (additions and corrections to Ward's *Index*).

D. Franke, 'Probleme der Arbeit mit altägyptischen Titeln des Mittleren Reiches', *GM* 83 (1984), 51-2 (additions and corrections to Ward's *Index*).

D. Jones, *An Index of Ancient Egyptian Titles, Epithets and Phrases of the Old Kingdom*, Oxford 2000.

S. Quirke, *Titles and Bureaux of Egypt 1850-1700*, London 2004.

W.A. Ward, *Index of Egyptian Administrative and Religious Titles of the Middle Kingdom*, Beirut 1982.

Viziers

M. Valloggia, 'Les Vizirs des XIe et XIIe Dynasties', *RdE* 74 (1974), 123-34.

A. Weil, *Die Veziere des Pharonenreiches: chronologisch angeordnet*, Strasburg 1908.

Treasurers

S. Desplancques, *L'Institution du Trésor en Égypte des origines à la fin du Moyen Empire*, Paris 2006.

W. Grajetzki, *Two Treasurers of the Late Middle Kingdom*, Oxford 2001.

P. Vernus, 'Observations sur le titre [*imy-ra htmt*] "directeur du Trésor"', in S. Allam (ed.), *Grund und Boden in Altägypten*, Tübingen 1994, 251-60.

Other officials

F. Arnold, 'The high stewards of the Early Middle Kingdom', *GM* 122 (1991), 7-14.

R. Buongarzone, '*La rw(y).t e il mr rw(y).t*', *EVO* 18 (1995), 45-63.

S. Quirke, 'The regular titles of the late Middle Kingdom', *RdE* 37 (1986), 107-30.

S. Quirke, 'State and labour in the Middle Kingdom', *RdE* 39 (1988), 83-106 (on the 'great compound').

M. Valloggia, 'A propos du titres "Économe"', *BIFAO* 76 (1976), 343-6.

Military officials

G. Andreu, 'Les titres de policiers formés sur la racine schena', *CRIPEL* 9 (1987), 17-23.

P.-M. Cheverau, 'Contributions à la prosopographie des cadres militaires du Moyen Empire', *RdE* 42 (1991), 43-88.

P.-M. Cheverau, 'Contributions à la prosopographie des cadres militaires du Moyen Empire', *RdE* 43 (1992), 11-34.

D. Stefanović, *The Holders of the Regular Military Titles in the Period of the Middle Kingdom: Dossiers*, London 2006.

Provincial administration

N. Favry, *Le normaque sous le règne de Sésostris Ier*, Paris 2004.

D. Franke, *Das Heiligtum des Heqaib auf Elephantine* (SAGA 9), Heidelberg 1994.

H. Willems, *Dayr al-Barsha*, Leuven 2007, 83-110.

Second Intermediate Period

S. Quirke in M. Bietak & E. Czerny (eds), *Scarabs of the Second Millennium BC from Egypt, Nubia, Crete and the Levant: Chronological and Historical Implications*, Vienna 2004, 171-93.

Lives of officials

E. Feucht, *Das Kind im Alten Ägypten*, Frankfurt & New York 1995.

R. Janssen & J. Janssen, *Growing up and Getting Old in Ancient Egypt*, London 2007.

K. Szpakowska, *Daily Life in Ancient Egypt: Recreating Lahun*, London 2007.

Women

W.A. Ward, *Essays on Feminine Titles of the Middle Kingdom and Related Subjects*, Beirut 1986.

H.G. Fischer, *Egyptian Women of the Old Kingdom and of the Heracleopolitan Period*, 2nd edn, revised and augmented, New York 2000.

Bibliography and Abbreviations

ÄAT = *Ägypten und Altes Testament.*
ANOC = Abydos North offering chapel; refers to the list of objects in Simpson (1974).
ASAE = *Annales du Service des Antiquités de l'Égypte*, Cairo.
Berlin 1913 = *Aegyptische Inschriften aus den königlichen Museen zu Berlin*, Leipzig 1913.
BES = *Bulletin of the Egyptological Seminar*, New York.
BIFAO = *Bulletin de l'Institut Français d'Archéologie Orientale*, Cairo.
BMFA = *Bulletin of the Museum of Fine Arts*, Boston.
BMMA = *Bulletin of the Metropolitan Museum of Art*, New York.
BSEG = *Bulletin de la Société d'Égyptologie Genève*, Geneva.
BSFdÉ = *Bulletin de la Société Française d'Égyptologie.*
CG = Catalogue général des antiquités égyptiennes du Musée du Caire.
CRIPEL = *Cahiers de Recherches de l'Institut de Papyrologie et d'Égyptologie de Lille.*
Dahchour I = J. de Morgan, *Fouilles à Dahchour, mars-juin 1894*, Vienna 1895.
EVO = *Egitto e Vicino Oriente*, Pisa.
Fr. + number, see Franke, *Doss.*
GM = *Göttinger Miszellen*, Göttingen.
Gr. + number, see Grajetzki, *Beamten.*
HTBM = *Hieroglyphic Texts of the British Museum*, London 1911-.
JEA = *Journal of Egyptian Archaeology.*
MMA = Metropolitan Museum of Art, New York.
MMJ = *Metropolitan Museum Journal*, New York.
pBoulaq 18 = A. Scharff, 'Ein Rechnungsbuch des königlichen Hofes aus der 13. Dynastie (Papyrus Boulaq Nr. 18)', *ZÄS* 57 (1922), 51-68.
PM = B. Porter and R.L.B. Moss, *Topographical Bibliography of Ancient Egyptian Hieroglyphic Texts, Statues, Reliefs and Paintings*, vols 1-7 (1-3 now in 2nd edn), Oxford 1965-95; vol. 8 (*Objects of Provenance Not Known*), Parts 1 and 2 (*Statues*) Oxford 2000.
PSBA = *Proceedings of the Society of Biblical Archaeology*, London.
RdE = *Revue d'Égyptologie*, Paris.
SAGA = *Studien zur Archäologie und Geschichte Altägyptens*, Heidelberg.
SAK = *Studien zur Altägyptischen Kultur*, Hamburg.
ZÄS = *Zeitschrift für ägyptische Sprache und Altertumskunde*, Leipzig/Berlin.

Allen, J.P. (2003) 'The high officials of the early Middle Kingdom', in N. Strudwick & J. Taylor, *The Theban Necropolis*, London, 14-29.
Arnold, D. (1971) *Das Grab des Jnj-jtj.f, Band 1, Die Architektur*, Mainz am Rhein.
Arnold, D. (2008) *Middle Kingdom Tomb Architecture at Lisht*, New York, New Haven & London.

Arnold, F. (1990) *The Control Notes and Team Marks: The South Cemeteries of Lisht II*, New York.

Beckerath, J. von (1964) *Untersuchungen zur politischen Geschichte der zweiten Zwischenzeit in Ägypten*, Glückstadt.

Ben-Tor, D. (2007) *Scarabs, Chronology, and Interconnections: Egypt and Palestine in the Second Intermediate Period*, Göttingen.

Berlev, O. (1974) 'A contemporary of King Sewah-enRe', *JEA* 60, 106-13.

Blackman, A.M. (1931) 'The Stele of Thethi, Brit. Mus. No. 614', *JEA* 17, 55-61.

Bolshakov, A.O. & Quirke, S.G. (1999) *The Middle Kingdom Stelae in the Hermitage*, Utrecht & Paris.

Boorn, G.P.F. van den (1988) *The Duties of the Vizier*, London & New York.

Borchardt, L. (1899) Der zweite Papyrusfund von Kahun und die zeitliche Festlegung des mittleren Reiches der ägyptischen Geschichte, *ZÄS* 37 (1899), 89-103.

Bosticco, S. (1959) *Le Stele Egiziane dall'antico al Nuovo Regno, Museo Archeologico di Firenze*, Rome.

Bourriau, J. (1988) *Pharaohs and Mortals: Egyptian Art in the Middle Kingdom*, Cambridge.

Brunner, H. (1957) *Altägyptische Erziehung*, Wiesbaden.

Brunner-Traut, E. & Brunner, H. (1981) *Die Ägyptische Sammlung der Universität Tübingen*, Mainz am Rhein.

Collier, M. & Quirke, S. (2004) *The UCL Lahun Papyri: Religious, Literary, Legal, Mathematical and Medical*, Oxford.

Couyat, J. & Montet, P. (1912) *Les inscriptions hiéroglyphiques et hiératiques du Ouâdi Hammâmât*, Cairo.

Davies, N. de Garis (1913) *Five Theban Tombs, being those of Mentuherkhepereshef, User, Daga, Nehemawäy and Tati*, London.

Davies, N. de Garis (1920) *The Tomb of Antefoker, Vizier of Sesostris I, and of his Wife, Senet (no. 60)*, London.

Delange, E. (1987) *Catalogue des statues égyptiennes du Moyen Empire*, Paris.

Doxey, D.M. (1988) *Egyptian Non-Royal Epithets in the Middle Kingdom*, Leiden, Boston & Cologne.

Farout, D. (2005) 'Le monument abydénien du général en chef Amény engendre pour Qebou', *Egypte, Afrique & Orient* 37, 25-32.

Favry, N. (2004) *Le normaque sous le règne de Sésostris Ier*, Paris.

Fay, B. (1996) *The Louvre Sphinx and Royal Sculpture from the Reign of Amenemhat II*, Mainz.

Feucht, E. (1995) *Das Kind im Alten Ägypten*, Frankfurt & New York.

Fischer, H.G. (1976) *Egyptian Studies I, Varia*, New York.

Fischer, H.G. (1997) *Egyptian Titles of the Middle Kingdom, A Supplement to Wm. Ward's Index*, New York.

Franke, D. (1983) *Altägyptische Verwandtschaftsbezeichnungen im Mittleren Reich*, Hamburg.

Franke, *Doss.* = D. Franke (1984), *Personendaten aus dem Mittleren Reich (20.-16. Jahrhundert v. Chr.), Dossiers 1-796*, Wiesbaden.

Franke, D. (1991) 'The career of Khnumhotep III of Beni Hasan and the so-called "Decline of the Nomarch"', in S. Quirke (ed.), *Middle Kingdom Studies*, Whitstable, 51-67.

Franke, D. (1994) *Das Heiligtum des Heqaib auf Elephantine (SAGA* 9), Heidelberg.

Freed, R.E. (1996) 'Stela workshops of Early Dynasty 12', in P. der Manuelian (ed.), *Studies in Honor of William Kelly Simpson*, Boston, 297-336.

Bibliography and Abbreviations

Garstang, J. (1907) *The Burial Customs of Ancient Egypt as Illustrated by the Tombs of the Middle Kingdom*, London.

Gasse, A. & Rondot, V. (2007), *Les inscriptions de Séhel*, Cairo.

Gayet, A.J. (1889) *Stèles de la XIIe Dynastie*, Paris.

Geisen, C. (2004) *Die Texte des verschollenen Sarges der Königin Mentuhotep aus der 13. Dynastie*, Wiesbaden.

Goyon, G. (1957) *Nouvelles inscriptions rupestres du Wadi Hammamat*, Paris.

Grajetzki, W. (2000), *Die höchsten Beamten der ägyptischen Zentralverwaltung zur Zeit des Mittleren Reiches*, Berlin.

Grajetzki, W. (2001) *Two Treasurers of the Late Middle Kingdom*, Oxford.

Grajetzki, W. (2006) *The Middle Kingdom of Ancient Egypt*, London.

Gratien, B. (1991) *Prosopographie des Nubiens et des Egyptiens en Nubie avant le Nouvel Empire*, *CRIPEL* Supplément 3, Lille.

Habachi, L. (1984) 'The family of the vizier Ibi and his place among the viziers of the Thirteenth Dynasty', *SAK* 11, 113-26, pls. 4-6.

Habachi, L. (1985) *Elephantine IV: The Sanctuary of Heqaib*, Archäologische Veröffentlichungen 33, Mainz am Rhein.

Hayes, W.C. (1947) 'Horemkhauef of Nekhen and his Trip to It-towe', *JEA* 33, 3-11.

Hayes, W.C. (1953) *The Scepter of Egypt I*, New York.

Hayes, W.C. (1955) *A Papyrus of the Late Middle Kingdom in the Brooklyn Museum*, New York.

Hein, I. & Satzinger, H. (1989) *Stelen des Mittleren Reiches I: einschliesslich der I. und II. Zwischenzeit*, Mainz.

Hein, I. & Satzinger, H. (1993) *Stelen des Mittleren Reiches II: einschliesslich der I. und II. Zwischenzeit*, Mainz.

Helck, W. (1958) *Zur Verwaltung des Mittleren und Neuen Reiches*, Leiden & Cologne.

Hintze F. & Reineke, W.F. (1989) *Felsinschriften aus dem sudanesischen Nubien*, Berlin.

James, T.G.H. (1974) *Corpus of Hieroglyphic Inscriptions in the Brooklyn Museum I*, Brooklyn NY.

Janssen, J. (1946) *De Traditioneel Egyptische Autobiografie vóór het Nieuwe Rijk*, Leiden.

Jaroš-Deckert, B. (1984) *Das Grab des Jnj-jtj.f. Die Wandmalereien der XI. Dynastie*, Mainz.

Jaroš-Deckert, *Wien* = Jaroš-Deckert, B. (1987) *Statuen des Mittleren Reiches und der 18. Dynastie*, CAA Kunsthistorische Museum Wien, 1, Mainz.

Jørgensen, M. (1996) *Catalogue, Egypt I (3000-1550 BC), Ny Carlsberg Glyptotek*, Copenhagen.

Kitchen K.A. & Conceição Beltrão, M. da (1990) *Catalogue of the Ancient Egyptian Monuments in the National Museum, Rio de Janeiro: Catálogo de coleção do Egito Antigo do Museo Nacional no Rio de Janeiro*, Warminster.

Lacau, P. (1939) *Une stèle juridique des Karnak*, Cairo.

Leiden, stela = Boeser, P.A.A. (1909) *Beschreibung der Aegyptischen Sammlung des Niederländischen Reichsmuseums der Altertümer in Leiden: die Denkmäler der Zeit zwischen dem alten und mittleren Reich und des mittleren Reiches I*, Stelen, Haag.

Lepsius, K.R. (1849-56) *Denkmäler aus Aegypten und Aethiopien*, 12 vols, Berlin.

Lichtheim, M. (1988) *Ancient Egyptian Autobiographies chiefly of the Middle Kingdom*, Freiburg/Göttingen.

Lloyd, A.B. (1922) 'The great inscription of Khnumhotep II at Beni Hasan', in *Studies in Pharaonic Religion and Society in Honour of J. Gwyn Griffiths*, ed. A.B. Lloyd, London, 21-36.

Lüscher, B. (1990) *Untersuchungen zu den ägyptischen Kanopenkästen*, Hildesheim.

Mariette, A. (1875) *Karnak: étude topographique et archéologique avec un appendice comprenant les principaux textes hiéroglyphiques découverts ou recueillis pendant les fouilles exécutées à Karnak: planches*, Leipzig.

Mariette, *Mastabas* = Mariette, A. (1889) *Les mastabas de l'Ancien Empire: fragment du dernier ouvrage de A. Mariette, publ. après le manuscript de l'auteur par G. Maspero*, Paris.

Martin, *Seals* = Martin, G. (1971) *Egyptian Administrative and Private-Name Seals*, Oxford.

Martin, G. (1979), 'Private name seals in Alnwick Castle collection', *MDAIK* 35 (1979), 215-26.

Martin, G. (2005) *Stelae from Egypt and Nubia in the Fitzwilliam Museum, Cambridge, c. 3000 BC-AD 1150*, Cambridge.

de Meulenaere, H. (1981), 'Contributions à la prosopographie du Moyen Empire', *BIFAO* 81s (1981), 77-85.

Morgan, J. de, Bouriant, U. & Legrain, G. (1894) *Catalogue des monuments et inscriptions de l'Egypte antique. Première série, Haute Egypte. Tome premier, de la frontière de Nubie à Kom Ombos*, Vienna.

Morgan, J. de (1895) *Fouilles à Dahchour, mars-juin 1894*, Vienna.

Morgan, J. de (1903) *Fouilles à Dahchour en 1894-1895*, Vienna.

Nash, W. L. (1914), 'Notes on some Egyptian Antiquities', *PSBA* 36, 249-52.

Newberry, P.E. (1893) *Beni Hasan I*, London.

Newberry, P.E. (1893) *Beni Hasan II*, London.

Newberry, P.E. (1895) *El Bersheh I*, London.

Newberry, P.E. (1895) *El Bersheh II*, London.

Page, A. (1976) *Archaic to Saite, from the Petrie Collection*, Warminster.

Parkinson, R.B. (1991) *Voices from Ancient Egypt*, London.

Parkinson, R. & Quirke, S. (1992) 'The coffin of Prince Herunefer and the early history of the Book of the Dead' in A.B. Lloyd (ed.), *Studies in Pharaonic Religion and Society in Honour of J. Gwyn Griffiths*, London, 37-51.

Petrie, W.M. Flinders (1888) *A Season in Egypt 1887*, London.

Petrie, W.M. Flinders (1890) *Kahun, Gurob and Hawara*, London.

Petrie, W.M. Flinders (1891) *Illahun, Kahun and Gurob*, London.

Petrie, W.M. Flinders (1903) *Abydos II*, London.

Petrie, W.M. Flinders (1909) *Memphis I*, with a chapter by J.H. Walker, London.

Petrie, W.M. Flinders, Brunton, G. & Murray, M.A. (1923), *Lahun II*, London.

Pilgrim, C. von (1996) *Elephantine XVIII, Untersuchungen in der Stadt des Mittleren Reiche und der Zweiten Zwischenzeit*, Mainz.

Philip-Stéphan, A. (2008) *Dire le droit en Égypte pharaonique en Égypte pharaonique*, Brussels.

Quirke, S. (1990) *The Administration of Egypt in the Late Middle Kingdom*, Whitstable.

Quirke, S. (2004) *Egyptian Literature 1800 BC: Questions and Readings*, London.

Quirke, S. (2004) *Titles and Bureaux of Egypt 1850-1750 BC*, London.

Reisner, G.A. (1923) *Excavations at Kerma I-V. Harvard African Studies 5.* Cambridge, MA.

Richards, J. (2005) *Society and Death in Ancient Egypt*, Cambridge.

Roccati, A. (2003) 'Quattro Stel del Medio Regno', in S. Quirke (ed.), *Discovering Egypt from the Neva: The Egyptological Legacy of Oleg D Berlev*, Berlin, 111-21.

Ryholt, K.S.B. (1997) *The Political Situation in Egypt during the Second Intermediate Period c. 1800-1550 BC*, Copenhagen.

Sadek, A.I. (1980) *The Amethyst Mining Inscriptions of Wadi el-Hudi I*, Warminster.

Sadek, A.I. (1985) *The Amethyst Mining Inscriptions of Wadi el-Hudi II*, Warminster.

[Sams, J.] (1839) *Ancient Egypt: Objects of Antiquity forming parts of the extensive and rich collections from Ancient Egypt brought to England by, or now in the possion of J. Sams*, London.

Schneider, T. (2003) *Ausländer in Ägypten während des Mittleren Reiches und der Hyksoszeit, II, Die ausländische Bevölkerung*, ÄAT 42, Wiesbaden.

Simpson, W.K. (1963) *Papyrus Reisner I*, Boston.

Simpson, W.K. (1974) *The Terrace of the Great God at Abydos: The Offering Chapels of Dynasties 12 and 13*, New Haven/Philadelphia.

Simpson, W.K. (1988) 'Lepsius Pyramid LV at Dahshur; the mastaba of Si-Ese, vizier of Amenemhat II', in John Baines (ed.), *Pyramid Studies and Other Essays Presented to I.E.S. Edwards*, London.

Simpson, W.K. (1991) 'Mentuhotep, Vizier of Sesostris I, Patron of Art and Architecture', *MDAIK* 47, 331-40.

Simpson, W.K. (1995) *Inscribed Material from the Pennsylvania-Yale Excavations at Abydos*, New Haven & Philadelphia.

Spalinger, A. (1980) 'Remarks on the family of Queen Ha.s-nbw and the problem of kingship in Dynasty XIII', *RdE* 32, 95-116.

Stefanović, D. (2006) *The Holders of the Regular Military Titles in the Period of the Middle Kingdom: Dossiers*, London.

Strudwick, N. (1985) *The Administration of Egypt in the Old Kingdom*, London.

Trope, B.T. (2005) *Excavating Egypt: Great Discoveries from the Petrie Museum of Egyptian Archaeology*, Atlanta.

Tylor, J.J. (1896) *The Tomb of Sebeknekht*, London.

Verbrovsek, A. (2004) *'Als Gunsterweis des Königs in den Tempel gegeben ...': Private Tempelstatuen des Alten und Mittleren Reiches*, Wiesbaden.

Vernus, P. (1986) *Le surnom au moyen Empire*, Rome.

Ward, W.A. (1982) *Index of Egyptian Administrative and Religious Titles of the Middle Kingdom*, Beirut.

Ward, W.A. (1986) *Essays on Feminine Titles of the Middle Kingdom and Related Subjects*, Beirut.

Wegner, J. (1998), 'Excavations at the town of Enduring-are-the-Places of Khakaure-Maa-Kheru-in-Abydos: a preliminary report on the 1994 and 1997 seasons', *JARCE* XXXV, 1-44.

Wegner, J. (2007) *The Mortuary Temple of Senwosret III at Abydos*, New Haven & Philadelphia.

Willems, H. (1988) *Chests of Life*, Leiden.

Willems, H. (1996) *The Coffin of Heqata (Cairo JdE 36418)*, Leuven.

Willems, H. (2007) *Dayr al-Barshâ*, Leuven.

Žába, Z. (1974) *The Rock Inscriptions of Lower Nubia*, Prague.

Index